RICHARD STRAUSS

AND

ROMAIN ROLLAND

★

CORRESPONDENCE

RICHARD STRAUSS
& ROMAIN ROLLAND
★
CORRESPONDENCE

Together with
Fragments from the DIARY
of Romain Rolland
and other essays
and an Introduction by
Gustave Samazeuilh

Edited and Annotated
with a Preface
by
ROLLO MYERS

UNIVERSITY OF CALIFORNIA PRESS
BERKELEY AND LOS ANGELES · 1968

University of California Press
Berkeley and Los Angeles, California

Originally published in French by Editions
Albin Michel, Paris, 1951 in their series
Cahiers Romain Rolland (*Cahiers* 3) under
the title *Richard Strauss et Romain Rolland,
Correspondance, Fragments de Journal*

Printed in Great Britain

CONTENTS

Preface by Rollo Myers vii

Introduction by Gustave Samazeuilh . . . 1

PART I

Correspondence 13
Notes 105

PART II

Fragments from Romain Rolland's Diary . . 109
Notes 169

PART III

Two Essays:
1 Richard Strauss 175
2 French Music and German Music . . . 197

APPENDIX

Romain Rolland and Music by Gustave Samazeuilh . 219
Index 233

PREFACE

Richard Strauss and Romain Rolland, who were almost exact contemporaries, Strauss having been born in 1864 and Rolland in 1866, were linked by a friendship based, it would seem, on Rolland's side more on this fastidious critic's admiration for an outstanding talent than on any deeper feelings of a more personal nature; while on Strauss's side there was, above all, grateful recognition of such influential support, especially in so far as it seemed likely to help him in his career and open doors to him in a country traditionally allergic to Germanic art. Fundamentally, however, the two men were very different in character, outlook and education, and had little in common on which a true friendship could have been founded, apart from that love of music that united them, albeit on different levels, the one creative and the other critical.

They first became acquainted in 1899, and in the same year began the correspondence, now published for the first time in English, which gives a fascinating picture of musical Europe from the turn of the century down to the last years of the first world war. From 1910 to 1917, however, no letters appear to have been exchanged, although from the few that have been preserved from the post-war years (1924–1926) it is clear that their feelings towards one another remained unchanged.

Supplementing the *Letters*, and covering almost exactly the same period, the *Diary* in which Rolland has recorded his impressions of Strauss and his own reactions towards the man and his music also appears here now for the first time in English, and makes equally fascinating reading.

vii

We have to remember, however, that although one party to this correspondence, the musician, needs no introduction to the reader of today, there must be many, especially of the younger generation, who, if they have ever heard of Romain Rolland, have only the haziest notion of who he was or of the place he occupied in the world of letters and musicology in the early years of this century. Therefore, in order to appreciate at their just value this Diary and this correspondence it is essential to know something about the background and achievements of the man who did perhaps more than any other to make the music of Richard Strauss known and appreciated in France at a time when this young and, as it then seemed, revolutionary composer was battling for recognition outside his own country.

*　　*　　*

Romain Rolland was in some respects a typical nineteenth-century French intellectual, with this difference—that in addition to his academic interests (he was a product of the Ecole Normale Supérieure and a Professor at the Sorbonne) he was a distinguished man of letters, a keen student of international affairs and not only a great lover of music, but a pioneer in the field of musicology in France. He gained his Doctorate in fact (in 1895) with a thesis on '*Les origines due théâtre lyrique moderne: historie de l'opéra en Europe avant Lulli et Scarlatti*'; lectured on the history of music at the Sorbonne, and was the author of a number of books on music which the reader will find listed in the concluding essay in this book: *Romain Rolland and music*.

But the book which made him famous, and by which he is most likely to be remembered today, was *Jean-Christophe*, an inordinately long and somewhat sententious novel, with a German musician as its hero, which was published in ten volumes between 1904–1912 and created a considerable stir in musical circles at that time. In this book Rolland describes the thoughts and adventures of a young German musician working in Paris at the turn of the century, his object being

to show how 'genius conquers adversity by refusing material-
ism', and also to contrast, not always to the advantage of his
own country, the respective musical achievements and aspirations of France and Germany.

Idealistic and romantic in tone, it can still be expected
to appeal to a young reading public today, and is, in
fact, being reissued in a four-volume paper-back edition
by the publishers of this volume. In so far as it embodies
the author's ideas about the relative merits of French
and German music, and is evidence of that lofty detachment and supra-national outlook which was later, as we
shall see, to make him so unpopular, even detested, in his
own country, the novel certainly cannot be ignored.

From earliest youth Rolland had been an ardent advocate
of international understanding, the enemy of 'chauvinism'
in any shape or form, and had never attempted to conceal
his admiration for the art and literature of Germany. This
was all very well up to a point, but when he went so far as
to make a German musician the hero of his novel, and even
to suggest that German music was superior to French, public
opinion in France, which was not at that time very favourable to Germany, was frankly offended. And when, soon
after the publication of the last volume of *Jean-Christophe,*
war broke out in 1914 and Rolland issued from Switzerland
his notorious and ill-timed manifesto *Au dessus de la mêlée,*
feeling against him rose to fever point and he was attacked
on all sides. Among his bitterest critics were writers like
Henri Massis, Charles Maurras, Anatole France, Paul
Souday (literary critic of *Le Temps*) and André Gide. The
latter denounced *Jean-Christophe* as a sort of monument of
'anti-France literature', and even maintained that its author
'had everything to gain from a disaster to France and from
the disappearance of the French language and French taste
and culture'. '*Le désastre final de la France*', he wrote in his
Journal and republished later in *La Nouvelle Revue Française*
(June 1919), '*donnerait à son Jean-Christophe la plus grande et
définitive importance.*'

The climax came when he was nominated by the Swedish

A*

Academy for the Nobel Prize in 1915. The intention was to honour him, not, as was widely supposed in France, as a pacifist, but purely for his literary achievements; but the proposal met with so much oppositon, and provoked so much vituperous abuse of Rolland in the French press, that the Swedes (who in any case were distrusted in France for their alleged Germanophil leanings) were obliged to withdraw the nomination. Nevertheless, in the following year Rolland was finally awarded the prize, despite all opposition and the rival candidature of Charles Péguy who, in the opinion of most Frenchmen, would have been a worthier recipient of the honour. The campaign against Rolland was now intensified; he was denounced as the 'only neutral Frenchman', and accused of having deserted his country in her hour of greatest danger, preferring the safety of neutral Switzerland where, as a writer in *Le Matin* scoffingly proclaimed: 'he writes articles in the Swiss papers praising German *Kultur,* and commiserating with the poor Germans involved against their will in a war which they had never wanted. Does this mean that M. Romain Rolland is a German Swiss? Not at all: M. Rolland is a Frenchman—a Professor at the Sorbonne . . . etc. . . . '*

With regard to *Au dessus de la mêlée,* in which Rolland apparently dissociated himself from the conflict in which his country was engaged, it is understandable that such an utterance, however idealistic and disinterested its purpose may have been, was bitterly resented in France and in England and in general among their Allies who, though doubtless sharing Rolland's detestation of war on principle, were nevertheless fighting for their freedom, and had no doubts whatever that their cause was just, and that German aggression must be halted at all costs. The Allies, in fact, were in no mood for sermons, and Rolland's superior and aloof attitude to the struggle in which they were engaged

*Quoted by Monsieur René Cheval in his *Romain Rolland, l'Allemagne et la Guerre*: *Presses Universitaires de France,* 1963, a most interesting and exhaustive study of the man and his period to which I am greatly indebted for much of the information in this essay.)

seemed intolerably sanctimonious and priggish. In England, though approved in some quarters, notably by the extreme Left and the I.L.P. and, strangely enough, *The Times* (which called Rolland's manifesto 'the expression of the noblest soul of modern France'), the appeal was in general very badly received, and denounced, notably, by the *Westminster Gazette*, the *Manchester Guardian* and the *Evening News*. M. René Cheval* recalls that H. G. Wells, in an open letter to Romain Rolland in the *Daily Chronicle* of March 17, 1916, with the sub-title *The Lament of a Pacifist*, expressed the very strongest disapproval of the manifesto coming at such a time, and did not conceal his irritation at what he described as Rolland's 'sanctimoniousness', with especial reference to the opening words of *Au dessus de la mêlée* addressed: 'To my enemies: they may hate me; they will not succeed in teaching me to hate.'

There is no doubt that one result of the manifesto was to make Rolland *persona non grata* in Britain, both in political and academic circles. Thus, the British Academy, which had invited him to speak on Shakespeare during the anniversary celebrations in 1915 before he had published his appeal to the warring nations, began by postponing the visit to the following year and ended by cancelling it altogether.

To sum up, then, the publication of *Au dessus de la mêlée* did Rolland far more harm than good; indeed, it did much to tarnish his reputation as a writer, both in his own country and abroad; and to the end of his life he tended to be looked upon as a man without a country, if anything more German than French in his affinities and general outlook on life.

I have thought it necessary, in order to 'place' Rolland in the right perspective, especially in the context of his friendship with and admiration for Richard Strauss, to explain in some detail the reasons why he was never, in any sense, a popular figure in his own country, either as a writer or a thinker. But there is another side to the picture, and it is time now to examine this, and see whether our subject

*Loc. cit.

cannot be made to appear in a more favourable light. I think it will emerge that he was one of those men who are born to be misunderstood, and that although he was perhaps his own worst enemy, he had many admirable qualities, not always apparent on the surface. He himself supplied what may very well be the key to a proper understanding of his character when he noted in his *Journal des années de la guerre* (1914) that he always felt isolated from the rest of mankind, and asked, rather sadly; 'How is it that I can never associate myself with any of the great movements of humanity?'. It was surely this fundamental spiritual loneliness, coupled with a high idealism which guided all his actions, that inevitably resulted in what seemed to the man in the street a kind of priggishness, a 'holier than thou' attitude, which was bound to make him unpopular, especially when it led him to express views that ran counter to ingrained national prejudices. There was nothing really Olympian about his apparent detachment from his country's cause, in his anxiety to see all round the questions at issue, and his unwillingness to believe that Germany was *wholly* in the wrong. But that he was 'pro-German' in any political sense which might have induced him, for example, to condone German atrocities, is simply not true. He had, however, since early youth, been a keen student of German art and literature, and above all of German music, and was unwilling to believe that the country that had produced Beethoven and Goethe could be wholly bad, however fervently that opinion was held by all good patriots in the heat and excitement of war. Nevertheless, when it was clear that atrocities had been committed, he did not hesitate to write to his old friend Gerhard Hauptmann an open letter inviting him to join in protestation against actions that dishonoured Germany, and was deeply shocked when Hauptmann replied in an article in the *Frankfurter Zeitung* defending Germany and attacking Rolland for his intervention. This was the signal for a concerted attack on Rolland in the whole German press which resulted, paradoxically, in Rolland, the alleged 'pro-German', being classed among the enemies of Germany, along with d'Annunzio, Barrès, Anatole France, Kipling, Shaw, Gorki, etc., while there were critics who denounced *Jean-Christophe* as a caricature, and prayed to be preserved from 'all our false friends'. Rolland was profoundly shocked, too, by the famous *Manifesto* signed by 93 German 'Intellectuals' defending the actions of their Army and their Government against all criticism; and, for the record, it is interesting to recall that among those who signed this document were such eminent personalities as Max Reinhardt, Max Planck, Gerhard Hauptmann, Röntgen, Sudermann, Humperdinck, Weingartner and Siegfried Wagner. His old friend Stefan Zweig also rejected Rolland's plea for a return to sanity, saying there was no place in the world today for beauty, but that hate must rule. (Article in the *Berliner Tageblatt*, September 20th, 1914.) Might it not then have been as a last despairing appeal to the belligerents to listen to the voice of reason before it was too late that Rolland sat down to write his famous and ill-fated manifesto?—which, as it turned out, did more harm than good, and failed signally in its purpose.

Up to now we have been examining the attitude of Romain Rolland during the 1914 war; but before we turn to the circumstances which had led to his making the acquaintance of Richard Strauss in the pre-war years, and the correspondence which the two men subsequently carried on, it might, I think, be helpful to consider briefly how it was that Rolland, from an early age, had always been attracted by certain aspects of German life and culture with which he felt himself in sympathy. He has admitted to three main influences: his adoration of Beethoven and other German masters; his love for the Rhineland, its scenery and atmosphere (the hero of his novel *Jean-Christophe* he made a Rhinelander); and last but not least, the influence and friendship of an old German Huguenot lady whose acquaintance he made in Rome when he was a young man of 23 and she already in her seventies. This was Malwida von Meysenbug who received in her salon in Rome such celebrities as Wagner, Liszt, Nietzsche, Ibsen, Turgeniev, etc., and was herself a writer and a highly cultured woman as well as being a keen musician. A friendship sprang up between the youth and the old lady, who admired in Rolland what she called his 'profound intelligence' and his great musical gifts; while he, on his side, looked upon her as 'a second mother', and spoke of her later as '*la lumière de mes vingt ans*'. When Rolland left Rome (he had gone there with a Fellowship to the French School of Archaeology and History) they began a correspondence which lasted for some years, and has since been published.*

It is still not easy, from the somewhat conflicting evidence outlined in the preceding pages, to determine the exact nature of Rolland's Germanic affinities. There is no doubt, I think, as I said above, that he was attracted by *certain aspects* of German life and culture; at the same time there is abundant evidence (from his own writings) that he was often revolted by German coarseness and lack of finesse; he even speaks of the 'physical revulsion' he experienced as a young man when in too close proximity with the beer-swilling, boisterous Teutons among whom he found himself on his first visit to Bayreuth. Despite his admiration for the music of Richard Strauss, there were times when he was struck by the 'barbarity and decadence' of certain pages; and it is interesting to see how, in his correspondence with Strauss, he was not afraid to criticise his bad taste (in *Salomé*, for example) and suggest that he was worthy of better things. And although he was sometimes almost fulsome in his praise in his letters to Strauss, his references to him in his *Diary* are often far from complimentary.

The truth is, I think, that Rolland, who was a highly cultured and extremely fastidious scholar, and fundamentally French in his hatred of vulgarity in any form and instinctive respect for good taste, yet somehow felt that these qualities were not enough in a work of art; and it was precisely for this reason that French music did not entirely

Lettres à Malwida von Meysenbug; *Cahiers Romain Rolland* No. I. Albin Michel, Paris 1945).

satisfy him. He felt the need for a fresh injection of vigour
and vitality, and found what he was looking for in the
music of the young Strauss whose early Tone Poems,
especially *Heldenleben* and the *Sinfonia domestica* seemed to
Rolland to be bursting with the strength and vitality for
which he was seeking in vain elsewhere. For despite his
inborn fastidiousness and refinement (which come out
clearly both in the Letters and the Diary) Rolland also had
a perhaps subconscious respect for force (it was not for
nothing that his hero Jean-Christophe was surnamed
Kraft); and it was this quality that he admired both in German music and the German temperament. At the same
time he was always ready to defend French music against
foreign critics, and was irritated, as the reader will see
from many passages in his letters to Strauss and in the
Diary, at the German composer's inability to understand
French music, and especially his obtuseness with regard
to *Pelléas et Mélisande*. Not only was Strauss insensitive to
the beauty of Debussy's music; he even went so far as to
criticise his setting of French words! This was too much for
Rolland who replied (see Letter of July 16, 1905) with a
withering attack on German insensibility in general and
Strauss's in particular. 'You Germans really are astonishing',
he wrote; 'You don't understand anything about our poetry,
not a thing, and you pass judgment on it with imperturbable
complacency . . . I can see very well that you have no feeling
for our literary French language at all. You imagine that
it's like yours . . . At the moment you are too arrogant in
Germany. You think you understand everything, and you
don't take any pains to understand. So much the worse for
you . . . ' And much more in this strain, and no punches
pulled. And yet Rolland took infinite pains to correct
Strauss's prosody in setting Wilde's *Salomé* (see especially his
letter of 5th November, 1905), and did his best to initiate
him into the subtleties of the pronunciation and inflexions
of spoken French. The reader will find these pages rewarding.
He will also not fail to be struck by the examples, recurring
again and again throughout the *Letters* and the *Diary*, of that

ambivalence in Rolland's love-hate attitude towards Germans and everything German to which I have already drawn attention in these pages in an attempt to clarify his complex character; and, in this context, a reading of the last pages of the essay on Strauss reproduced from *Musiciens d'aujourd'hui* at the end of this volume is to be recommended, because in them it is Romain Rolland the music critic speaking, and revealing with deadly accuracy and strict impartiality the essential strength and weakness of the young musician whom, amongst his contemporaries, he most admired and whose friendship he had enjoyed.

* * *

Romain Rolland lived to see another war, with Germany again in the villain's role. He was outspoken in his condemnation of Hitler and National Socialism in the pre-war years, but remained silent during the Occupation. But by then he was 74 and in feeble health, and living in retirement at Vézelay, in his native Burgundy; and it was there that he died in December 1944. If a personal reminiscence is not out of place, I was asked by the BBC a few days later to broadcast in the French service a brief tribute to his memory in which I spoke of his *'probité intellectuelle'*, and of the way in which, in all that he wrote, *'il avait fait preuve d'un si grand attachement à la vérité.'*

In the pages that follow it will be evident, I think, that in all his judgments about music and musicians a desire to arrive at the truth was not the least of his preoccupations.

ROLLO MYERS.

P.S. The author of the introductory essay that follows, Gustave Samazeuilh [b. Bordeaux 1877], is a distinguished French composer and writer on music. An ardent Wagnerian and a lifelong friend and admirer of Richard Strauss, he has written studies of both composers, and in the year after Strauss's death published in the *Revue Musicale* [Jan. 1950] his *Souvenirs sur Richard Strauss*.

INTRODUCTION

Following the publication of Romain Rolland's sensitive and moving letters to Malwida von Meysenbug,[1] and his *Correspondence* with Louis Gillet, in which the fine quality of two very different natures stands out against the events of an already disturbed epoch, here, assembled and translated, are a series of significant documents: letters, fragments from a diary and various studies, concerning the friendship and mutual admiration which united Richard Strauss and Romain Rolland from their very first meeting. They are both now, alas! departed; their independence, influence, and example could have been so beneficial in this unbalanced world.

I had only just left school, more than half a century ago, when I had the good fortune to get to know them both, and to appreciate the value of their long-suffering friendship. Since that time, I have always kept in touch with them, visiting them whenever I could and enriching myself by this contact with them, with their works and with their respect for other people's freedom of thought . . . Indeed, that is, I think, the only reason which could have induced Madame Romain Rolland to ask me, a simple musician, to introduce this new volume to the numerous and faithful readers of the *Cahiers*, by gathering together here some of my recollections.

It was during my two first visits to Germany in order to study there, in 1894 and in 1897–8, that I first became acquainted with Richard Strauss. My father, Fernand

1

Samazeuilh, a great traveller, a man of wide culture, a great music lover, and an admirer of Richard Wagner, (whom he had known in Lübeck in 1867, and of whom he had been one of the first French supporters), had taken me to Bayreuth and to Munich . . . Richard Strauss, then barely thirty years old, had just married the singer Pauline de Ahna, and was at that time making a most brilliant *début*, conducting *Tannhäuser* at the Festspielhaus, and then *Tristan* and Mozart's *Don Giovanni* at the Königliche Opera and the Residenztheater of the Bavarian capital where he had been born. Apart from the products of his early youth, written under the influence of the classics, of Schumann and of Brahms, of whom his father, the famous horn player Franz Josef Strauss, was a somewhat exclusive advocate, Richard Strauss had already produced his symphonic poems *Macbeth*, *Don Juan* and *Tod und Verklärung*, and his first musical drama, *Guntram*, which were conceived in a new atmosphere, inspired by the works of Liszt and of Wagner, which he had got to know and appreciate through his friend Alexander Ritter.[2] In these early works of Strauss the inventive gifts and precocious mastery of instrumentation which had rightly struck Hans von Bülow, Hermann Levi, and Cosima Wagner, stood out. Cosima Wagner made no secret in her own circle of the value she attached to this 'rising star', to whom she would have readily entrusted the heaviest tasks.

Two years later, having returned to central Europe for a more prolonged stay, I was present, at the Museum concerts in Frankfurt, at the first performance, which Strauss himself conducted, of his symphonic poem based on Nietzsche: *Also sprach Zarathustra*. The whole of him is to be found in this work, his high poetic aspirations, and that harmonic and orchestral audacity which, in 1897, was shocking those neo-classical circles beyond the Rhine whose gods were Brahms and the famous violinist Joachim. *Don Quixote*, which followed shortly afterwards, was not calculated to please them—far from it. Already at this epoch, as I can bear witness, Richard Strauss was following the

2

development of our music with interest, and showed himself to be well-disposed, encouraging, and accessible to young foreign tyro-composers, who felt somewhat lost at the beginning of their stay because of their insufficient familiarity with the German language. He was, as was Humperdinck, the author of *Hänsel und Gretel,* one of the first to applaud and to support Vincent d'Indy, who had come to Frankfurt to conduct *Wallenstein* and, at the Mannheim festival, his *Symphonie sur un chant montagnard,* with Edouard Risler at the piano,—Edouard Risler who was then in charge of singing at Bayreuth, and the author of a skilful concert transcription for piano of *Till Eulenspiegel* which, by the end of the year, had already been round the world. It was not Strauss's fault that *Fervaal,* also by Vincent d'Indy, was not performed in Munich, after the great success of the first performance in Brussels in 1897; it was thanks to him that later on *Benvenuto Cellini, Carmen, Samson et Dalila, Briséis, Istar* and *Louise* were all performed in Berlin.[3]

It was shortly afterwards, in 1899, during a stay in Berlin and later in Düsseldorf, that Romain Rolland, whose first books had already revealed to me all the nobility of his mind, made the acquaintance of Richard Strauss. He was one of the first Frenchmen to understand his complex nature, by turns impulsive and reserved, his poetic and expressive potentialities, and the great promise shown in his works, which already at this period, were the faithful reflection of his personalty. The uninhibited correspondence, the fragments of the Diary, and the essays which are collected together in this volume, will show, much better than I could myself, how his friendship, as always disinterested, was, also as always, shrewd, and how, when occasion arose he did not shrink from outspoken frankness. For proof I need look no further than his criticism of certain episodes in *Don Quixote* and in *Heldenleben,* the literary synopsis of the *Sinfonia domestica,* and the libretto of *Guntram.* But this did not prevent him from estimating these vast sonorous frescoes at their true worth, nor from discerning the popular pungency of *Feuersnot,* nor, whatever might be the manifold objections raised by the choice of Oscar Wilde's poem, from praising the force and the power which, from the very outset, made *Salomé* command attention, even from those who despised it.

In this book will also be found the excellent directives which Romain Rolland gave to Richard Strauss, at the latter's request, about the drafting of the French version of *Salomé*. Like all adaptations of this sort made as an afterthought, this raised, almost in every bar, the most delicate problems of stress and of declamation which the musician, in view of his then very imperfect knowledge of our language, would never have been able to resolve alone . . . The same could be said of the unfortunate Mariotte affair[4] which—I was told by both the composers themselves,—would have been easily settled between them if other people who were incompletely informed had not intervened to confuse and to embitter the issue.

It was the same when Richard Strauss first heard *Louise,* and above all *Pelléas et Mélisande.* Romain Rolland, while not concealing his personal preferences for a different operatic conception, understood so well the respective meanings of these works, their novelty in very different fields, that he was able to modify the first inevitably cautious impressions of a foreign musican with a different background. It was the same with the works of Paul Dukas; later on, at the Festival of the Coopération Internationale des Compositeurs at Vichy in 1935, three months after the death of the author of *Ariane et Barbe-Bleue,* Richard Strauss made a point of honouring his memory before the microphone as one of the great masters of French music by conducting the dazzling *Apprenti Sorcier,* unconcerned by the fact that by so doing he was bound to incur the displeasure of the Nazi régime, the official representative of which refrained from attending the concert.

It is to be deeply regretted that after such a solid beginning, the correspondence of Romain Rolland and Richard Strauss should, as a result of circumstances independent of their will, have become less frequent, without their reci-

4

procal feelings ceasing to be the same; the last letters
published here testify to this, in particular those written in
1917 during the first world war, during which Richard
Strauss refused to sign the Manifesto of German Intellectuals which was directed against France. There is no doubt
that their points of view would have drawn even closer
together since then, in a common condemnation of the
manifold excesses which were to lead a great country to
its ruin . . . I would here cite the dedication, reproduced in
this book, (p. 102) to the beautiful piece of music which
Richard Strauss composed as a setting to a text by Goethe
for the *Liber Amicorum*, published in 1926 in Zürich at the
initiative of Georges Duhamel, Maxim Gorki and Stefan
Zweig, on the occasion of Romain Rolland's sixtieth birthday.
In its spirited breadth—if I may thus express myself—it
forms almost a direct prefiguration of the hymn for the
reconciliation of the nations which, ten years later, was to
bring to a close in such a moving way the opera *Friedenstag*,
which prophetically stigmatises the useless cruelty of wars.

Cut off myself from all regular contact with Romain
Rolland during his long stay in Switzerland, and knowing
that, since the occupation, he had been immobilized at
Vézelay by the ever-precarious state of his health, I wrote
to inform him of a cruel bereavement which had just
befallen me, and to ask him for news of himself. He answered
me at once in the most sensitive and understanding manner,
and added: 'Who would have said, forty years ago, that we
would be the last survivors—or very nearly—of the great
musical epoch which was then in its prime! It's true that
one must add that old master Richard II[5] with whom we
have both been friends, and whom I envy you having been
able to see again . . . I am quite sure that events have done
nothing to alter the calm and rather contemptuous independence of his character, or his inspired good nature . . . It
is some time now since I heard any of his works. But I often
pick out the old ones again on my ancient piano in Vézelay.'

From another letter, written some while later, I copy the
following lines: 'Gregor's book on Strauss, which I thank

5

you for having sent to me, is very interesting. (I confess, however, that his ideas on the "metaphysics of rococo" are to a French mind,—even one that is familiar with German thought—somewhat surprising: If Jean-Christophe had known about it, he would have added some pages to *La Révolte*). I have heard Strauss's works up to, and including, *Die Frau ohne Schatten* and *Schlagobers*, at the celebrations of his sixtieth birthday in Vienna. I would very much like to get to know *Daphne* and *Friedenstag*. I am quite sure that he would send me the scores, if it were possible to get them to me. My friendship dates, as does yours, from the last century; and on my side, it is unchanged . . .'.

Taking advantage of the fact that a mutual friend was crossing the demarcation line, I was able to send Romain Rolland the scores he desired. In September 1943 he replied to me: 'I had great joy in reading them, and especially *Daphne* which seems to me to be one of Strauss's purest and most melodious works. It's wonderful to see how that old man grows younger with each new year. And it even seems as if his music gushes from an ever fresher source. It is becoming increasingly related—without resembling them—to the great classics, of whom Wagner is still for him the last and the closest.'

*　　*　　*

Written in a more spontaneous form, the fragments from Romain Rolland's diary which are published here concern his various musical visits to Germany, the concerts and various celebrations which he attended, Richard Strauss's visits to Paris in 1900, at the time of the first performance of Gustave Charpentier's *Louise*[6] and also, some years later, at the time of the first performances, which the composer conducted, of *Salomé*. The publishers of this book, in agreement with the families of the two people concerned, have thought it preferable to postpone publication of some passages of the text, in any case of secondary importance, in which various people are mentioned, some of whom are still alive, as they rightly considered that the Romain Rolland we knew and admired at the time of his death, with his generous nature, wise in the experience and trials of life, would not have wished that his frank comments on certain private remarks made in his presence, or certain of his own personal reactions, might, against his will, risk being wrongly interpreted.

Vincent d'Indy as early as 1897, had told me in Frankfurt and Mannheim where we met, what a high opinion he had of Richard Strauss and had advised me to visit him if I should have an opportunity during my stay in Germany for my studies; but there is no doubt, as we shall see, that his reservations with regard to the subject matter of *Salomé* and spirit of Oscar Wilde's literature were no less genuine than those of Romain Rolland himself. But as in his case, too, more often than it is generally believed, musical considerations took precedence over all others, he did not hesitate to ask his pupils at one of his composition courses at the *Schola*, which I was then attending, for a detailed analysis and a reasoned appreciation of *Salomé*. The author of these lines can here bear witness that his remarks which, while freely expressing certain reservations about the libretto, paid tribute to the intense life, to the dramatic power of the music, and to the mastery of the orchestration, did not expose him to any criticism. André Messager, Gustave Charpentier, Alfred Bruneau, Claude Debussy, Gabriel Pierné, Alfred Bachelet, Paul Dukas, Maurice Ravel, and others too, who, from the very beginning, had come under the sway of Strauss's exceptional temperament, continued to take an interest in and follow the inintermittent production of the author of *Der Rosenkavalier*. Rolland, from his very first reading of the score which, as will be seen, he was only to hear in the theatre very much later, was able to estimate this work at its true worth. He subsequently did the same with *Elektra, Ariadne auf Naxos, Die Frau ohne Schatten* and *Die ägyptische Helena*. It would have been interesting to have known his opinion of the evolution of Richard Strauss's work during these last twenty years, of the influence

7

of the Mozartian spirit which came little by little to add itself so curiously to that Wagnerian ascendance which he never repudiated. I am thinking of *Arabella,* of *Die schweig-same Frau,* of *Die Liebe der Danae,* of *Capriccio,* and above all of the astonishing series of 'training exercises' or 'posthumous works'—as Richard Strauss called them—written in Switzerland since 1944. Side by side with the *Suites* for wind instruments[7] the *Concerto* for oboe, the *Duet Concertino* for clarinet and bassoon, full of brilliant freshness, and the four Late Songs for voice and orchestra, but outshining them all, we recall most vividly the *Metamorphosen,* that profound meditation for twenty-three solo string instruments, that review of a whole lifetime, of the misfortunes of the world. No one would have felt more keenly than Romain Rolland the moving grandeur, the lofty kinship with Beethoven, so apparent in that heart-rending and at the same time resigned peroration which is a masterpiece.

The essays which follow the *Diary* in the present volume, reproduced by kind permission of Hachette, the publishers, form part of the collection *Les Musiciens d'Aujourd 'hui* (*Musicians of Today*) which appeared in 1908. They will enable the reader to appreciate with what perspicacity Romain Rolland knew, even as long ago as that, how to 'place' Richard Strauss's message in contemporary music, but not without questioning certain of its aspects. As to the pages on *Romain Rolland et la Musique* which the publishers have kindly added as an appendix, they were written shortly after Romain Rolland's death for a special number of *La Revue Musicale,* the publication of which has been postponed to a date still undecided.[8] It seemed to me preferable to leave them as they are, their sole aim being to remind readers of the *Cahiers* how much music and great musicians of all epochs owe to the sensitive fervour of the author of *Jean-Christophe.*

Finally, it would surely have been a supreme consolation to Romain Rolland to see the ample evidence which Richard Strauss provided of his attachment to France, once he really knew that country—an attachment which continued to the end of his long life. For Romain Rolland had, not so long before, contributed so much to the correction of some of Richard Strauss's preconceived ideas, and certain hastily formulated youthful opinions on this subject—as will be seen in the *Letters* and the *Diary*. Richard Strauss returned to Paris several times before the war in order to conduct his works both in the theatre and the concert hall, and it was with regret that during the Exhibition of 1937 he was obliged for the first time, as a result of an unfortunate attack of 'flu, to give up taking part in the German week and to hand over to his friend and favourite interpreter, Clemens Krauss, the conducting of *Der Rosenkavalier* and *Ariadne auf Naxos* at the Théâtre des Champs-Elysées. When, in June 1939, the deterioration in the international situation which he had been fearing for a long time, prevented him from conducting the 100th performance of *Salomé* at the Paris Opéra and from being present at the first performances of *Daphne* and *Friedenstag*, for which the rehearsals were far advanced, he nevertheless did go to Luxembourg in order to preside at a Gabriel Fauré competition, honouring the memory of one of our great musicians, whose support at the time of the first performances in Paris of *Heldenleben* and *Salomé* he had not forgotten. It was in France, in a château in the vicinity of Versailles, that Richard Strauss set his two last works for the theatre, which were written during the last war: the divertissement, *Verklungene Feste* based on pieces by Couperin which he had orchestrated, and the remarkable *Capriccio*, so sensitive and lively, the action of which takes place at the time of the *Guerre des Bouffons*[9] and is the occasion for a series of pastiches which are treated with astonishing virtuosity. It was to France that, in 1944, he presented the original manuscript score of his *Alpensinfonie* at present in the collection of the musical section of the Bibliothèque Nationale, as a token of gratitude to our government for having restored to him certain manuscripts which had remained in Occupied France . . .

From 1945 onwards he stayed in Switzerland, successively

in Baden, Lausanne and Montreux, and only left this voluntary retreat once in order to take part in a festival organised in London, in October 1947, by his friend, Sir Thomas Beecham, during which he conducted two concerts. On the eve of his eighty-fifth birthday he was preparing to attend and to take part in the celebrations given in his honour in May 1949 in Paris by the Opéra, the Société des Concerts du Conservatoire, and Radiodiffusion Française, during which *Friedenstag*, which remains one of his greatest works, was performed in France, at the same time as it was in Brussels. Ill-health prevented him at the last moment from realizing his desire. In the letter in which he begged me to express to everyone his great regret at finding himself obliged, against his will, to follow the advice of his doctors, he expressed this wish: 'The fact that the broadcast of *Friedenstag* happens to coincide with the meeting of the Foreign Minister's Conference seems a sign of destiny, and I want to consider it as a good omen that my artistic vision of 1938, conjuring up that peace so much desired, which would give happiness to everyone, can radiate over the world from the city of light that is Paris.'

This idea of peace between men was, as it was with Romain Rolland, one of the principal preoccupations of Richard Strauss during all his long life. He was expressing it already in the text of his first musical drama, *Guntram*. On his return to Bavaria he went back to it again,—a few moments before the heart-attack which was to carry him off on 8th September, 1949,—in a letter destined for Monsieur André François-Poncet. Here is the text, as it was sent to him by Dr. Franz Strauss, the composer's son, in accordance with his father's wishes: 'Your Excellency, Allow me to express to you the profound satisfaction which I felt on learning that you, one of the most deserving of Europeans, are to assume the office of High Commissioner in Germany. You have devoted a considerable part of your life's work to the Franco-German Entente, and it is for me, in the evening of my own existence, a comforting thought to know that you are invested with that office, so heavy with responsibilities. I am, unfortunately, ill, and cannot tell you as fully as I should have liked all that fills my heart when I think of Germany, of France, of the future of Central Europe. My thoughts on this subject have always been linked with yourself, and it is to you that my hopes were attached during all the catastrophic years that we have lived through. I would like to talk to you about all this at greater leisure. I hope that one day soon you will find your way again to Garmisch, where we were so happy to welcome you and your wife during the First Olympiad.'

Thus ended an existence entirely devoted, as was that of Romain Rolland, to serving great ideas, to creating great works. Thanks to this glorious privilege, the memories of the authors of *Friedenstag* and *Jean-Christophe*, who all their lives knew how to defend noble causes in all sincerity, are assured of survival, and of being honoured with men's gratitude. May this certainty soften the sorrow of their families, and of those who were their friends, and who often benefitted from their valuable advice . . . Through their messages, which are for us of universal validity and which faithfully reflect their personalities, they remain alive amongst us . . .

GUSTAVE SAMAZEUILH

NOTES

1. *Lettres à Malwida von Meysenbug*. Edited by Rolland's widow, published in *Cahiers Romain Rolland* (Paris, Albin Michel, 1945).
Malwida von Meysenbug was a German Huguenot, novelist, playwright and critic, and a friend of Wagner and Nietzsche, with whom Rolland had started to correspond after meeting her in Rome towards the end of her life. Louïs Gillet (1876-1943): Art historian.

2. Alexander Ritter (1833-1896). He married Richard Wagner's niece Franziska, and founded the *Rittersche Tafelrunde* (Knights' Round Table) for the propagation of the new German music. Himself the author of two operas—*Der faule Hans* and *Wem die Krone?*, he first met Strauss in 1883 when the latter was working under Hans von Bülow at Meiningen.

3. *Benvenuto Cellini* was Berlioz' first opera, produced in Paris in 1838; *Briséis,* an unfinished opera by Emmanuel Chabrier, of which the one completed act was performed at the Paris Opera, after his death, in 1899. *Istar,* by Vincent d'Indy, is a set of Symphonic Variations on the Babylonian legend of Ishtar, descriptive of her descent into limbo shedding her garments as she went, each variation representing the successive stages of her disrobing. A peculiarity of the work is that the theme does not appear until the end. It was first performed in Brussels in 1897.

4. Antoine Mariotte (1875-1944), conductor and composer and a pupil of Vincent d'Indy, had written an opera *Salomé,* on Oscar Wilde's original French text which, although not produced (in Lyons) until 1908 (i.e. three years *after* the *Salomé* of Richard Strauss) was actually written earlier, as the composer was able to prove after having been accused of plagiarism, unjustly as it turned out. See also *Letter* from Strauss to Rolland of 5.5.'09-[p. 89].

5. Richard Strauss, who succeeded Richard Wagner.

6. *Louise* was Strauss's favourite French opera, which he much preferred to *Pelléas.* When Rolland objected that *Louise* was crude and meretricious in comparison, Strauss replied: 'But, my dear friend, that's Montmartre. The French are like that. Great gestures, fine words, exaggeration and rhetoric. That is the picture we have of you in Germany; and very good and very true it is too. Every people has its faults. These are yours . . .'. [See *Diary* March 5th, 1900, p. 128].

7. The reference is to the two Sonatinas for 16 wind instruments No. 1 in F. (1943) and No. 2 in E flat (1944-5).

8. The *Revue Musicale* suspended publication between 1940 and 1946, and I have been unable to trace any Special Number devoted to Romain Rolland.

9. Name given to the feud which divided the partisans of French and Italian opera in the eighteenth century, and was brought to a head by the production in Paris in 1752 of *La Serva Padrona* by Pergolese. Rameau and his followers represented the French school, while J. J. Rousseau and the Encyclopaedists favoured the Italian.

PART I

Correspondence

I

Correspondence

To RICHARD STRAUSS

76, Rue Notre-Dame des Champs.
Sunday, 14th May (1899).

Dear Mr. Strauss,

I was obliged to come back to Paris for my work earlier than I had expected, and it was a grief to me not to be able to go to your concert at Düsseldorf. But I have just persuaded the *Revue de Paris* to send me there as correspondent, and I shall have the pleasure of seeing you and hearing your compositions at the end of this week. I hope to be able to chat with you a little. Since I met you in Berlin I have been living with your thoughts every day, and I think I have progressed towards their inner meaning. I want to clear a way for the Heros[1] whom your imagination has created and with whom my heart is in sympathy.

Yours very sincerely,
ROMAIN ROLLAND.

To ROMAIN ROLLAND

Marquartstein, Oberbaiern.
27th July, 1899.

Dear Monsieur Rolland,

Your interesting letter, and the kind invitation to take part in the Congress with which you honoured me, gave me great pleasure; I am happy to put my poor capacities at

15

your disposal and at the disposal of your distinguished colleagues.[2] Thank you so much for having thought of me. I wish your splendid and most disinterested venture the greatest success. There is *a great deal* to be discussed and even more *to be done* in order that our art may be developed in a really profitable way. The reform of our theatres, the theatrical repertory which no longer feeds itself on anything but established values and speculative routine! The encouragement of general culture in musical academies, where so many musicians of working-class origin are being educated, and so on! It would also be extremely profitable if Richard Wagner's ideas of reform, which have as yet unfortunately so little hold on our artistic life, but which nevertheless have been given expression and put into effect in such an exemplary way in the festivals at Bayreuth, should find fresh impetus in Paris. I consider the invitation to collaborate on these lines with my distinguished French colleagues a great honour: you can certainly count on me!

I can't remember at the moment if I have already thanked you for your extremely fine article, full of feeling and so true, which appeared in the periodical.[3] I think I did. If not, let me assure you today that never, so far, has a critical study of my personality and of my works touched me in such a beneficial way. Doubly beneficial, since your article combines in a most excellent way an undeniable heart-felt kindred feeling with the most acute critical understanding and the clearest artistic judgment. It is also a real pleasure, and one that is unfortunately all too rare, to be able for once to learn something from a friend. I only know one other man to whom I owe the same gratitude: he is the General Secretary of our new Society of Composers, Friedrich Rösch, who is a man highly cultured in philosophical and artistic matters, whom Vincent d'Indy also greatly appreciates, as I know.

I am awaiting more news from you with interest, and I also hope to bring an appreciable contribution to your Congress (perhaps in collaboration with Friedrich Rösch whom I've just mentioned to you?)

But which other German musicians should take part in it? Meanwhile, I send you my most cordial greetings, and remain your sincerely devoted

RICHARD STRAUSS.

When an opportunity arises give my regards to M. d'Indy. In September I shall conduct Saint-Saëns' *Samson and Dalila* in Berlin.[4]

*   *   *

(Postmark: 1900)

Cher Monsieur,

If you will allow me, I shall come to luncheon with you at your house tomorrow, Thursday, at about 12.30 p.m.

Yours,
RICHARD STRAUSS.

To RICHARD STRAUSS

Monday, 27th May (1901).

Dear Friend,

My thoughts have been drawn to you by some concerts which Nikisch has just conducted here, and in which he gave several of your works, *Till Eulenspiegel* amongst others. I am struck by the spirit, the zest and the sense of the theatre which your music has. What a pity that you can't write musical comedies and get them performed! I would love you to have a sort of German *Pantagruel* in which you could find employment for that force of laughter and humour which is, perhaps, the rarest thing in the world in light music.

I should very much like to know all about your new works. Of all the composers of Europe you are—I say it sincerely—the one whom I appreciate and admire the most at the moment; and I am very anxious to know in what way your thought and your art are going to develop. In Paris it is impossible to keep up with German musical publications—you would be very kind if you would tell your

17

publisher to send me one or other of your new compositions from time to time—those which you value the most. I shall write about them in the *Revue d'histoire et de critique musicale*, of which I am one of the directors.

Won't you be coming to Paris next winter? I no longer dare mention this year, for the season is practically over. In any case we have been overwhelmed with concerts conducted by German Kapellmeisters, most of whom were not particularly interesting. Each one felt himself obliged to give a new interpretation of the classics, and a different dumb-show. There have also been attempts to convert us to Brahms: there was some resistance; but the public is so snobbish that one can expect anything. I hope that you are continuing your campaign, by means of banter and force, against the *Widersacher des Helden*.[5]

Yours affectionately,
ROMAIN ROLLAND.
162, Boulevard Montparnasse.

To ROMAIN ROLLAND

Charlottenburg, Knesebeckstr. 30.
29th May, 1901.

Dear Friend,

Heart-felt thanks for your kind letter: I am sending you herewith the programme of the musical festival at Heidelberg; in it you will find the names of the best young composers which Germany has at the present time. It would be delightful if you could come to Heidelberg!

Perhaps *Béatrice et Bénédict*, which is to be performed on 5th June at Karlsruhe, would also interest you, as well as the art exhibition at Armstadt, which is also very near.

I shall be at Heidelberg from Friday, 31st May onwards, and I shall be staying with Professor Philipp Wolfrum[5a] (the conductor of the Festival). I think that it is going to be very interesting; do come!

I finished this winter a fairly sizeable comic opera in one act: *Feuersnot*. The first performances of it will be given in

Dresden and in Vienna during November. I am having sent to you the latest of my works to appear.

Good-bye then until, I hope, Heidelberg: I can recommend the Hotel Victoria there to you.

My best wishes to your wife.

Your faithfully devoted,
RICHARD STRAUSS.

To RICHARD STRAUSS

Saturday, 1st June, 1901.

Dear Friend,

On the spur of the moment, when I received your letter, I rushed to the post office and sent a telegram to M. Wolfrum to tell him that I was coming. But a minute later I was forced to consider some engagements which detain me in Paris, and to send another telegram cancelling the first one. How annoyed I am not to be able to spend those four or five splendid days of music with you! If only I had known the date of the concerts earlier! I would certainly have come—Well, regrets don't help—one must try to be more fortunate another time.

Thank you for your nice letter. Thank you for your charming *Lieder,* which I have already looked at, and in which I rediscover what I love most in you. I see from the dates that they are May flowers and September fruits; and they really are fresh and fragrant like the two seasons. How I love the tenderness and melancholy of *Rückleben* and *Winterweihe*! But so far I have only skimmed through both collections. They exude a breath of youth—the most beautiful of all beautiful things—'*gioventú primavera della vita*'. I greatly hope you will have it always. As for me, I've made up my mind to lose it only with my life.

Good-bye, I hope we shall meet soon. I am pleased with the news you give me about this comic opera which you have composed. I should like to succeed in ridding myself for a year of all the ties which hold me here, in order to live in Berlin and everywhere in Germany where there is music. But so long as one has not achieved success one cannot leave the battlefield; I must stay in Paris because of articles to be written, campaigns to be launched, plays to be acted. Patience! I shall surely succeed in freeing myself.

Please give my kindest regards to Dr. Wolfrum, and I hope he'll forgive the cavalier way in which I treated him.

Yours affectionately,
ROMAIN ROLLAND.

162, Boulevard Montparnasse.

What must one do in order to belong to the *Allgemeinen Deutschen Musikverein?*[6]

To ROMAIN ROLLAND

(Telegram)   (Postmark: 13th January, 1902).
Rolland, Paris.
162, Boulevard Montparnasse.

Am conducting *Feuersnot* tomorrow, Frankfurt, Opernhaus, Wednesday *Heldenleben* Karlsruhe STRAUSS.
(In French)

To RICHARD STRAUSS

Sunday, 16th February (1902).

Dear Friend,

Thank you so much for your charming *Lieder*, which I have just been enjoying. I don't suppose you want me to read the score of *Feuersnot* or discuss it until I've heard it.—But I have read it, and I shall speak about it all the same, just to punish you. Dukas has lent me the score. (Do you know Paul Dukas? He's the best French composer after d'Indy. I consider him greatly superior to our friend Charpentier. Do try to read the score of his Symphony in C, and his piano sonata; I should be surprised if they don't give you pleasure)—Well, I've read the score of *Feuersnot*, and I was entranced. I don't know what they say about it in Germany, and I would very much like to know. But you can take it from me: it is greatly superior to *Guntram*, and equal to your best works, and what's more—it has a richness, zest, and joy, which are infectious. A thing which surprises and amuses me in you is the way certain musical phrases are closely linked with you; you carry them about every-where, in the same way that one bears everywhere the same face, the same forehead, the same eyes: it seems that certain phrases *are you*. I've never seen this to such an extent in other composers. I was also very amused by the allusions of 'hehre Herrscher der Geister', and of 'böser Feind, den triebt Ihr mit aus, der stellt sich Euch immer auf's Neue zum Strauss'. What did the 'Reich in der Isargau' think about it?[7] I'm sorry that the niceties of the local dialect make it a bit difficult for me to understand the text. If there are any other allusions in the text or in the music, do put me a bit on their track, won't you. I well know that you're not fond of writing; but you could really make a little effort for me. I assure you that you won't very often find a foreign friend who likes your works so much, and who understands them, in so far as it's possible for anyone, especially a foreigner, to understand you.

If *Feuersnot* were to be performed in about April or May, I should very much like to be notified a month in advance. I need to make arrangements with the *Revue de Paris* for these little trips, and I can't do it at a moment's notice.—If a performance of *Feuersnot* or a recital of some of your new works could roughly coincide with the date of the Rhine festival or the Beethoven concerts at Bonn, I should be pleased. I must have the pretext of an article in order to get away from Paris, where I am held by so many things. Where and when will the youth festival of German music be this year?

Good-bye for the present. You are a fortunate man. You have joy in you.

Your affectionate friend,
ROMAIN ROLLAND.

162, Boulevard Montparnasse.

I know that you are apt to dismiss old music when people talk to you about it—it seems a bit musty-dusty and pedantic to you. But I wish you would look at—if you don't know it—a *Biblical Sonata* by Johann Kuhnau: 'Saul's fury, soothed by David's harp'. It's a descriptive poem of admirable audacity and intensity of expression. It dates from 1700. It has just been published in the *Denkmäler deutscher Tonkunst* (*J. Kuhnau: Klavierwerke*).

To ROMAIN ROLLAND

Posen, 18th February, 1902.

Dear Friend,

If I haven't written to you, it's not from laziness, but because I'm terribly busy with my work as a conductor, with my journeys, with concerts of new works in Berlin, all of which genuinely give me no respite. All the same, I am taking advantage of a little free time, before a concert at Posen, to give you the information which you require.

I am really delighted that you like *Feuersnot*. The first performance in Berlin will take place in March or, at the latest, at the end of April; after that it will remain in the repertory and be performed once a week until June.

On 19th and 20th May (Whitsun) I am conducting Liszt's *Faust-Symphony* at the Rhine Festival at Düsseldorf; the programme will also include the B minor Mass of Bach and other works. The Assembly of Musicians at Crefeld will take place from 7th-10th June. Programme: Liszt's *Christus*, Mahler's Third Symphony, works by Schillings, Hausegger, Thuille, Alexander Ritter, etc. If you can manage to come to Düsseldorf at Whitsun, then to Berlin at the end of May (*Feuersnot*), then to Krefeld on your way back, you will have heard a great deal of modern German music, and you'll have material for three books on the subject.

Could you persuade M. Dukas to send me his Symphony (the score)? It is so difficult to find French scores for reference.

22

Apart from the drinking songs, there are no other allusions in *Feuersnot*.

Here are the drinking songs:

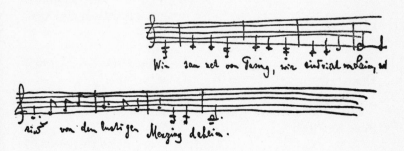

This is also a reminiscence of the giant's motif in *Das Rheingold*. And then:

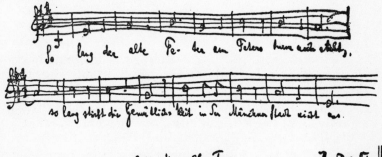

(Translations)

1. We do not come from Pasing, we don't come from Laim, we are from gay Memzing.

2. As long as old Peter remains at Peter's tower, good humour in the town of Munich is not dead.

3. Good-morning, Mr. Fischer, Mr. Fischer, good-morning.

That's enough for today.

Good-bye till we meet in May. At Düsseldorf, Berlin, Krefeld. My warmest wishes to yourself and your dear wife.

Yours,
RICHARD STRAUSS.

*　*　*

(Postmark: 27.III.1903)

Dear Friend,

I am very ill and I cannot go out.

But I hope to see you at the rehearsal, Saturday 9 a.m. (new theatre).

Yours sincerely,
RICHARD STRAUSS.

C/o Mr. W. Rosenberg,
57, Boulevard des Batignolles.
(In French)

*　*　*

Julius Bard Verlag

Berlin W.
23rd June, 1903
Bülowstrasse 88.

Dear Sir,

The undersigned publishing house has the honour to inform you, in this letter, of a new and important venture.

A series of monographs on aesthetics and biographies of musicians will shortly be published periodically under the editorship of Mr. Richard Strauss, Conductor to the Court.

All manner of questions concerning musical aesthetics, the characteristics of the great masters of the art of music, as well as monographs on the towns which music has made famous, will be presented in this series in an up-to-date way, and set forth in a form which is accessible to the general public.

The volumes in this series will be of the same importance as those in the *Die Kunst* series, which is published by the same firm under the editorship of Richard Muther (approximately 60–80 printed pages, small 8vo).

24

We, the undersigned, take the liberty of asking you, Sir, to collaborate in this series. If you agree, when sending your assent and if possible by return of post, would you be kind enough to send us a choice of themes about which you would envisage writing; could you also tell us if the MSS could be delivered before the autumn?

Hoping shortly to receive a favourable reply,

We remain, my dear Sir,

Yours faithfully,
RICHARD STRAUSS,
Editor of the Series,
Julius Bard Verlag, E.

My honoured friend! Would you feel like letting me have a short volume (Royalties 400 marks)? *Paris, City of Music*,[8] would be a splendid theme, or any other fine thing that's in a spirit of progress!

If you write the book in French, we will have it translated. Kindest regards.

Yours,
RICHARD STRAUSS.*

*　　*　　*

(Post Card)
Marquartstein, Oberbaiern.

9th August, 1903.

Dear Friend!

Agreed: *Paris* in April or May 1904. It would be very good with original illustrations. I will inform the publisher, and am waiting for your decision as soon as possible.

All best wishes

Yours,
RICHARD STRAUSS.
Since yesterday Doctor honoris of the
University of Heidelberg.

(In French)

---

*These lines in R. Strauss's handwriting, are added at the foot of the letter, which is typed.

25

B*

To RICHARD STRAUSS

Thursday, 10th November, 1904.

Dear Friend,

You will probably be visited in the near future by a charming Parisian concert artist, Madame Wanda Landowska, who is going to give two piano and harpsichord recitals at the Königliche Hochschule on 19th and 26th November. Don't let the words 'piano' or 'harpsichord' frighten you! Firstly, the pianist (or harpsichord player) is extremely pretty, which doesn't do any harm. And she is very intelligent and well-read. The programmes for both these concerts are rather original. The first is devoted to French and Italian harpsichord masters of the eighteenth century; especially Couperin, whom Madame Landowska likes and understands particularly well. The second is a 'sequence of voltes, laendler and waltzes" from William Byrd and Praetorius down to the present day. Do you know what you should do? You should give her one of your own waltzes with which to end her programme! I commend Madame Landowska to your good offices. I don't think she knows anyone in Berlin. She is very well-known here, where she often plays at the concerts at Vincent d'Indy's *Schola cantorum.*[9]

I would be very pleased to have a word from you giving me your news. Are you coming to Paris to conduct your *Sinfonia domestica?* At the moment I am writing a novel about a musician's life.[10] The first volumes have already been published; I don't remember now if I sent them to you.

Do you know Albéric Magnard's works?[11] His Third Symphony has just been played at Chevillard's, and is altogether interesting. Together with Dukas and Debussy he appears to me to be the most original of young French composers; and perhaps there's something stronger and more trenchant about him than the other two. He has already composed a great deal: an opera, *Guercoeur,* three Symphonies, a Quintet, a Quartet which was performed last year at the Société Nationale, symphonic poems, a Sonata for piano and violin, etc. I would like particularly to draw your attention to him, if you don't know him.

I also wanted to ask you if you have ever had any relations with Hugo Wolf. Don't you like his *Spanisches Liederbuch* and his Lieder to Michelangelo's poetry? What, according to you, is most interesting in the young German school?

Good-bye, dear friend, I hope we shall meet soon. Why aren't you in a more southern part of the world! I would go and visit you. But the winters in Paris make me suffer as it is, and I'm afraid of your climate.

Yours affectionately,
ROMAIN ROLLAND.

162, Boulevard Montparnasse.

*　　*　　*

Monday, 29th May, 1905

My dear Friend,

I didn't see you again at Strasbourg, and I regretted it. I didn't want to bore you by talking to you again about the luncheon with Schweitzer (who is, moreover, an interesting man, a fine type of Alsatian: he would have shown you in the old Bach the father of programme music).

As to your *Sinfonia domestica,* I didn't want to say anything to you about it after the rehearsal which I attended: to tell the truth (I always want to do so with you: perhaps it'll be a change for you from the majority of your friends), I was rather shocked by your 'programme': it prevented me from judging the work itself. It was only in the evening, at the concert, that I really heard it, forgetting the whole programme; and I can tell you that then it seemed to me the most perfect and the most unified work of art which you have written since *Tod und Verklärung,* with a quite different richness of life and art. The first part in which the themes are stated is perhaps rather dry and schematic; but the Adagio is wonderful; and above all the Finale is full of a joy and breadth such as you have rarely attained, and which I can find nowhere else in contemporary music.

But, if you are going to have the work performed in Paris, believe me, don't publish the programme. What's the use of the programme, which diminishes the work and makes it puerile? One can so well do without it. It's quite enough to call it *Sinfonia domestica*, without any other indication. It's a regular symphony. You're quite at liberty to draw up whatever programme you like. But why publish it? In a programme one only has some rather mediocre *facts*. What makes the work interesting is not the expression of those facts, but powerful internal forces which those facts conjure up. The programme can only distract one's attention, and falsify the character of the work. The longer I live, the more I believe that a man like you, who is the foremost symphonist of Europe, should definitely give up these analytical programmes, and that would not prevent your music from being most strictly, most scruplously realistic, nor would it prevent it from depicting precise feelings and scenes. It's up to other people to understand you if they can. Let music keep its mystery. Let the sphinx keep its smile.

You are very fortunate to have such joy in you. I am pleased. The *Sinfonia domestica* seems to me to mark more definite progress than *Feuersnot*.

Yours affectionately,
Romain Rolland.

162, Boulevard Montparnasse, Paris.

What, actually, is *Taillefer*, which I see mentioned in the catalogues?[12]

But, between ourselves, isn't German music 'in a bad way' (as we say here). I was very disappointed by Mahler's Symphony.[13] Which contemporary compositions do you consider interesting? I have the greatest desire to do justice to German works; but I must confess that I find very few being produced at the moment that are worthy of interest. It would be very kind of you to point out to me those of which you have a high opinion.

28

To ROMAIN ROLLAND

Marquartstein, Oberbaiern.
5th July, 1905.

Dear Friend!

Many thanks for your letter. Perhaps you are right so far as the programme of the *Domestica* is concerned; you agree entirely with G. Mahler, who completely condemns the very principle of programme music. But firstly, I have not attached any programme to the *Sinfonia domestica*, and secondly, I think that you are yourself rather mistaken about the aim of such a programme.

In my opinion, too, a poetic programme is nothing but a pretext for the purely musical expression and development of my emotions, and not a simple *musical description* of concrete everyday facts. For that would be quite contrary to the spirit of music. But so that music should not lose itself in pure abstractions and drift in limitless directions, it needs to be held within bounds which determine a certain form, and it is the programme which fixes these bounds. And an analytic programme of this kind should be nothing more than a starting-point. Those who are interested in it can use it. Those who really know how to listen to music doubtless have no need for it.

I shall gladly take your advice not to provide any programme in Paris. But do you think that the Parisian public is sufficiently mature to listen to a symphony which last three-quarters of an hour without landmarks pointing the way?

Now, a request: you know that I have finished a *Salomé*, adapted from Oscar Wilde. The composition concerned is a setting of a French text. Oscar Wilde originally wrote *Salomé* in French, and it is his original text which I want to use for my composition. I cannot entrust this work to a translator, but I wish to preserve Wilde's original, word for word; that is why the musical phrases must be adapted to the French text. When I have finished it, who will be able to check that I haven't done violence to the French language? I am enclosing a sample with this letter: from the alterations you

29

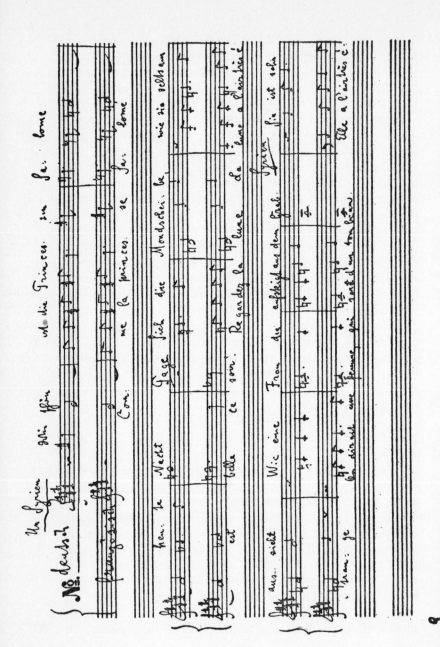

30

31

will be able to see whether I have grasped the stresses in French correctly.

Another question: when singing in French, must mute syllables at the end of words be stressed? Com*me*, princes*se*, or can one stress them as one likes? Sometimes stress them and sometimes not? Can one substitute for *Comme la princesse Salomé est belle ce soir* (the original) '*Comme est belle ce soir, la princesse Salomé ! !*'

Or even by: *Comme elle est belle ce soir, la pr. S!*

My best thanks in advance, and warmest wishes.

Yours sincerely,
Dr. RICHARD STRAUSS.

*   *   *

To RICHARD STRAUSS

Sunday, 9th July, 1905.

Dear Friend,

Thank you for your nice letter. The mute e̲ is one of the great difficulties of the French language. One must really be careful not to eliminate it: it is one of the principal charms of our poetry; but it is very rare for a foreigner to have a real feeling for it. It's not so much a sound as a resonance, an echo of the preceding syllable, which vibrates, hovers, and gently dies away in the air.

Because it is credited with having a uniform quantity, and one which is equal to the preceding syllable, the mute e̲ is considered monotonous. But it is nothing of the kind: it is part of the music of our language; it gives, as it were, an 'aura' to the word; it surrounds it with a liquid atmosphere. If you take it away, there's nothing left but the dry bones:

'On dirait un' femm' . . . '
'Ell' ressemble a un' petit' princesse᷅'

That's no longer French, it's slang. Of course, it would be even worse to stress the mute e̲ too heavily than to do away with it. These are very delicate shades, all in half tones.

32

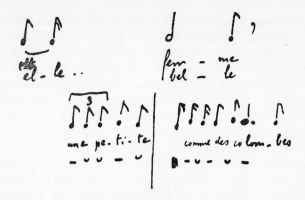

As to the rest of your declamation, it seems to me to be very good.

Unfortunately, I am leaving Paris for a few months; and I am going to shut myself up somewhere in the mountains in order to write a book; otherwise I would gladly have offered to look through your French text. When leaving I would have told you of other French writers who, like me, would have been glad to help you. But everyone is going away for the holidays now, and will only be back in October. If you have other difficulties which are holding you up, please do tell me: it will be a pleasure for me to reply to you.

If you have not already got the score, I urge you most strongly to get hold of *Pelléas et Mélisande* by Claude Debussy, the music of which follows Maeterlinck's text very closely indeed—or the *Chansons de Bilitis,* also by Debussy, settings of three poems by Pierre Louÿs. They are marvels of 'speaking' French in music, and true models of their kind, whereas the declamation of Bruneau and Charpentier is constantly incorrect, heavy, with no connection with true French pronunciation—I mean, with the beautiful language of graceful conversation, which must be the language of your *Salomé,* as of Debussy's *Pelléas.* Do order these works from Durand's in the Place de la Madeleine. They will tell you more than all the friends to whom you may have recourse; I am quite sure that they will interest you.

I am very pleased with what you tell me about programme music, and I see that I had indeed misunderstood your intention. But if the Scherzo, Adagio and Finale of the *Domestica* are or can be heard as pure music, which has its origin in definite personal emotions, don't you think that the Introduction to the *Domestica* contains a more descriptive element, in any case a more objective one? You want to set three characters, three people in it: that seems to me no longer to be reticent emotion nor pure music. In your characterisation of the man, the woman and the child, you are forced to introduce something which is alien to music; it is a rather arbitrary assumption, from which everything else follows. Whereas in *Heldenleben*, with or without a programme, the starting point is a feeling of fervour and heroic joy (no matter who the person may be in whom these passions may be stirring),—in the *Domestica*, the starting point seems to me to be less objective and lyrical, than subjective and descriptive: it looks as if at the beginning of it you wanted to sketch in a schematic way three individual figures (or at least, two: for the child has a less definite, more general character). I think that this would not be very clear if one hadn't got the literary programme for it; and that is why I like that part less than that which follows; and the more the music which follows is independent and rich, the more I like it,—right on to the Finale, brimming over with power and joy, which I think is wonderful.

The French public has made great progress in the last fifteen years. Vincent d'Indy and Albéric Magnard have made it accustomed to long symphonies.—If you do retain a programme, I think in any case that the shorter it will be, the better. For example, for the Scherzo: '*Family greetings, children's games*' (or '*The Child*'); for the Adagio: '*Night*' seems to me to be enough. For the Finale I could very well do without any indications: *Finale and Double Fugue* is, I think, preferable to any other commentary. Only the first piece, the Introduction, seems to me to need a sort of little thematic index of the three characters.

Yours affectionately,
ROMAIN ROLLAND.

162, Boulevard Montparnasse.

To ROMAIN ROLLAND*

Marquartstein, Oberbaiern,
Villa De Ahna.
15th July, 1905.

My Dear Friend,

Well, I have had the Debussy score sent to me (*Pelléas et Mélisande*), but here too I find the same unconcern about declamation which has always so much surprised me in all French music. Why do the French sing differently to the way they speak?

When speaking, do you say: le terráin or le terrain?
Then why does Debussy declaim:

Why?

Does one say then: petíte or petít(e).
Debussy writes:

It's not possible for this to be right: Elle m'entend?
I gladly accept what you say about the mute e! But this

*Letter addressed to "Monsieur Romain Rolland, poète, 162, Boulevard Montparnasse, Paris."

irregular way of pronouncing and stressing mute and weak syllables is quite contrary to the feeling of the meaning of the language.

Does one say, then: Je / ne peux pas le / dire!

or Je ne / peux pas le / dire!

Once again I ask, why do the French sing differently to the way they speak?

These are atavisms of an ossified tradition!

Here in Germany, Wagner has revived a feeling for the sense of language. France seems to me to be still bogged down in the artificiality of eighteenth-century tragedy in buskins.

Do teach me please, if you can, how one should free oneself from old habits!

With my best wishes,

Yours,
RICHARD STRAUSS.

To RICHARD STRAUSS

Sunday, 16th July, 1905.

Dear Friend,

First of all, I'm not a poet—(nor a writer, nor a critic, nor a teacher)—I am, and I only want to be, Romain Rolland. I am only a poet in so far as I can be of help to you.

Secondly, I hardly know how to reply to you. I would have too much to say, and I would be afraid of being rather harsh. May I say it in a friendly way? You Germans really are astonishing; you don't understand anything about our poetry, not a thing; and you pass judgement on it with imperturbable complacency. You may tell me that we do the same thing in France? No. We don't pass judgement on your poets, we don't know them. But it's better not to know something at all, than to think you know when you don't.

You say to me: '*Why do the French sing differently from the way they speak?*' But who are the French? The French from which part of France? And what do you mean by the French language? Which French language do you know? In Germany generally you either know the Swiss French (?) pronunciation, or the pronunciation of Montmartre, neither of which are anything but slang. Go to Laon, Noyon, Coucy, in the Ile-de-France, to the heart of the French nation, and there, in the countryside you will hear the pronunciation which you think literary and artificial, and which is none other but the real French language, the French of the race which has deservedly conquered all the other races in France, pure French, which we defend against all manner of jargons. The French language is our most beautiful work of art, and you maintain that we break it ourselves? In France we are too artistic. Our language will die only when we do ourselves.

Besides, do you yourselves write and sing in the same way as you talk? What is this text of Wilde's which you've chosen? Isn't it literary jargon as far removed from the truth as can be? And you want to give to poetry by a decadent Anglo-Belgian[14] the realistic declamation of the slang of Montmartre? You must be logical. If you have to make a dauber from Montmartre speak, take the accent of Montmartre. If you have a peasant from Savoy or Auvergne on the stage, take the accent of Savoy or Auvergne. But if you are depicting in music Princess Salomé (or Mélisande), who are literary creations, you should use literary accents.

I can see very well that you have no feeling for our literary French language at all. You imagine that it's like yours. Our language has no connection with yours. You have very marked stresses, very strong and continual contrasts between the – and ◡, between the strong and the weak syllable. With you, it's either all one thing, or all the other. And it's precisely in the interval which separates the – from the ◡, the f from p, that our poetry lies. It has an infinite number of shades in the half-tone—accents much less stressed than yours are, but much more varied, more supple, more flexible.

What you call 'unconcern about declamation' is suppleness and psychological truth. We have not got just one way of stressing a word, once and for all: it is stressed differently, according to the meaning of the sentence, and above all according to the character of the person who is speaking.

'*Je ne peux pas le dire*' can be stressed either:

(1) '*J́e ne peux pas le dire*' (if it's *obstinacy*)

(2) '*Je ne ṕeux pas le dire*' (if it's really *impossible*).

(3) '*Je ne peux ṕas le dire*' (if the character is tired of answering, if there is *weariness*).

Why, you ask, does Debussy stress:

'*Sélon le t́errain ét le vent*'?

Because it is the *rhythm* of the phrase and of the person who is speaking. Hasn't everyone got his own rhythm, measured by his breathing? In this case the breathing is short and rather panting.

Why:

'*Élle ne ḿentend pas?*'

In reality, there is no stress here on the word '*Elle*' (The bar-line does not mean anything.) It has to be said very quickly: Golaud is merely establishing the fact: that is why the only important word here is '*entend*'. But I imagine that if Golaud had been in love and his girl had not wanted to reply to him, the stress could have been:

'*Élle ne ḿentend pas*'

The stress on the first syllable, then continuing and growing weaker, as if discouraged, until the end.*

You will say to me perhaps that this way of stressing is arbitrary. Not in the least. There are general rules about the

---

*As to: '*Une ṕetite f́ille*'; the stress certainly is slight, even in ordinary language. (Unless one is speaking workman's slang and says: '*un' petit* '.)

38

value of words; but they are broad enough to allow each individual genius to stamp his mark on the rhythm and accentuation: and it is such individual genius which makes all French styles of any value interesting.

That should show you how extremely difficult it is for a foreigner to take note of all these shades. What do you expect? One has enough difficulty in mastering one's own mother-tongue in a lifetime. If one really knew it through and through, one would be a very great man. For the infinite number of shades in a language like the French language, which is the product of ten centuries of art and of life, are the very shades of the soul of a great people. It is very frivolous to pass judgment on it, as you do in Germany, according to a formula: '*Buskined Tragedy*'. If only you understood it, the tragedy, with or without buskins! Do read Nietzsche—he really did understand it.

At the moment you are too arrogant in Germany. You think you understand everything, and you don't take any pains to understand. So much the worse for you, if you don't understand us! We exist all the same, and we shall go on existing for a long time to come, I hope.

You see that I speak to you with complete frankness. My deep affection for you must excuse everything.

Yours.
ROMAIN ROLLAND.

To ROMAIN ROLLAND

Marquartstein.   July, 1905.

Dear Friend,

I thank you cordially for your very interesting letter, which has at last enlightened me in a satisfactory way about an error of long-standing.

How could you think that I might be vexed with you for being 'rather harsh'?

But if you think that I, like other Germans, am 'too arrogant', that is not fair. Even if I am proud of our Richard Wagner (I know very well that for young people in France that seems 'ridiculous'), I nevertheless appreciate French culture much too highly not to try to the best of my ability, to penetrate it more deeply than the average German.

Unfortunately, I don't know the language well: but I have, I dare say, learnt more than you think from French music, from the delicacy and the crystalline clarity of a score by Bizet or Berlioz; if you follow the development of my orchestral style carefully, this study which I have made must be apparent to you.

Anyway, thank you very much for your directions, which will always be for me a document of lasting value for my study of the French language. But one more request: tell me the names of those French composers whose declamation is typical and current, so that I can continue to study the differences. Gounod, Bizet, Bruneau, Charpentier?

Debussy, therefore, can serve as a model for the language? Isn't that so? Of what does the difference between his declamation and that of Bruneau and Charpentier consist? Or of Berlioz?

Is Wilde's *Salomé* in bad French? In what style should it be musically declaimed?

In my country there is *no* difference between 'good declamation' and what you call 'realistic declamation'.

In German 'she' on the strong beat of a bar is absolutely impossible. For example, in a bar of 4/4, the first and the third beat have always a necessary stress which can only be made on the radical syllable of each word. Since Wagner, of course! Before him, one didn't attach so much importance to it, so long as the melody was beautiful.

Nowadays, in order that a phrase may keep its rhythm, a melody must originate from the spoken tonic accent. Otherwise, it is better to play the phrase on the violin. This is moreover the case for almost all Brahms' Lieder, which all have instrumental melodies in them.

And now, yet once more my best thanks and kindest regards.

Yours sincerely,
RICHARD STRAUSS.

I think that *Salomé* would suit the Opéra-Comique *very well·* That is why I would like to give it the foundation of a perfect adaptation of the music to the French text. Who could help me with this?

To RICHARD STRAUSS

Hôtel Mont-Barry par
Bulle (Switzerland).   Thursday, 3rd August, 1905.

Dear Friend,

Thank you for your very friendly letter. Forgive me for not having answered it before, and for not answering it, even today; for this is only a note written in haste; in a few days' time I hope to be able to write to you more fully, and at my leisure.

During the last fortnight I was engaged in examining at the Sorbonne, where I am a professor. After that. I escaped into the mountains. Tomorrow I am going to the Wine-growers' Festival at Vevey; it is one of the most beautiful folk festivals of Switzerland, which takes place at open-air performances with crowds of from 1,500–2,000 actors and singers. The festival takes place every twenty years; and as I have some reason to believe that I shall not be at the next one, I am taking advantage of my stay here to see this one. The music is by a young composer, Gustave Doret,[15] who has talent, and who is to have a work based on a Swiss subject performed this winter at the Opéra-Comique in Paris.

You ask too many questions in your letter for me to answer them today. I will do so soon from Felsenegg (Zug), where I am going to settle down on Saturday for some weeks.

I would only like to draw your attention to the tendency— both instinctive and at the same time deliberate—that exists amongst young French musicians (and young French musical critics) to free themselves from the tyranny of the bar with fixed stresses, and to make musical rhythm as much as possible the closest possible copy of spoken rhythm. For this the model is ancient French popular melody, and above all Gregorian chant, as restored by the Benedictines of Solesmes and popularised during the last ten years in Paris by the Chanteurs de Saint-Gervais. (Do you know those Benedictine editions? There are melodic jewels amongst them of the most unrestricted freedom.) In the sixteenth century, too, one finds examples of some of our French masters, amongst others of Claude le Jeune, who set to music the verses of Baïf preserving the old metrical scanning in which he displayed admirable imagination and grace.[16] In short, I really think that the present movement for freedom of rhythm, and against the inflexible regularity of the bar, is in accordance with the old French tradition, before our music was conquered in the seventeenth century by Italianism.

I can't write any more to you today. I hope to see you soon, and remain your affectionate friend.

ROMAIN ROLLAND.

(Hôtel Felsenegg par Zug—Suisse.)

Forgive this letter written in a rush and full of crossings-out.

To ROMAIN ROLLAND

Marquartstein, Oberbaiern.   31st July, 1905.

Dear Friend,

Just a question of linguistics: do the French pronounce double vowels like *noir*, *pied*, *paupière*, *rien*, on one note or on two short notes?

How does one declaim: Babylone
                       Arabie
                       Hérodias
                       Iokanaan.

Babylone   or two accented syllables?   Babylone

        Arabie   or   Arabie

        Hérodias   or   Hérodias

        Iokanaan   or   Iokanaan?

Je baise-rai ta bou-che, Jo. Ka: na: an

or

Jo: Kana an

or

J: o· Kana an.

Do let me have some brief particulars.

Does one say: regarderai or regarderai.

Les mines de Moab?

        Moab   or   Moab?

In general, I am managing the adaptation of the text and
the transcription very well.

Could I send you the latter when it is ready, so that you

could revise it? I thank you warmly in advance, and send you my kindest regards.

Your sincerely devoted
DR. RICHARD STRAUSS.

Salome?   or Salome?   or   Salome?

Marquartstein, Oberbaiern.   2nd August, 1905.

Dear Friend,

Yesterday I again read some of Debussy's *Pelléas et Mélisande*, and I am once more very uncertain about the principle of the declamation of French when sung. Thus, on page 113, I found:

Page 115

Cheveux, cheveux, de cheveux.

For heaven's sake, I ask you, of these three ways there can all the same only be *one* which is right.

And another question:

ils viennent

ils veulent

qui ⎰ demeurent
    ⎱ annoncent
    ⎱ réservent

44

Isn't *ent* an entirely mute syllable? Does one nevertheless pronounce it in song, and if so, how?

In Debussy, on page 115, I find:

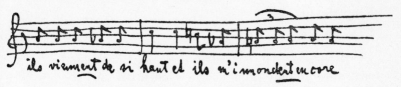

How does one pronounce here inond<u>ent</u> encore?

       inonde tencore

       innond encore, or innonde encore?

I beg you to let me have these brief particulars as well. The principle is still not very clear to me.

Has the fact of making the verse scan, which of all rhythms is the most boring and the most monotonous (it would be preferable to say that it is the opposite of rhythm) such importance in your country, or do you think it so beautiful that, in order to preserve an iambic or trochaic rhythm, you sacrifice the whole force and vigour of all the roots and radical syllables?

In Debussy, do you consider that eternal and monotonous rhythm of triplets continually on *the same note* beautiful or poetic? To my German way of thinking it's purely and simply a distortion of the language by the composer. But of course, we Germans are 'too arrogant', aren't we? I must modestly keep silence.

Kindest regards, and thanks in advance.

Yours,
RICHARD STRAUSS.

To RICHARD STRAUSS

Hôtel Felsenegg (Zug)
    Switzerland.   Wednesday, 9th August, 1905.

Dear Friend,

I shall try to reply to some of your questions. I only received your letters yesterday evening.

1. Noir is only *one* syllable. In no case should it be set to two notes.

Pied: id.

Paupière: id.

Rien: id.

2. Ils vie*nnent*,—ils veul*ent*, ils demeur*ent*,—ils inond*ent* . . . etc., must be fully pronounced. That is not only the law of French prosody, it's the law of good speech, which rules

that one should pronounce: 'ils m'i-non-de-ten-core'. No one who speaks properly will ever leave out the liaison with the *t*. (Naturally, it must be very soft and very swift, so as just to

make the mute syllable which precedes it (de) rebound.) *In no case* can one say: '*inond' encore*'.

3. *Les cheveux*.

Here, I shall make so bold as to remind you of a remark which I have made to you before about the alteration of the value of certain syllables, according to the rhythm and the emotion of the sentence in which the word is set.

The natural value of '*cheveux*' is: che-veux. But a man in love will, when saying this word, put quite a special stress

on it: 'tes che-veux'. There is a sort of slight, imperceptible quiver of the voice and lips (the stress remains very faint, what's more, even then). It's as if he were saying 'tes *chers* cheveux'—'your *dear* hair'.

You see: the great difficulty with our language is that for a very large number of words, the accentuation is variable,— never arbitrarily, but in accordance with logical or psycho-

logical reasons. When you say to me: 'Von diesen 3 (cheveux)

kann doch nur *eines richtig sein*', 'of these 3 (cheveux) *only one can be right*', what you say is doubtless true for German, but not for French. In French there are a certain number of words which have an absolutely fixed stress: they form

46

the skeleton of the language. The others are fluid and Protean; they obey and yield to circumstances which are logical, psychological, etc.

You say that you do not understand the monotony of our French rhymed hexameter. That does not surprise me at all. I don't know of any foreigner who has any suspicion of what it really is; and I would add that none of us Frenchmen have known how to make them understand it. (There are so few people, even in this country who are really sensitive to French poetry, and who know how to analyse the pleasure they derive from it.) I shall try to put you on the right track by a remark which I don't think anyone has made so far, and which, in my opinion, is the key to our traditional poetic system:

You have just seen the extraordinary power which the majority of French words have to change, to alter their stress. This characteristic enables our language to produce the most supple prose that exists. But it would be a serious obstacle to the formation of poetry, if this extreme freedom, which tends towards anarchy, were not strictly held within fixed limits. You only notice these limits, which are nothing but the framework of French verse. But we, we no longer see, or scarcely see, the framework. You have no suspicion of the infinite variety of rhythmic combinations which follow one another in the hexameters of Hugo or Verlaine. Without the law, which the spirit of the race imposes, instinctively, on itself I believe we should head straight for rhythmic prose or free poetry. You see: the strong laws of reason usually only appear in nations which need them in order to combat and curb their natural instincts, which are too strong and too dangerous. Quite recently Kipling demonstrated that the biblical hypocrisy of the English, with which one so often reproaches them, is an absolute necessity for them in order to live: without this brake all that is savage and wild in the English nature would lead the nation into the worst excesses. The wig and the strict laws of society in the age of Louis XIV were the masks and brakes which a brutal and passionate society, which was afraid of its own instincts, was obliged to wear. (Read Funck-Brentano's curious book: *L'Affaire des Poisons*: you will see what fierce passions seethed in that bewigged court.) That is really for us the interesting thing—of which you have no suspicion—about Racine's tragedies, that we find in them the same ferocity hidden beneath the same apparent politeness. You consider this artificial. And I, on the contrary, would be inclined to see in it one of the summits of human civilization: all the primitive animal nature still preserved in its purity, and veiled only by the most refined form. Well, the iron law which governs our poetry comes, I think, from the same need to bring to heel a language which is too free and too fluid, which escapes and runs away just when one thinks one grasps it.

4. The stresses for the proper names which you mention to me are rather difficult to indicate: they are foreign names, which are pronounced rarely, if ever, in France: therefore the stress has no great importance. I don't think a Frenchman has ever pronounced the name of *Iokanaan*, and you can mark it as you wish:* it is nevertheless preferable to bring out the final an. Generally speaking, we in this country are familiar with Hérodi*ade* and not Hérod*ias*. (You know that we scarcely ever aspirate the *H*; and we would pronounce *Hé* short in Hérodias, if anything; but you have every right to lengthen it, in order to accentuate the archaic uncouthness of the name.) *Arabie* forms a sort of < in a half-tint: *Arabie-Babylone* (Parisian pronounciation). *Babylone* (pronounciation of the North and East of France): you can choose.—*Moab*. (But the *o* is also lightly stressed). *Salomé*. (At any rate that

*Io in one syllable. I prefer this version:

48

is how one pronounces the name when it belongs to a contemporary. But, I repeat, the 'local colour' permits you to do what you like with these proper names. Sometimes changing their stress is a way of removing them from their natural element.)

I think that is about all that you asked me.

No, it isn't, though. I find there's still the word *'regarderai'* about the stress of which you ask me. I would refer you to the article: *cheveux,* etc. The normal and, if I may so call it, lackadaisical stress of the word is: regarderai: but it can become: regarderai, if the person speaking puts special vigour into the word. 'Je regarderai la mort en face'.

There, this time, it's the lot. You don't like Debussy's musical declamation, my friend? It's a bit flabby for my taste, too. But as refined, aristocratic, society French declamation, it is perfect. Of course, there's nothing popular about it (in any case, Maeterlinck's *Pelléas* requires a certain monotony of diction); but it has opened up the way to true French musical declamation. If you do not like this kind of recitative with its very efficient lines,* bear in mind that Wagnerian declamation seems barbarous to us—I mean, of course, when it is applied to our language. A French middle-class man, or even a working-class man, never uses those vocal leaps which one finds all the time in the *Meistersinger.* Bear in mind that I who love and always will love Wagner deeply (whether 'young people in France' consider him 'ridiculous' or not—it's young people in France who are ridiculous if they hold this opinion)—bear in mind that I myself love Wagner not *because* of his declamation, but *in spite* of it. I grind my teeth when I hear those heavy recitatives in the *Meistersinger,* which seem to me to be 'forced' (like German pronunciation) and which prevent me from hearing the superb orchestral music. I know perfectly well that I am mistaken, and that what seems false to a French-

*(It was already Monteverdi's system in his admirable *Orfeo.*)

C

man is true for a German. But you see how careful one must be in these judgments of one nation by another.

Good-bye for the present. Believe me, I remain with all my heart

Yours,
ROMAIN ROLLAND.

Don't send me your translation. I am still travelling about, and it might risk going astray. If you have any more questions to ask me, write to my Paris address (*Please forward*).

To ROMAIN ROLLAND

(Postmark: 7.IX.05.

Dear Rolland,

Would you say: vous avez juré?

or: vous avez juré?

Dansez pour moi?

or Dansez pour moi?
Is that all right?

Versez or versez?

demandez or demandez?

Would you be kind enough to give me a brief reply?

So far as the rest goes, I think I am doing my transposition quite well, for I am recomposing almost all the vocal

part, and I hope you will be pleased with your sincerely
devoted

Dr. RICHARD STRAUSS.

It must become a real French opera: not a translation ! ! !

To RICHARD STRAUSS

Hôtel Belvédère.
Mont Pèlerin-sur-Vevey (Vaud)
Switzerland.   Saturday, 9th September, 1905.

My dear Strauss,

1. 'Vous avez juré (stress on vez and ju).

2. 'Versez' (with the stress on the first syllable, if the word
is followed by other words: 'Versez encore! . . . etc.' If the
word 'Versez' ends the phrase, the stress is on the last
syllable.)

3. 'Dansez' (I would put the stress on the first syllable, but
it is not a mistake to do as you have done, and I would
reproach myself if I were to make you change your rhythm.
In the word 'dansez', the musical rhythm has every right
to carry the stress with it).

4. 'Demandez' (if the verb is followed by another word:
'que demandez-vous?' If, on the contrary, it finishes the
phrase in an interrogative way: 'Vous demandez?' the stress
would be on the last syllable.)

When you want to ask me about a stress, *tell me the whole
sentence.*

ROMAIN ROLLAND.

I shall be at this address all this month.

To ROMAIN ROLLAND

Until 30th September:
Marquartstein, Bavaria.
From 1st October:
Berlin W, Joachimsthalerstr. 17.

13th September, 1905.

Dear Friend!

I have just finished the French transcription of *Salomé*. May I once more appeal to your kindness and ask you to examine and to correct the phrases noted on the back of this,* the declamation of which I am not yet quite sure about.

Then I shall make a fair copy of the whole piano score, and I hope you will allow me to send it to you towards the end of October (where? to Paris?) before giving it to the printers. As Wilde's original text for *Salomé* is in French, I would like to achieve a quite special French edition of my opera, which does not give the impression of being a translation, but of being a real setting of the original. Will you help me with this? I think that *Salomé* would suit the Opéra-Comique perfectly.

We are leaving tomorrow for a fortnight in Northern Italy: Brescia, Verona, Vicenza, Padua, Venice (Hôtel Brittania).

With my kindest regards and thanks.

Yours,
DR. RICHARD STRAUSS.

*   *   *

Marquartstein.

29th September, 1905.

Dear Friend!

Did you get my last letter? Would you be kind enough to send me an answer as soon as possible to Berlin W., Joachimsthalerstr. 17, where I am going tomorrow.

*See illustrations pp. 55–75.

I shall probably conduct the *Sinfonia domestica* at Colonne's this winter.

Kindest regards and many thanks.

Yours,
DR. RICHARD STRAUSS.

Berlin W., 15,
   Joachimsthalerstr. 17.   23rd October, 1905.

Dear Friend,

I am sending you herewith my piano score with the French text.

Would you be kind enough to read it, and to correct in pencil everything which seems bad to you?

Would it be possible for you to send me back the score, which I would ask you to keep strictly secret and not to show to anyone, before 5th November, to the following address:

> Musikverlag Adolf Fürstner.
> Berlin W., Kronenstrasse 16?

Thank you in advance for everything! I hope you will not be too displeased with my French *Salomé!*

With my kindest regards.

Yours,
RICHARD STRAUSS.

To RICHARD STRAUSS

Sunday, 5th November, 1905

My dear Friend,

I have finished reading through your score with great attention. I can't send it back today, because it's Sunday;

53

but I'll put it in the post tomorrow, addressed to M. Fürstner.

As you doubtless won't receive it for five or six days (since it took such a long time to reach me) I am sending you at once by letter a list of my remarks, so that you can make your corrections without waiting.* On the whole, the French stresses are fairly correct; only the declamation is in general rather emphatic, and has more wide gaps for the voice than in ordinary French declamation; but there are very few real faults of stress and of pronunciation.

—And now I must tell you how much pleasure reading your work has given me. Firstly, the libretto, as you have arranged it, is admirably suited to the stage; it is at the same time picturesque, and compact, concentrated: it is a dramatic *crescendo* from beginning to end. And the music has the same qualities. It is not only always alive and brimming over, it moves towards an end, it flows towards the climax like a river to the sea. It is, without any doubt, your most powerful work from the theatrical point of view. The simplification of line and severity of construction make it have something more classical about it than its predecessors have.

May it have all the success that it merits! (Isn't it the first night tonight?) I am afraid that a good many passages of the dialogue, and the sensual ferocity of the ending, may frighten our Opéra-Comique; and I don't know how the ending can be staged. As it's impossible in the theatre to give an impression of the true horror of it, there is a risk it may arouse irony.

I hope to see you soon in Paris! Thank you for giving me your work to look at, and

Yours affectionately,
ROMAIN ROLLAND.

*As it is not possible to make a typographical transcription of Romain Rolland's phonetic and musical indications, we give here the rest of the letter in facsimile.

5 novembre 1905

p. 5. [Dans l'indication de scène :] "Un énorme escalier"
        J'aimerais mieux : "un escalier colossal."

[On aurait pu mettre les indications de
nuances et de mouvements en français, et non en
italien, puisque le texte est en français — Mais
c'est un détail.)

p. 8. 1re ligne.] Comme est belle la princesse
        Il serait mieux de dire : "Comme elle est belle, la
                                                    princesse

p. 8   6e ligne] Comme est belle !
        Ici il faut absolument : Comme elle est belle.
                    ou bien :   qu'elle est belle !

p. 9   dernière ligne en chantant] : Je ne sais pas
            Il serait plus correct d'avoir une ? ? ? ?
        Il serait plus correct, tout en laissant l'accent
sur le mot : sais, de le faire une croche, comme
les trois autres mots. La voix ne met pas d'arrêt
dans la phrase :

p. 11   Je ne suis pas digne même de dé-li-er
                    Dé-li-er est un peu trop long. En
réalité, on le prononce assez vite, avec accent sur le
            dernier : délier.

55

p. 13 (avant dernière mesure du chant)
   " Une grande foule de disciples "

; Il faut accentuer disciple et non disciple .
L'arrêt entre la 1ère et la 2e syllabe est désagréable .

   p. 16 . [Manque une note au haut de la page]

p. 19   " Qui a crié cela ? "

      Cri-é est en 2 syllabes ⌣ ‾ "

p. 21   " Nous ne comprenons . "

      Com - pre - nons beaucoup trop lourd .
   ? Il faudrait : Nous ne comprenons jamais /
      ⌣ ⌣   ⌣ ⌣ ⌣   ⌣ ⌣

p. 21 (dernière ligne du chant)

      " Le tétrarque vous prie de retourner au festin "

      Re - tourner   Accentuation très fausse .
on prononce de Retourner ., et il serait mieux
de mettre des ⌣ ⌣ ⌣ ⌣

p. 22   " Est-ce / un / vieillard ? "
      C'est une grave faute de compter ici le mot : ce
comme une syllabe ; il s'élide devant la voyelle suivante,
on prononce : Est-ç'un /

56

p. 27   « Page 5 "Oh! qu'est-ce qui va arriver ? Je suis
sûr qu'il va arriver un malheur …".

C'est un peu naïf comme expression, et je crains
que cela ne prête au sourire. Cela aurait pu être sup-
primé facilement, d'autant plus que la même formule :
"Je suis sûr qu'il va arriver un malheur" est répétée dans
le cours de la pièce, et que cela finit par avoir l'air
d'un refrain, qu'on ne prend pas très au sérieux.

p. 35 .   « Dans l'indication de mouvements de la
3ᵉ scène) : Andante ne me semble pas du tout
correspondre à Breit. Vous auriez, je crois, en français,
plus facilement l'équivalent : Large . Ne
pensez-vous pas ? -

     p. 35   "La coupe d'abominations"
        Il vaudrait mieux, compter pour 2 syllabes
la fin du mot : abominati - ons
                    ᴗ ᴗ

p. 36   "De celui qui a crié dans les déserts"
        Cri-é   doit être en 2 syllabes.
        ᴗ ᴗ

p. 37   "Où est celle qui ayant vu des hommes .. etc.
qui l'est lassée … "

Il faut supprimer le 1ᵉʳ qui : il n'est pas français,
et il n'est pas non plus harmonieux : Il faut écrire :
        "Où est celle, ayant vu des hommes . . . , qui
l'est lassée"

   (N.B. – Ne pas mettre sur les "y" de petits accents
        ou les points, comme vous en avez
            l'habitude

p.39 . [Pour l'impression :] écrire: <u>inces — tueuse</u>
et non pas : <u>ince — stueuse</u>

p.40 écrire : <u>Sei — gneur</u>
et non pas : <u>Seig — neur</u>
(id. p. 59)

p.42 [Dans l'indication de scène :]
" Narraboth : <u>toujours plus exagéré</u> "
Exagéré voudrait dire qu'il ne parle pas sincère-ment. Il faut plutôt mettre, je crois : " toujours plus ins.3?"

p.42 <u>Dernière ligne du chant</u>
" Il ressemble à une mince / image / d'ivoire.
très mal accentué. Il faut tout au contraire
appuyer ~~sur~~ la dernière syllabe de <u>mince</u> et abréger la
dernière syllabe d'<u>image</u> . Voici la prononciation seule
correcte : une <u>mince</u> image

p.42 [Dernière ligne]
" Je suis sûre qu'il est <u>chaste</u> / autant .. "
La dernière syllabe de <u>chaste</u> doit s'élider doucement
devant la voyelle suivante. On prononce :
chast' autant

p.43 " Sa chair doit être très froide, froide
comme l'ivoire "
Tous ces mots ne sont pas prononcés avec les
inflexions françaises. Ils sont beaucoup trop alourdis,
ralentis. On prononcerait : " très froide / comme l'ivoire. "

58

p. 43   " Je veu / le regar / der de / près. "

    La prononciation est mauvaise. Ce devrait être :
    Je veux / le regarder / de près. /

p. 45   " Ta mère / a - - "

    La dernière syllabe de mère s'élide nécessairement devant a ; mais comme le son n'est pas très agréable (" ta mèr' a "), il serait mieux de mettre la syllabe muette sur une note également muette :

Ta mè - re / a

p. 57   " Il n'y a rien au monde . . . "

    Quand il est possible de changer : " Il n'y a rien " en " Il n'est rien ", il vaut mieux le faire ; car le son : " Il n'y a " n'est pas très agréable en français ; et malheureusement, il revient fréquemment au cours du livret.

p. 60   " serpents qui se tortillent "

    qui se tordent, vaudrait mieux.
    Comment prononcez - vous : noirs, sur 2 notes ? c'est une seule syllabe, qu'il faut prononcer d'une façon très nette.

p. 63   : " le vermillon dans les mines de Moab, que les rois leur prennent. "

    Ce n'est pas français. Il faudrait, (si je comprends bien le sens de la phrase) : " que les rois prennent dans les mines de Moab. "

p. 69   [Pour l'impression] : écrire : Pros - terne, et non pas : Pro - sterne

59

p. 79 : Hérodias : "Il ne faut pas la regarder"

Voilà encore une formule qui revient bien souvent et qui paraît d... un peu comique. (Voir dans les ver- sieres du page et de Narraboth)

p. 80. "une femme hystérique qui va /"

que qui va est excessivement désagréable. Il faudrait : "une femme hystérique.../ qui va /"

p. 83 "Le jeune Syrien."

Il serait mieux de prononcer : Sy/ri/en

p. 91 "Je trouve qu'elle a bien raison"

Cette déclamation est un peu trop lente en français.

p. 92 "Mordez un tout / petit morceau"

Déclamation fausse. Il faut :

Mordez / un tout petit morceau /. A la rigueur, on peut séparer très légèrement : petit de : mor... mais on ne peut pas séparer : tout de : petit.

p. 94 "Aussi, c'était un voleur"

Cela voudrait dire : "C'était un voleur, parcequ'il gardait des chameaux." Je suppose que ce n'est pas le sens que vous avez voulu ; et que vous vouliez dire prenez le mot : aussi dans le sens de : également. Alors il faut dire : "C'était aussi un voleur." Ou, plus simplement : "Et c'était un voleur."

p. 96 "Aussi, c'est un très grand prophète."

Même observation : Cela voudrait dire : "C'est un très grand prophète, parcequ'il n'a rien dit contre vous." — Il faut écrire "C'est aussi un très grand prophète." Ou mieux : "Et c'est un très grand prophète."

p. 98 [Dans] 5 novembre 1908

« Il se cache, et par conséquent il y a
de grands malheurs dans le pays. »

Ce n'est pas très clair ; on ne comprend pas la
logique de la phrase.

p. 101 (1ère ligne) "Ses voi-es sont très mystérieuses"

Voi-e ne peut pas se prononcer en deux syllabes.
Il faut mettre l'e sur une note muette.

$$\frac{Voi-e}{L-L}$$

p. 104.105 . Écrire : "Il y a de grands malheurs"
et non pas : "Il y a des grands malheurs"

p. 106 Voi-es
même observation que p. 101.

p. 109 qu'Iokanaan ---

qu'Iokanaan , d'Iokanaan est un peu
– Il eût été peut-être mieux de
etc : que Iokanaan , de Iokanaan (On n'élide
les e muets devant les noms propres, en général). Mais
n'est pas une observation très importante

p. 111 [dans l'indication de mouvement]
"più tranquillo che prima"

Est-ce qu'en italien, on dit : più ... che , ou :
... di ? Je ne me souviens pas très bien, en ce moment ;
il me semble que c'est di.
(Comme il eût été mieux de mettre les indications
françaises : "Plus tranquille qu'avant.")

61

p. 120   " Le soleil deviendra noir comme un sac de poil."

Qu'est-ce que c'est que cette comparaison ?!! Est-ce que c'est oriental ? — En français, elle paraît bien saugrenue.

p. 122 . " Salomé, fille d'Hérodias "

fil — le   accentuation désagréable sur la dernière syllabe, qui devrait être comme sousentendue..

p. 138 : " Je veux qu'on | m'apporte | présentement —

A aucun prix, il ne faut conserver cette coupe de la phrase, qui est incorrecte, et prétieux [?] aux ridicule. Il faut séparer ainsi les mots :

" Je veux | qu'on m'apporte | à présent

(la dernière syllabe de apporte s'élide devant à présent)

p. 140   « quoi que cela puisse | être

Prononciation défectueuse. La dernière syllabe de puisse s'élide nécessairement devant la voyelle de être. Il faudrait :

     puisse être

ou :   puiss' être

p. 144   (Une note manque à la fin du chant
          d'Hérode, à la 2ᵉ ligne.)

p. 144   Hérode : "Non, je ne veux pas"
               Salomé : " Oui, vous avez juré."

     Il faut : "Si ! vous avez juré." Si s'oppose
à non. Oui ne s'oppose pas ; il ne fait que confirmer
ce qu'on vient de dire.

     p. 145   "la tête de cet homme"
                                          appuyé sur le muet
Trop souvent, dans la partition, revient l'accentuation (?)
qui n'est pas très correcte.

     p. 145   Hérodias : "On voit qu'elle a... me beau-
-coup sa mère."
          La phrase est un peu comique en français.
Il vaudrait mieux quelque chose ; comme : "Elle m'aime
je le vois."

(p. 147   "la tête d'une homme décapité"
(Ce n'est pas français. Littéralement, cela voudrait
dire : "La tête d'un homme sans tête." Il faut changer
cela ; cela ferait sourire. On pourrait mettre à la
place, par exemple : "La tête d'un homme, --- une
                        ou : une tête - - - - -
tête coupée. - - - : c'est une chose lourde -- "
     p. 148   "N'est-ce pas que voulez cela ?"
(Ce n'est pas français. Il faut : "N'est-ce pas que vous
voulez cela ?" (ou : "que vous la voulez")

63

p. 151   "mes pafons, mes beaux pafons"

Très grosse faute de prononciation. On prononce paon en une syllabe (& cela fait le son : pan)

p. 153   " avec vos pafons " &

Même remarque que ci-dessus

p. 161   "Qu'on lui donne ce | qu'elle demande !"

Mal accentué. Il faut :

"qu'on lui donne | ce qu'elle demande ! |

p. 163   "Je suis sûr qu'il va arriver un malheur à quelqu'un "

Encore ! Cela fait la 4ᵉ ou 5ᵉ fois. Et cette fois-ci, cette façon de parler est tout à fait comique ? Il est évident qu'il va arriver un malheur à quelqu'un puisque St Jokanaan va avoir la tête coupée. Je sais bien que ce n'est pas à Jokanaan que pense Hérode. Mais le public y pensera ; et cela a l'air d'une mauvaise plaisanterie.

p. 164-5 : " J'entends rien "

Ce n'est pas français, cela ne peut pas se dire. Il faut : "Je n'entends rien."

p. 165   "Si quelqu'un cherchait à me tuer."

Non français. Il faut : "cherchait à me tuer "

                    aussi [tuer en une syllabe]

64

p. 165 : « Je crie/rais ».

Mauvaise accentuation. Il faut : « Je crie/rais »
crie (en une syllabe)

p. 166 « Il y a un silence .. »

y (a, un) est bien désagréable, comme sonorité,
en français ; et malheureusement, ce n'est pas la seule
fois que cette forme est employée ici.

p. 166 « C'était l'épée l'é-pé-e du bour-reau »

Il faudrait ainsi partager la phrase :

« C'était l'épée | du bourreau »

De plus, on ne peut pas prononcer : épé/e . Il
faut : é/pée/
        é é
ou : é/é/
     é é é

p. 167 « Il n'ose pas le tu/er/

tuer est en une syllabe. Il est désagréable, et
correct de prononcer tu/er/ .

p. 168 « Il n'y a pas en assez morts »

?? Cela ne veut rien dire en français. Il
r changer le texte .

p. 174 : « Soulève tes paupières »
Mauvaise accentuation : Il faut : « Soulève
                                      é f

65

...174 [Dans l'indication de nuances]

"Corto e duro"

Est-ce que : Breve ne vaudrait pas mieux ?

p.175 "que la vipère rouge ne remuet-e/plus ?"

Il faut prononcer : remuet

ou

L'e muet, quand il fait suite immédiatement à une autre voyelle, s'agglomère avec elle : cela fait une pâte sonore.)

p.176 "de Hérodias"

En français, nous disons d'habitude : d'Hérodias (ou plutôt : d'Hérodiade ; car c'est ainsi que le nom est toujours écrit chez nous). Mais cela n'a pas grande importance ; car on permet beaucoup de licences dans l'orthographe et la prononciation des noms propres anciens

p.179 : " d'ivoi – re sur un.."

Cette dernière syllabe muette de ivoire, formant la 1ère note d'un triolet, est d'une accentuation incorrecte. faudrait : " d'ivoi...re / sur un so...de / d'argent /

p.181 "une musique/etrange

Il faut absolument élider la dernière syllabe de musique
· une musiqu' étrange

p.184 [une note manque, au haut de la page.]

p. 184   ne pourrai – ent éteindre`

Il faut changer cette accentuation – raient est
une seule syllabe :   ne/pour/raient/é/teindre

p. 185   [Dans l'indication de nuances]
    Più lento che prima

même observation que plus haut – Dit-on en italien :
Più che , ou Più di .

p. 188   "Cachez la lune, cachez les étoiles"
Je ne comprends pas très bien.

p. 188   [Dans l'indication de ~~ce~~ mouvement,
         au bas de la page)

"traînez ! "

Il vaudrait mieux : "traîner la voix" ; mais ce
n'est pas encore bien bon. – Ici, il serait peut-être
préférable de mettre ~~une~~ indication en italien, si vous
~~savez~~ ~~décemment~~.

    (N. B. En tout cas, ne mettez jamais
un point d'exclamation (!) après une indication . C'est
une habitude allemande, mais ce n'est jamais français ;
c'est même à ce trait que nous reconnaissons tout de suite
l'Allemand dans une lettre, ou un livre : par exemple,
quand il nous écrit : "cher Monsieur ! " (Nous écrivons :
"cher Monsieur, "]

p. 191   " Tu /es cette /femme ! "
    Tuez est en une syllabe ; Il faut :
        Tuez/ cette femme /   Ce sera,
                              d'ailleurs, beau-
                              -coup plus énergique.

67

5th November, 1905.

p. 5. (Stage direction): 'Un énorme escalier'—I would prefer: 'un escalier colossal.'

(The tempo indications and marks of expression might have been in French and not in Italian since the text is in French. But that's only a detail.)

p. 8. 5th line: 'Comme est belle la princesse' . . . It would be better to write: 'Comme elle est belle, la princesse'.

p. 8. 6th line: 'Comme est belle!' Here it must absolutely be: 'Comme elle est belle', or else: 'qu'elle est belle!'.

p. 9. (Last line of voice part): 'Je ne sais pas'. It would be more correct here, while preserving the accent on the word '*sais*', to make it a quaver, like the other three words. There is no pause for the voice in this phrase.

p. 11. 'Je ne suis pas digne même de dé/li/er'. Dé-li-er is rather too long. Actually, it is pronounced rather quickly, with the accent on the last syllable: délier.

p. 13. (Penultimate bar of voice part): 'Une grande foule de disciples'. This should be simply: disciples (evenly stressed) and not: disciples. The pause between the first and second syllable is disagreeable.

p. 16. There is a note missing at the top of the page.

p. 19. 'Qui a crié cela?'—Crié has two syllables: ♩ ♩

p. 21. 'Nous ne comprenons'—Com-pre-nons is much too heavy. It should be: 'Nous ne comprenons jamais'/

p. 21. (Last line of voice part): 'Le tétrarque vous prie de retourner au festin'—Re-tourner: this accentuation is quite wrong. One would say: de re/tourner, and this would be better in quavers:

p. 22. 'Est/-ce/un/vieillard?'—It is a serious fault to treat the word ce here as one syllable; it is elided before the vowel that follows, and is pronounced: Est/-ç'un/.

p. 27. Page 5. 'Oh! qu'est-ce qui va arriver? Je suis sûr qu'il va arriver un malheur'. This remark is rather naive, and I'm afraid it might raise a laugh. It might have been omitted altogether, all the more because the same phrase: 'Je suis sûr qu'il va arriver un malheur' is repeated several times in the course of the piece and almost becomes a refrain, not likely to be taken very seriously.

p. 35. (Tempo indication in Scene 3.): Andante doesn't seem to me to correspond to Breit. A better equivalent in French, I think, would be: Large. Don't you agree?

p. 35. 'La coupe d'abominations'. It would be better to count as two syllables the ending of the word 'abominati-ŏns̄'.

p. 36. 'De celui qui a crié dans les déserts'. Crĭ/-é has two syllables.

p. 37. 'Où est celle qui ayant vu des hommes . . . etc. qui s'est laissée . . .'. Here you must get rid of the first 'qui'; it's not French, and doesn't sound well, either. It should be: 'Où est celle, ayant vu des hommes . . . qui s'est laissée . . .' N.B. Don't put any little accents or dots over the letter 'y' as you are accustomed to do.

p.39. (For the printers): Write: inces-tueux, and not: ince-stueux.

p. 40. and: Sei-gneur, and not: Seig-neur.

p. 42. (Stage direction): 'Narraboth: toujours plus exagéré'. Exagéré is intended to mean that he does not speak sincerely. It would be better, I think, to put: 'toujours plus insistant'.

p. 42. (Last line in voice part): 'Il ressemble à une mince/image/ d'ivoire.' The accents are all wrong. The last syllable of mince must be elided, and the last syllable of image shortened. The following is the only correct pronunciation: une minç' image.

69

p. 42. (Last line): 'Je suis sûre qu'il est chaste|autant . . . ' The last syllable of chaste must be softly elided before the vowel that follows, thus: chast' autant.

p. 43. 'Sa chair doit être très froide, froide comme l'ivoire . . . '. None of these words have the right French inflexions. They are much too heavy and dragged . . . The correct pronunciation would be: 'très froide|comme l'ivoire'.

p. 43. 'Je veux/le regar/–der de/près'. The pronunciation is bad. It should be:
'Je veux/le regarder/ de près.'

p. 45. 'Ta mère|a . . . '. The last syllable of mère must be elided before a; but as it would not sound well (ta mèr'a) it would be better to place the mute syllable over a note that is also silent, thus: ta mè–re/a.

p. 57. 'Il n'y a rien au monde . . . ' If it is possible to change 'il n'y a rien' to 'il n'est rien', this should be done, because 'il n'y a' has a disagreeable sound in French and, unfortunately, recurs frequently in this libretto.

p. 60. 'serpents qui se tortillent'; qui se tordent would be preferable. How do you manage to spread 'noirs' over two notes? It is only one syllable and must be pronounced sharply.

p. 63. 'le vermillon dans les mines de Moab, et que les rois leur prennent'. This is not French. It should be (if I understand the meaning of the phrase rightly); 'que les rois prennent dans les mines de Moab.'

p. 69. (For the printers): should be written: Pros–ternez and not: Pro–sternez.

p. 79. Hérodias: 'Il ne faut pas la regarder' Here again is an expression which recurs often and seems slightly comic. (cf. the scenes with the page and with Narraboth).

70

p. 80. 'une femme hystérique qui va'. que qui va is extremely

disagreeable to the ear. Instead: une femme hystérique–/ qui va/.

p. 83. 'Le jeune Sy/rien'. Sy/ri/en would be better.

p. 91. 'Je trouve qu'elle a bien raison'. This declamation is rather too slow in French.

p. 92. 'Mordez un tout/petit morceau'. False declamation. It should be: Mordez/un tout petit morceau/. If necessary one could make a slight break between petit and morceau, but tout cannot be separated from petit.

p. 94. 'Aussi, c'était un voleur'. That would mean: 'He was a thief because he looked after the camels'. I presume that's not the meaning you wanted, and that you are using the word aussi in the sense of as well. In that case it should be: 'C'était aussi un voleur'. Or simply: Et c'était un voleur.

p. 96. 'Aussi c'est un très grand prophète.' Same as above; the meaning would be: 'He's a very great prophet because he has said nothing against you'. It should be: 'C'est aussi un très grand prophète. Or better still: 'Et c'est un très grand prophète.'

p. 98. 'Il se cache, et par conséquent il y a de grands malheurs dans le pays.' This is not very clear; I don't understand the logic of this sentence.

p. 101. (First line): 'Ses voi/es sont très mystérieuses'. Voi–e cannot be pronounced as two syllables. You must place the e over a note that is not sounded: voi–e.

p. 104, 105. 'This should be: 'Il y a de grands malheurs', and *not* 'Il y a des grands malheurs'.

p. 106. Voi–es. See above p. 101.

71

p. 109. 'qu'Jokanaan, d'Jokanaan is rather harsh. It would perhaps be better to write: que Jokanaan, de Jokanaan. (The
silent e is not generally elided before proper names). But
this is not a very important point.

p. 111. (Tempo indication): 'più tranquillo che prima'. Does
one say in Italian: più . . . che, or più . . . di? I can't for
the moment remember, but I would have thought di.
(How much better it would have been to put the direction in French: 'Plus tranquille qu'avant'!).

p. 120. 'Le soleil deviendra noir comme un sac de poil.' What
sort of a comparison is this ! ! ! Is it Oriental? In French
it sounds grotesque.

p. 122. 'Salomé, fille d'Hérodias'. fil–le: unpleasant accent on
the last syllable, which ought to be merely hinted at.

p. 138. 'Je veux qu'on/m'apporte/présentement . . .'. Under no
circumstances can this phrase stand as so divided; it is
both incorrect and open to ridicule. The words must be
divided as follows: 'Je veux/qu'on m'apporte/à présent'
(the last syllable of apporte is elided before à présent).

p. 140. 'quoi que cela puisse|être'. Incorrect pronunciation. The
last syllable of puisse must be elided before the vowel in
être: thus: puisse être, or: puiss' être.

p. 144. There is a note missing at the end of Herod's air, 2nd
line).

p. 144. Herod: 'Non, je ne veux pas'; Salomé: 'Oui, vous avez
juré'. This should be: 'Si! vous avez juré'. Si is the
opposite to Non. Oui does not contradict, but merely
confirms what has just been said.

p. 145. Herodias: 'On voit qu'elle aime beaucoup sa mère'. This
sounds slightly comic in French. Something like: 'Elle
m'aime, je le vois' would be better.

72

p. 147. 'la tête d'un homme décapité'. This is not French.
Literally it means: 'The head of a man without a head"
This must be changed; it might raise a laugh. Instead
one could say: 'la tête d'un homme . . . une tête coupée
. . . c'est une chose laide . . . '.

p. 148. 'N'est–ce pas que voulez cela?' This is not French. It
should be: 'N'est–ce pas que <u>vous</u> voulez cela?' (or:
'que vous la <u>voulez</u>').

p. 151. 'mes pa–/ons, mes beaux pa/–ons'. Very bad pronunciation. Paon is pronounced as one syllable (sounding as: <u>pan</u>).

p. 153. 'avec mes pa–/ons. See above: same mistake.

p. 161. 'Qu'on lui donne ce / qu'elle demande!' Wrong accentuation. It should be: 'qu'on lui donne / ce qu'elle
demande/'.

p. 163. 'Je suis sûr qu'il va arriver un malheur à quelqu'un . . .'.
Once again!—for the 4th or 5th time. And this time this
expression is altogether comic. It is obvious that 'someone is going to be in trouble' since Jokanaan is about to
have his head cut off. I am aware that Herod is not
thinking about Jokanaan, but the audience is; and the
remark sounds like a joke in very bad taste.

p. 164-5. 'J'entends rien'. This is not French and cannot be
allowed. It should be: 'Je n'entends rien.'

p. 169. 'Si quelqu'un cherchait me tuer'. Not French. Should
be: 'cherchait à me tuer'. (tuer as one syllable).

p. 165. 'Je cri/e/rais'. Bad accentuation. Should be: 'je crie/rais'
(crie as one syllable).

p. 166. 'Il y a un silence' . . . y/a/un/ does not sound at all well
in French; and unfortunately this is not the only time
it occurs.

p. 166. 'C'etait/l'é–pé–e du bourreau'. The phrase should be
divided thus: 'C'était l'épée / du bourreau'/. Moreover,
é–pé–e is wrong. It should be: é–pée.

73

p. 167. 'Il n'ose pas le tu / er/'. Tuer is one syllable. It is both disagreeable and incorrect to pronounce it as tu / er.

p. 168. 'Il n'y a pas eu assez morts' ? ? This is meaningless in French. The text must be changed.

p. 174. 'Sou / lève tes paupières'. Bad accentuation. Should be: 'Soulève'.

      ſ ſ

p. 174. (Expression indication) 'Corto e duro'. Would not Breve be better?

p. 175. 'que la vipère rouge ne re / mu/–e / plus?'. This should be re / mue/

      ſ ſ

or ſ ſſ

e mute when it follows immediately another vowel, is merged with it, thus forming one sound.

p. 176. 'de Hérodias'. In French we should say: d'Hérodias (or rather: d'Hérodiade as that is how we always write the name). But it is not important, for considerable licence is allowed in the spelling and pronunciation of ancient proper names.

p. 179. 'd'ivoi– re sur un . . .'. To make the last mute syllable of ivoire form the first note of a triplet is incorrect. It should be written: 'd'ivoí–re / sur un só–cle / d'argeńt.

p. 181. 'une musique / étrange'. Here the last syllable of musique must be elided: une musiqu' étrange.

p.184. A note is missing at the top of the page.

p. 184. 'ne pourrai-ent éteindre'. As . . . raient is one syllable, this should be: ne / pour/–raient / é / tein–/dre.

p. 185. (Expression indication) Più lento che prima, Same remark as above (p. 111): Più che, or Più di?

p. 188. 'Cachez la lune, cachez les étoiles' I don't quite understand this.

p. 188. (Bottom of the page, tempo indication): Trainez!

'Trainez la voix' would be better, but this is not very good either. Here perhaps it would be better in Italian, if you know the right expression. (N.B. In any case, never put an exclamation mark after an indication. This is a German custom, but is never done in French, and it's one of the things that enable us to recognize immediately the hand of a German in a letter or a book. For example, where a German would write 'Cher Monsieur!', we say simply: 'Cher Monsieur').

p. 191. 'Tu/–ez cette / femme!' Tuez is one syllable; the correct accentuation would be: Tuez / cette fémme/, which is also much more forceful.

*   *   *

To ROMAIN ROLLAND

Berlin W., 15,
    Joachimsthalerstr. 17.   10th November, 1905.

Dear Friend,

Heart-felt thanks for all your devotion and all the trouble you have taken over my Salomé, and I am very happy that you are on the whole pleased with my transcription, and that you like the work. You will not appreciate the scope of my work until you have the German edition, and will be able to compare how I have modified the rhythm and melody according to the character of the French language. In this way I hope to a certain extent to have opened the way, for in it I have for the first time demonstrated that it is only the composer who can, if he is sufficiently familiar with the foreign language, or if he has the benefit of help as kindly as yours, undertake a transposition of this kind. How the best French operas of Berlioz, Boïeldieu (and also particularly those of Auber and Meyerbeer) suffer in our country from abominable translations! And Meyerbeer, who was so rich and who, what's more was German himself, should really have taken care that his operas were not performed in Germany in such shameful transpositions. I have paid attention to most of your remarks: most of the things which you have marked 'mal français' (in French in the original—i.e., 'mauvais français'), are word for word in Wilde's original, and I didn't think I had the right to correct Wilde's anglicisms.

The numerous repetitions: *il va arriver un malheur* (in French in the original) etc., are also in Wilde's text, and even repeated far more often, they are almost part of his style, so that I did not want to avoid them completely, and I have preserved them here and there.

Salomé: *Je veux qu'on m'apporte* . . . etc.

I chose this incorrect declamation on purpose, to make it sound somehow demoniacal and perverse. Should I change it, or can I in this case leave it as it is? In any case, I thank you whole-heartedly for all I have learned thanks to this interesting correspondence with you.

A few day ago I received a very good engraved reproduction of my portrait: would it give you pleasure if I were to ask you to accept it as a small token of my gratitude?

With kindest regards.

Yours sincerely,
DR. RICHARD STRAUSS.

I am conducting at Colonne's on 25th March.

To RICHARD STRAUSS

Sunday, 12th November, 1905.

Dear Friend,

On no account keep the false declamation of Salomé's phrase: 'Je veux . . . etc.' I quite understand your intention; but the sound of the phrase, cut up in this way, has an unfortunate double-meaning; and I know the coarseness of the public too well not to be sure that it would be spotted. If you want this phrase to have something demoniacal about it, you could adopt a rapid and very jerky declamation such as:

Je veux/qu'on m'apporte/dans un bassin/d'argent

or:

Je . . . veux . . ./qu'on m'apporte . . ./dans un bassin
d'argent

(The two first parts of the phrases being said very quickly and *with bursts of anger* on *veux* and ap*porte*; and the last part of the phrase being said all in the same tone, without a pause, fairly quickly, all the syllables being dwelt on angrily.)

As to Wilde's anglicisms, I understand your scruples. When it's only a question of expressions which 'aren't very French', keep them, if you wish to. But when there are 'mistakes in French', don't hesitate to correct Wilde's original. However remarkable Wilde's knowledge of French may have been, it is nevertheless impossible to consider him as a French poet.

I entirely share your opinion as to the necessity for composers to translate their libretti themselves when they want their works to be properly judged abroad—or at any rate to keep a close eye on their translations. But very few are capable of following your example; for very few know a foreign language as well as you do.

Nothing has done Wagner more harm, and nothing has so much contributed to the movement of anti-Wagnerian reaction which is taking shape now, as the colossal absurdity of his translations. They are neither French, nor even intelligible in any other language. They inspire me with such disgust that I scarcely ever go to hear Wagner at the Opéra.

You would give me the greatest pleasure by sending me your portrait. You know what affection I have for you, and how happy I am to witness the development, which is so rich and alive, of your personality. I should also be very pleased if you would tell your publisher to send me the score.

Is it really true then that the censorship has forbidden your play in Germany? Please tell me whether, as people say, *Salomé* is to be performed in Italy, and where and when. In Paris I know several of the principal critics who are taking an interest in it, and who might plan to go to the first night. They asked me for information about it, which I was unable to give them. Would you keep me informed?

Yours affectionately,
ROMAIN ROLLAND.

162, Boulevard Montparnasse.

In spite of your repugnance to giving fragments of your musical dramas at concerts, couldn't you take out the final scene of *Salomé* for the Colonne concert on 25th (not in a transcription for orchestra alone, like the funeral scene of *Feuersnot*, but with voices?) I think that it would make a great effect. Who knows, even? Perhaps it would be even more striking at the concert: for I am afraid of the realization of this scene in the theatre (St. John's head, etc.).

*   *   *

Monday, 27th November, 1905.
Dear Friend,

You have given me great joy by sending me your portrait. It's a superb engraving, done with profound incisive vigour. You are very alive in it, and just as I've seen you sometimes when you are absorbed by your thoughts. As to the dedication, really I'm ashamed that you speak of 'collaboration' in connection with the few small comments which I wrote to you: that was not worth mentioning, and it was a double pleasure for me: that of doing you some small service, and that of reading your *Salomé!*—I thank you with all my heart for your friendly gift.

78

I played some of its own music to your 'head' on its
arrival, some music from *Guntram* and *Feuersnot*.

Yours affectionately,
ROMAIN ROLLAND.

I couldn't read the engraver's name. When you write, do
tell me his name. He has done a beautiful piece of work.

To ROMAIN ROLLAND

Paris, Hôtel Bellevue,   21.III.06.
   Avenue de l'Opera.

Dear Friend!
    When can I see you?
    Perhaps you'll come to the dress rehearsal on Saturday
at 9 o'clock at the Châtelet? If so, will you come and fetch
me at the hotel on Saturday at 8.30?
    All best wishes.

Yours sincerely,
DR. RICHARD STRAUSS.

To RICHARD STRAUSS

Saturday, 1st December, 1906.

Dear Friend,
    I am writing you a word which is entirely confidential
and *about which I beg you not to say anything, above all to any
of the French you will see shortly in Berlin.*
    Your *Salomé* is creating the devil of a row in that little
provincial town, the Paris-that-matters of the theatres and
boulevards. You should know about it: the question which
is being discussed at the moment is much less a question of
Art than a question of actresses, who are quarrelling in
advance over the part of *Salomé*. Each has her adherents.
And what is comic is that both sides, fancying (I can't think
why) that I have some influence with you, have come to
see me to ask me to bring my influence to bear on you in
the way they wish.
    I needn't tell you that if I had to take action, it would be

neither for the one nor the other, but for you. I am writing to advise you to be very cautious, and to mistrust all the fine phrases and solicitations with which you can't fail to be besieged; for I don't doubt that one or other of the two parties—(or both of them at the same time)—will try to outwit you. It is most unfortunate that you can't judge for yourself, without having to rely on the judgment of other people who have all more or less taken sides in the affair, and for different reasons. I can't unfortunately advise you about the two actresses, for I only know one of them; and I am leaving Paris shortly for several months.

Bear in mind, too, that the licence of the Director of the Paris Opéra is to be renewed in about a fortnight's time—(so I've heard)—and that it is very possible (even probable) that Gailhard will not be renominated, and that Carré[17] or Messager will be nominated instead of him. Perhaps it would be to your advantage,—whichever way you may decide—to postpone your final answer to Gailhard, (if you have not yet given it) until this question has been finally settled. If it should be Carré who is nominated, it would then be up to you to decide if it would not be better to postpone performances of *Salomé* in Paris for a year, and to negotiate with the new management (which would begin only in January 1908)—or if you would prefer to have it performed at once, and to make the best of Gailhard. I don't conceal the fact from you that I would prefer for you someone like Carré as producer; for I have little confidence in Gailhard's taste. In the event of it being definitely the latter with whom you would have to deal, it would be a good thing if you could keep a fairly close eye on the work of production and rehearsals—or that, in your absence, a friend whom you trust could look after it for you,—but a friend from Germany, who would be quite outside all the little Parisian cliques. And whenever you have the possibility of seeing, hearing and judging things for yourself, do it, don't rely on others. There are always too many interests involved in Paris. Practically no one is free.

(*All this strictly between ourselves.*)

80

—As I was saying, I am leaving Paris for four or five months. I have taken a year's leave from the Faculty of Literature because I am rather tired, and above all because I want this year to write a novel and a play which I have in mind in peace. Perhaps we shall meet in Italy, where I shall probably stay until Easter. After that I think of going to Spain for a month or two, and coming back at the end of May to Paris, where there is at the moment a plan for an open-air performance in the square of the Hôtel de Ville of my play: *The Fourteenth of July*, with a cast of 1,500 or 2,000 people. (This would take place on the very day of the 14th July holiday.) I should enjoy putting that on, with Gémier[18] who is an admirable handler of crowds.

Good-bye for the present.

Yours affectionately,
ROMAIN ROLLAND.

162, Boulevard Montparnasse.

Astruc[19] wrote to me that he had something to ask me on your behalf. I asked him to come and see me, or to write. But he has given no further sign of life.

To ROMAIN ROLLAND

(Postmark: 1907)

Dear Friend!

Rehearsal of *Salomé* tomorrow Saturday at 10 o'clock Sunday 9.30

You are always welcome. Tous l'autre personnellement (*sic*)*

Yours sincerely,
DR. RICHARD STRAUSS.

Paris, 3rd May.
Hôtel Bellevue.
(In French)

*This phrase is meaningless in French. Tr.

To RICHARD STRAUSS

Tuesday evening, 14th May, 1907.
(After the 3rd performance of *Salomé*)

My dear Friend,

If I have not yet seen you, it is because I was shaken by so many tumultuous and diverse emotions after hearing your *Salomé* for the first time, that I did not want to speak to you about it before hearing it again. Besides, I rather wondered if it was worth speaking about it. No criticism can teach a great deal to an artist so much master, so aware of himself, as you are. But as I know that you have often shown interest in knowing what I think, I have made up my mind to send you these friendly reflections, which I beg you to read with indulgence.

Your work is a meteor, the power and brilliancy of which commands the attention of everyone, even of those who don't like it. It has conquered the public. It has even got the better of certain antipathies of temperament. I saw a well-known French musician, who hated it, but who had just heard it for the third or fourth time: he couldn't tear himself away from it; he was grumbling, but he was caught. I don't think that one could find a more manifest proof of your power. That power is, so far as I am concerned, the greatest in musical Europe today.

Will you now allow me to regret that it spends itself on inferior libretti? Oscar Wilde's *Salomé* was not worthy of you. It isn't that I am insulting his play by putting it in the class of the majority of libretti of modern operas . . . which are solemn idiocies, or . . . of which the symbolism is soporific. In spite of the pretentious affectations of the style, there is an undeniable dramatic power in Wilde's poem; but it has a nauseous and sickly atmosphere about it: it exudes vice and literature. This isn't a question of middle-class morality, it's a question of health. The same passions can be healthy or unhealthy, according to the artists who experience them, and the personages by whom they are incarnated. The incest in the *Walküre* is a thousand times more healthy than the conjugal and legitimate love in such and such a dirty Parisian comedy, which I don't want to name. Wilde's Salomé, and all those who surround her, except that poor creature Jokanaan, are unwholesome, unclean, hysterical or alcoholic beings, stinking of sophisticated and perfumed corruption.—In vain do you transfigure your subject, increase its vigour a hundredfold, and envelope it in a Shakespearean atmosphere—in vain do you ascribe moving accents to your Salomé: you transcend your subject, but you can't make one forget it.

I fear—(forgive me if I am wrong)—that you have been caught by the mirage of German decadent literature. However talented these poets may be—(I don't want to enter into personalities here)—the difference between them and you is the difference between an artist who is great (or famous) at *one* time (a fashion)—and of one who is—who should be—great for *all* time.

Of course, one must be of one's own time, and reflect the passions of one's time.—But after all, isn't Shakespeare also of our time? Isn't he more so than Wilde,—or anyone else of his kind? I mention Shakespeare to you, because I was thinking of him while listening to *your* Salomé. In it you have spent a force of frenzied passion capable of filling *King Lear*! And I was saying to myself: 'Why isn't it *King Lear*? What a *King Lear* Strauss could write! One would never have seen the like.'

Above all, you love force. And I too love it above all else. Nevertheless, do not scorn another power too much: that of sympathy. There are forces which burn. There are others which fertilize—which communicate and which inspire love. In the *Domestica*, in *Tod und Verklärung*, in *Heldenleben*, these beneficial forces existed. In *Salomé* it seems to me that they are no longer there, in spite of the pity which you try to feel for your unfortunate heroine. Beware of your poets: they do not possess the generous power of sympathy which is the attribute of the greatest artists, and which is one of the principal causes of the lasting-quality of great works. Certainly there are geniuses who only inspire admiration.

83

But they do not have the universality and the quasi-eternity of those who inspire both admiration and love at the same time. Beethoven is only as great and universal as he is because of all the good he does with his prodigious force.

Another thing:

I know the love you have for the theatre. You have always wanted to write for the theatre, you told me once; and your dramatic symphonies were in a way only a poor substitute for you, for want of having a theatre at your disposal. Now you have got a theatre—you have conquered it, conquered it forever, and not only because in actual fact *Salomé* is a success: the victory is much more complete than that: *Salomé* is for me the proof that you can now write, when you wish to, other works which will have the same force and the same fortune: you have made yourself master of the musico-dramatic art; you know the way to subjugate the public; you have acquired that special mastery of the stage, that understanding of dramatic effect, which is often denied to the greatest musicians.

—And in spite of that, I wonder if music gains as much as the theatre does in this victory? The impression I have of you (I am perhaps mistaken) is that you are essentially lyrical. The only thing you *feel* with genius is your own personality (and everything that resembles it, either closely or remotely). As you have, besides your genius, great inteligence and will-power, you are always capable of *understanding* other passions or other characters, and of expressing them—but from the outside, without feeling them really deeply, on your own account. For example: Jokanaan. I have a very strong impression that you have not in any degree experienced that wild forerunner's faith. Nevertheless you have depicted him fairly and powerfully, but in a rather abstract way, with no truly personal touch about it. This state of mind sometimes even leads you to accept certain questionable melodies, which do indeed produce the dramatic *effect* which you want, but which are surely not the expression of real passions which you had to express. This is doubtless because you haven't really experienced them.

84

Mind you, I know very well that that is not a defect so far as the theatre public is concerned. One needs,—in order to please those thousands of people assembled together, who have so many differences betwen them,—one needs a truth and a feeling which are, as it were, an average between all the multifarious truths and the varied feelings of all those beings. The passions and the characters must be subordinate to the dramatic effect *in abstracto*. That was the secret of the triumphant success of certain operas of the last century which, though lacking musical genius, achieved this impersonal ideal and this special gift of effect.

You are, I believe, at the present time, the only musician in Europe capable of exercising this sway over the masses in the theatre,—and not only in Germany,—but in all countries. That is no small matter. But the danger is that this victory risks being won at the expense of the most personal qualities of your genius, and by subordinating your powerful internal lyricism to the objective representation of an external world, *for which you perhaps do not feel very warm sympathy*. When you speak in your own name, as in the *Domestica* or in *Heldenleben*, you attain a matchless intensity and fullness of feeling. When you speak in the name of Herod, or of St. John, you create a sturdily constructed work, but you do not, in my opinion, say eternal things. What seems to me to be most intense in *Salomé* (all the end of the drama, from the moment when St. John's 'decollation' is expected),—and in which you are most closely reflected,—that stupendous nervous tension, which is so characteristic of your genius: that is not the best, the purest that you have to give.

To sum up:

1. *Salomé* appears to me to be the most powerful of your dramatic works.

2. *Salomé* appears to me the most powerful of contemporary musico-dramatic works.

3. You are worthy of better things than *Salomé*.

You have triumphed over the Europe of our time. Now you must leave our Europe, raise yourself above it. There is, in the European world today, an unbridled force of decadence, of suicide—(in various forms, in Germany, in France)—beware of joining forces with it. Let that which must die, die,—and live yourself.

I'm ashamed of speaking to you at such length and in such a tactless way. Don't be annoyed with me. Don't see anything in this letter but my joy at knowing you to be very great, and my desire to see you even greater still.

Yours affectionately,
ROMAIN ROLLAND.

162, Boulevard Montparnasse.

I am not saying anything about your orchestration. There can be only one opinion about that: it's an artistic miracle. Wednesday, 15th May (1907).

This letter was already written when I received Marnold's[20] note communicating your desire to talk to me. I am sending you my letter all the same; for I shouldn't be able to speak to you of all this during our conversation. Don't you think it would be a good thing if you, Debussy, Louis Laloy[21] (who is one of the most intelligent musical critics in Paris, and editor of an important musical magazine,* and I were to meet one day? There would be no one else. It would be just between friends and without ceremony. We could meet (either for luncheon, or dinner, or after dinner) on any day you like next week, and where you like: in a restaurant or a brasserie, near where you're living—as you like. (Would you send me a word of reply about this?)

But this mustn't bore you, or tire you. Above all, look after yourself. I am distressed to hear that you're not well.

All you tell me about your impressions of Paris amuses and interests me very much; for they agree completely with those of the hero of my novel,—a young German musician who, in the next volume which I am at present writing, arrives in Paris, where he is forced to live. I shall look forward to talking to you more about this.

* *Mercure Musicale.*

To M. JEAN MARNOLD

Hôtel Bellevue,   Paris,
  39, Avenue de l'Opéra.   22nd March, 1908.

Dear Monsieur Marnold,
  I am sending you 2 tickets for the concert, one for you
and the other for Romain Rolland. As the two seats are
together, would you be kind enough to warn Rolland to
meet you at the theatre before the concert.

Yours sincerely,
DR. RICHARD STRAUSS.

(In French)

(Note added by Jean Marnold, addressed to Romain
Rolland).

Dear Friend, I've just received the above letter from
R. Strauss. Monsieur Otto Fürstner has been kind enough
to undertake to transmit it to you. The numbers of the
tickets are: orchestra stalls 203 and 205. I shall wait for
you outside the Châtelet at 2.15. If you are late I shall
give your name to the box-office and leave the number.
I shall be glad to see you again after so long.

All best wishes, yours
J. MARNOLD.

14, rue Laferrière.

To RICHARD STRAUSS

Sunday, 21st February, 1909.

Dear Friend,
  Thank you so much for your cordial dedication on the
score of *Feuersnot*. I had a great deal of pleasure re-reading
it, and I expect the work to be a great success here. I have
just spent the last few days reading the score of *Elektra*. It is
great. One is enveloped and swept along from one end of
it to the other by a tragic force. This, more than any other

of your works, will compel recognition in all the theatres of the world.

I am sending you two volumes: one, *La Foire sur la Place*, (one of a series of novels entitled *Jean-Christophe*) so that you can see that I'm not at all afraid of saying what I think to the Parisians. You will find in it (p. 91 and the following pages) some memories of an evening we spent together at a performance of *Pelléas et Mélisande*. The other volume is a book of plays. If you ever have time to glance at it, look only at the third act of *Danton* (the Revolutionary Tribunal), *Les Loups*, and the musical note on p. 150–1.

I hope, my dear friend, to see you again soon. I spoke of you a great deal this morning with one of the directors of the *Orfeo Català* of Barcelona, and with a young French composer, who has been living in Berlin for a year or two, who admires you so much that he doesn't dare to go to see you; his name is Edgard Varèse;[22] and he is talented; he seems to me above all to have a bent for the orchestra. I think he might interest you. He has what I believe you (like me) love above all else, and what is so rare nowadays: life.

Yours affectionately,
ROMAIN ROLLAND.

162, Boulevard Montparnasse.

To ROMAIN ROLLAND

(Postmark: 6.III.1909)

Dear Friend!

Many thanks for so kindly sending me your works. I hope to read them this summer, in so far as my poor knowledge of French will allow me. I am very well, I am getting ready to make a trip to Milan and Rome. I am really delighted that *Elektra* meets with your approval.

With my best wishes and kindest regards,

Yours sincerely,
DR. RICHARD STRAUSS.

*   *   *

88

Landhaus Richard Strauss.

Garmisch, 5th May, 1909.

Dear Friend!

Thank you so much for the kind lines you wrote me, and for your friendly solicitude on my behalf.*

But what am I to do? Do you know of a better means of fighting hate and envy than by maintaining a lofty silence? You know the story of Hercules and the hydra, don't you?

So far as the Cassandra-Elektra affair is concerned, I had already decided not to make any reply about it, so long as I was still unfamiliar with M. Tebaldini's publicity pamphlet, in which he boosts Gnecchi.[23] Now that I am familiar with it, I have all the more reason to remain silent. For the whole of this affair is really too idiotic, not to mention the base hints of a Chauvinistic nature which are clearly discernible in the Italian and French attacks against me, and in contrast to which one must always stress afresh the generous hospitality which Germany, more than any other country, offers to Italian and French art—hospitality for which our neighbours show so little gratitude. As to the Mariotte-Salomé case,[24] the situation has already once been clearly stated in the *Berliner Tageblatt*.

In order to set your own mind at rest, I will once again repeat the facts:

M. Mariotte asked Wilde's heirs to assign the musical composition rights for *Salomé* to him. Wilde's heirs told him in reply that these rights had already been assigned. In spite of that M. Mariotte concluded his composition.

In his first letter to me, M. Mariotte acknowledged that I had sole rights, and only asked me to authorize him to have his *Salomé* performed on two occasions. To that I replied to him: have your work performed where you like and as often as you like. In doing this, I had unfortunately forgotten that in the meantime the libretto for *Salomé* had become the property of my publisher, Adolf Fürstner of Berlin.

*This letter is a reply to a letter from Romain Rolland which has not been traced.

89

Herr Fürstner protested against the authorization which I had given to M. Mariotte.

After many efforts, I finally succeeded in persuading Herr Fürstner to authorize some performances of M. Mariotte's *Salomé* at Lyons, and in that way I was able to satisfy the first and only request which M. Mariotte made to me.

Ever since then I have unflaggingly done my utmost to obtain complete freedom for M. Mariotte's work from Herr Fürstner. On two occasions I almost succeeded: each time something stood in the way; first of all M. Lalo's very unfriendly article appeared, then a few weeks ago there was that contemptible pamphlet by M. Camille Mauclair, attacking me with such base insults, that M. Fürstner asked me explicitly to give up my plan, so that it would not look as if we had given in to the pressure of intimidation.

That's how things stand at the moment. M. Mariotte has only his friends to thank for not having yet been able to obtain the release of his work. For I shall not let myself be coerced by threats and insults, when right is on my side.

If M. Mariotte returns to the path of loyalty again and if, instead of inciting his friends to insult me, he addresses a polite request to my German good nature, I think that even now the question could be settled, and that my publisher, who is a true gentleman, would give in.

I leave it to your judgment, dear Friend, to do what you think fit with my letter, and I remain, with kindest regards,

Ever your faithful,
DR. RICHARD STRAUSS.

To RICHARD STRAUSS

11th May, 1909

Dear Friend,

Thank you for your kind letter and for the information which you asked M. Fürstner to send me. Since I last wrote to you I have obtained Tebaldini's article: it's a ridiculous story—like almost all these stories of so-called imitation in art, what's more: they usually only come from people who don't know what art is.

As to the Mariotte affair, your letter has made things clear once more. Right is on your side. Only I think that your publisher was rather lacking in tact. For one thing, it would have been more advantageous for him if he had shut his eyes to those performances of Mariotte's (who would not have competed with him in any way), instead of making a song and dance about them. And then, immediately after Lalo's article, he should have forwarded to *Le Temps* a reply which would have at once re-established the truth of the matter. One must never hesitate to clip the wings of rumours of that sort. As for you, it's not your business, you have more important things to do; but I think your publisher should have undertaken it on your behalf.

You can be sure that I shall certainly reply to this mischievous tittle-tattle in the next number of the International Music Society's periodical *S.I.M.* I will send you the number immediately. If an article on the Gnecchi-Tebaldini affair in one of the important Parisian newspapers, like *Le Temps,* were to come to my knowledge, I would send a reply on the spot.

Forgive me for having bothered you about all this. Don't think any more about it. I congratulate you on having so many enemies. I shall try to take some of them away from you for myself.

Your affectionate and faithful friend,
ROMAIN ROLLAND.

162, Boulevard Montparnasse, Paris.

*   *   *

Thursday, 29th June, 1909.

My dear Friend,

You have received the article which I published in the *S.I.M.* and you will have seen that in it I am supporting your cause as plainly as possible against the partisans of Mariotte and Gnecchi.

Today I have received a long reply from Mariotte, which

I shall arrange to have published in the next number of the *S.I.M.* There's nothing offensive about you in it. It is simply sad and dignified. Here are some extracts from it:

' . . . *I am not complaining about anything, not even about Strauss and his friends. I only regret that he did not do me the honour of believing me when, on two occasions, I gave him the assurance that I had nothing to do with the attacks that were levelled at him* . . . *My only dealings with the press were limited to asking the critics whenever I could to abstain from any attack. The papers of Lyons and Marseilles attest to this. When I was warned in time, I even prevented the publication of articles. (This occurred with a Parisian periodical and a Toulon newspaper). I declined offers which were made to me that I should publish fragments of my* Salomé *and even that I should give private performances of it. What more can you want to prove the peaceful good faith of my conduct? I don't know how to see into the future, and it was difficult for me to stop articles which appeared without warning, and which more often than not were signed by journalists whom I knew as little as you yourself know me* . . . '

And now, may I tell you how happy I would be to see you, of your own accord, grant M. Mariotte (who doesn't even ask for it any more) complete freedom to have his *Salomé* produced and published, where and when he wishes. It would be a fine gesture, which would put an end to this affair, in the course of which, as M. Mariotte again writes to me, 'the ridiculous reproach was never made to you [i.e. Strauss] that you were not strictly within your rights, but rather that, in view of the circumstances of the case, you were rather hard in the exercise of them'. I can assure you that M. Mariotte deserves every sympathy; he sacrificed his career as an officer to devote himself entirely to music; he has been a professor at the Conservatoire at Lyons since 1902; and he leads a life of great hardship.

So don't pay attention any more to the more or less venomous articles in the press,—even if new ones appear— and by performing this act of generous courteousness, show that you despise them.

If you make up your mind to do this, let me know as soon

as possible, *if needs be, by telegram*—so that I can have your decision published after Mariotte's very reply, in the next number of the *S.I.M.* (which is in the press). That will close the debate, in the most dignified way for everyone.

Don't see in all this anything but the great fellow-feeling I have for you, and believe me, I am

Yours affectionately,
ROMAIN ROLLAND.

162, Boulevard Montparnasse.

To ROMAIN ROLLAND

Dear Friend!

I'm hastening to announce to you that I today succeeded in obtaining from Herr Fürstner the release of M. Mariotte's *Salomé*. Herr Fürstner will communicate all the details about the necessary formalities direct to M. Mariotte.

Here we have 40 centimetres of snow, my fingers are cold and don't obey my pen. I hope that France is now satisfied with the "Barbarians'.

With my best wishes,

Your sincerely devoted
DR. RICHARD STRAUSS.

Mürren, Bernese Oberland.
12th July, 1909

To RICHARD STRAUSS

Wednesday, 14th July, 1909.

Dear Friend,

Thank you for your note, which gave me great joy. That's the real way to be in the right.

I send you my affectionate greetings,

Your devoted
ROMAIN ROLLAND.

You know that so far as I am concerned, I'm no more fond of the 'Barbarians' on this side of the Rhine, than of the 'Barbarians' on the other side. Since Goethe, how many men have there been in Europe who weren't 'Barbarians'?

93

The joke is that they cast this word in each other's teeth. It's as if, in order to insult one another, we were to call each other: 'Man!'

I hope you have some good mountaineering, and that you are making the ice of Mürren melt with your music. Beware of avalanches!

* * *

Wednesday, 9th November, 1910.*

My dear Friend,

Will you allow me to recommend to your kind attention two orchestral scores which my young friend Gabriel Dupont[25] should have sent you during the last few days. You are familiar with his name: he is the author of *La Cabrera* which won the prize in the Sonzogno competitition some years ago. Since then he has been very ill, he had a touch of consumption (of which he seems to be more or less cured now). His artistic personality is not yet completely formed; but it is poetical, sincere, and independent of the Parisian cliques. In any case during the last few years he has been living out of Paris, in Arcachon. His *Heures Dolentes* were composed when he was most gravely ill; at that time he was living in the same house as I was, on the floor below, and I used to hear him composing or trying it out on his piano. He admires you a great deal; and it would be a great consolation to him if you were to find what he writes of some interest, and if you were to be good enough to be a support to him in Berlin.

Forgive my bad writing. I am writing to you in bed, having been not at all well for the last fortnight. I was knocked down by a car, which broke my left arm in several places, and injured my right leg. It will take a long time to heal, and it is painful. But I'm not complaining, for with the blow I received, I should by rights have been killed.

I hope you're in good health, my dear friend. I am looking forward to getting to know your *Rosenkavalier* soon.

Yours affectionately,

162, Boulevard Montparnasse.   ROMAIN ROLLAND.

*For the next seven years no letters appear to have been exchanged.

To ROMAIN ROLLAND

Mythenstrasse 24, Zürich 2.   29.I.17.

Dear Friend,

I would not like to offend your artist's eye with my bad French, so I am asking your permission to tell you in my native tongue what pleasure it gave me to see from your letter to Hans Huber that you greeted my wish for a meeting in such a friendly way.

I shall arrive in Berne (Hôtel Bellevue) on Wednesday, 31st at 5.45 p.m. and I would be grateful if you would let me know where we could meet in private. May I hope that you will give me the pleasure of attending my *Ariadne* at 8 p.m. at the Théâtre de Berne? In any case I shall have a good seat reserved for you, the ticket for which you will find left in your name with the hall porter at the Hôtel Bellevue. Would you be kind enough to telegraph to me here to tell me if I may expect you at Berne, and if you will give me the pleasure of having supper with me in some quiet spot after the performance which, I hope, will give you pleasure? Then I will arrange everything in accordance with your wishes.

With my best wishes for your health,

Ever your faithful, respectful and devoted,
DR. RICHARD STRAUSS.

To RICHARD STRAUSS

Tuesday, 30th January, 1917.

Dear Friend,

I don't yet know if I shall be able to brave the cold to-morrow, because of 'flu. If I can come, you will find a telegram from me when you arrive in Berne. In any case, this letter comes to you as a token of my steadfast and affectionate friendship. I have thought of you very often during the last two years; and what I heard said about your lofty reserve and about your artistic work gave me pleasure. Above all, how much I should like to get to know your new symphony!*

*No doubt the *Alpensinfonie* (1915) Ed.

As far as the performance of *Ariadne* is concerned, my position is rather tricky. I am very much in the public eye, and I must not compromise what little good I am able to do by an error of tact which would immediately be noisily taken up. If tomorrow, Wednesday, when you arrive in Berne, you do not find word from me saying that I am coming, give the ticket you have reserved for me to someone else.

Yours affectionately,
ROMAIN ROLLAND.

If I come, I shall stay in Berne for the whole of Thursday.

*   *   *

Sierre, Hôtel Château Bellevue.

Friday, 2nd February, 1917.

My Dear Friend, I am so very sorry, but I still have some temperature as a result of influenza this morning, and they won't allow me to go to Berne today as I had hoped. It's a great disappointment to me. I would have liked to tell you that during this horrible epoch, in which the minds of Europe are raving and tearing each other to pieces like mad dogs, I feel nearer than ever to those very rare friends of mine who have remained free from the follies of the herd, in the serenity of eternal art. How much I would have liked to hear what you think, to know your precise spiritual attitude amongst your compatriots! I can but imagine it, but I don't know if I am right, and I would be happy if I could have a word from you, before you leave Switzerland, telling me about it.

Won't you be coming in this direction, by any chance, or in the direction of Lausanne?

I send you my affectionate greetings.

Your faithful friend,
ROMAIN ROLLAND.

Marnold is still splendid, very independent and courageous. Do you ever read his musical articles in the *Mercure de France*?

I am sending you two articles of mine which appeared recently.

To ROMAIN ROLLAND

Landhaus Richard Strauss, Garmisch.   12.2.17.

Dear Friend!

I so much regretted that your health prevented you a second time from coming to Berne. I am sure that my performances there would have given you some pleasure, and that perhaps *Ariadne* especially would up to a certain point have rectified your judgment on German music in general, such as I see it set forth in *Jean-Christophe*.

I hope that now the beautiful sunshine on Lake Geneva will bring you a speedy convalescence. I hope to return to Switzerland in May in order to conduct some Mozart there; perhaps I shall then have the pleasure of seeing you again.

I am looking forward to both pleasure and consolation as a result of a personal conversation, and especially one with you for, on reading your fine article, I see with satisfaction to what an extent we are agreed on so many questions of a purely humane kind, or questions of principle, in our affection for our respective countries, and in our admiration for our courageous armies in the battlefield.

Moreover, it is precisely we artists who should freely keep our gaze fixed on all that is beautiful and noble, and who should put ourselves at the service of truth which, like light breaking through the shadows, must after all, one day, emerge from the thick tissue of lies and falsehoods with which the world in delirium seems to be enveloped at the present time.

Unfortunately, I heard from many sides in Switzerland the most saddening news about the bad treatment inflicted on poor German prisoners, who are suffering terrible inflictions, insults, and even tortures, at the hands of your compatriots. What a contrast with Germany, England, and even Italy, from where one hears of no complaint!

I have always wished that men like you could, by personal investigation in enemy territory, ensure the continuation of their work of justice and of truth on a more solid and convincing basis. *Wouldn't you like to do this?* I have not so far spoken to anyone about this idea, but I think that, in view of my connections, it would be possible for me to invite you to Garmisch this spring, and there to offer you an opportunity to gain varied impressions of our nations at war.

I have asked the German Embassy in Berne to send on to me letters addressed there in my name, so you can simply send your letters to that address, in a double envelope.

With my best wishes for your prosperity, and kindest greetings,

Your very respectful
DR. RICHARD STRAUSS.

To RICHARD STRAUSS

Sunday, 11th May, 1924

Dear Friend,

In spite of my bad health, I wanted to come from Switzerland to be present at your festival. Unfortunately, I was only able to get here after the performance of *Der Rosenkavalier;* (and I'm inconsolable about it: for I know it only from reading the score, and I have a partiality for it). But at least I was at last night's concert, and I shall hear the rest of your works.

Twenty-five years ago at Cologne I heard *Heldenleben* for the first time and, carried away by the impetus of that great work, I went to see you in Berlin. Yesterday I recaptured quite intact the emotions I felt as a young man.

I want particularly to tell you of the constant admiration I have always had for you, and which has increased even more with each of your new works. Praise be to your genius, stupendously varied as it is, for the gift it has of illuminating with its rays of imagination and of poetic irony the miseries of the present time!

Yours affectionately,
ROMAIN ROLLAND.

C/o. Herrn Dr. Erwin Rieger
Linke Wienzeile 4.

To ROMAIN ROLLAND

Staatsoper
Mozartgasse 4.   12.5.24.

Dear Friend,
   I am delighted to know you are in Vienna, and I thank you
with all my heart for your kind letter. When can I see you?
Will you have tea with me at my house this afternoon at 4.30?
I am unfortunately on the point of leaving, but I must see
you all the same!

                                        With kindest regards,
                                              Yours ever,
                                        DR. RICHARD STRAUSS.
Telephone: 58109.

To RICHARD STRAUSS

Villeneuve (Vaud)
Villa Olga.   Tuesday, 10th June, 1924.

My Dear Friend,
   You will doubtless shortly receive a letter from Monsieur
André Cœuroy, of Paris, who will express to you his desire
to translate *Der Rosenkavalier* into French. I highly commend
his request to you. Monsieur Cœuroy is an excellent writer,
who knows the German language well (he was a pupil at the
Ecole Normale Supérieure and has a teacher's training
certificate in German), a valued musical critic, and secretary
of the *Revue Musicale* (the best and handsomest musical
periodical in Paris). His connections in the Parisian theatre
world will probably facilitate the production of your work in
France, and will assure it the support of some of the critics.
   I was very happy to see you again, looking so young still,
so strong. Nothing could express to you the joy which filled
me when I listened to the *Domestica* at your last concert in
Vienna. And I felt you were sharing that joy with us as you

conducted that masterpiece. My dear friend, do not completely abandon the symphony! I know very well that in the second part of the *Domestica* you have reached a summit to which it is not easy to reascend. One must await the great gust of wind that comes in its own good time. But this wind will blow again. Seize the moment.

Since I have re-read the score of *Schlagobers*, I am more convinced that a cabal has been set up against that work. Of course, the work is a game, but by what a player! The writing is so subtle and perfect that it should have been relished in Vienna if people had not certainly had personal motives for showing resentment to you.

All your recent works for the theatre (*Die Frau ohne Schatten, Ariadne,* etc.) are full of riches. I only regret that the great writer[26] who gives you such brilliant libretti too often lacks a sense of the theatre: his subjects, as in *Die Frau ohne Schatten,* mark time a bit too much, or else are cluttered up with obscure thought. I regret, too, that in the final version of *Ariadne* the comic characters have been eliminated from the end. Either one of two things; either you should have ended up with the Dionysiac frenzy of a Procession of Bacchus (chorus and full orchestra) or,—preserving the irony of the original basic idea— you should at the end have mingled high-flown tragedy and comic opera, adding a septet for the five comic characters, Bacchus and Ariadne: that would really have been the *nec plus ultra.* I have the feeling that Hofmannsthal begins each of his 'pastiches' of a past age with an ironic intention, but that his wonderful virtuosity brings them off so successfully that he always ends up by taking them seriously. And it's a pity: a pastiche-subject like *Ariadne* only gets its full value through irony; and this irony should above all blossom out at the end.

I spoke to you of a farce called *Liluli,* which I have written in the style of Aristophanes in order to satirize the follies of our time. I am sending you a copy of it. The work is to be published in a German translation by Rütten and Loening, in Frankfurt. The translation is very polished; but it is almost impossible to render the rhythms and assonances of the original French in another language. The play has been

100

produced in Paris in *avant-garde* theatres, partly with live characters, and partly with shadows. I know that there are plans to put it on in various theatres in Germany. But what musician will write for me the bird-song of Liluli, and the screech of the diabolic motorcar of the goddess Llôpih (opinion)?

Good-bye for the present, my dear friend, give my kindest regards to your wife and to yourself.

I hope that your son has completely recovered his health.

Romain Rolland.

Villeneuve (Vaud)
Villa Olga.   25th February, 1926.

My very dear friend,

How can I thank you for the joy you have given me with your regal gift of friendship—in the *Liber amicorum*—the triumphal song of the 'West-östlicher Divan'[27] (which is one of my favourite books), and the magnificent dedication! The radiance of your music illumines the whole volume, as it has enveloped my life since the first day (it'll soon be thirty years ago) when the jubilant fanfares of *Ein Heldenleben* made my heart dance.

Your friendship is one of the very greatest gifts that destiny has bestowed on me. And I am proud that through so many ruins of empires—and of friendships—ours has remained pure and unshaken—and I embrace you fraternally.

Your
Romain Rolland.

Please remember me to your wife.

P.S. I am taking the liberty of sending you—in a fine and rare edition—the first edition of my *Jeu de l'Amour et de la Mort*, one of my latest dramatic works.

101

Roman Rolland

dem großen Dichter und Hochverehrten Freunde,

dem heroischen Kämpfer gegen alle ruchlosen an Europas Untergang
arbeitenden Mächte

mit dem Ausdruck treuester Sympathie und aufrichtigster Bewunderung

Richard Strauss

Den 29 Januar 1926.

102

103

104

CORRESPONDENCE

NOTES

1. An allusion to *Heldenleben,* no doubt.

2. Rolland has invited Strauss to take part in a Congress on the History of Music organised at the Collège de France.

3. Presumably the *Revue de Paris* for which Rolland was then writing. (See previous letter.)

4. This project was apparently not fulfilled.

5. 'The Hero's adversaries.' Again an allusion to *Heldenleben?*

6. Founded in Weimar in August 1861 this was a society whose aim was 'the promotion of the art of music and protection of musicians'. It ceased to exist in 1937.

7. The allusions in these quotations from the text of *Feuersnot* though somewhat obscure, apparently relate to a certain rivalry between 'Richard I' (Wagner) and 'Richard II' (Strauss), with a pun on the word 'Strauss' meaning 'contest'. Hence, 'hehre Herrscher der Geister': 'lofty ruler of the spirits'; and the couplet that follows: 'The evil one you did not expel, still stands in your way to renew the strife.' 'Reich in den Isargau' should be: *'Fern aus dem* Reich . . .: 'Far from the Empire into the region of the Isar'—i.e. *Munich.*

8. *Paris als Musikstadt* appeared in 1905.

9. Wanda Landowska died in 1959. Her collected writings on music were published in London in 1965 under the title *Landowska on Music* (Secker & Warburg).

10. *Jean-Christophe,* Rolland's famous novel, (10 vols.) was published in England between 1904 and 1912, reissued in Jupiter Books 1967.

11. Magnard (1865-1914) was killed defending his home near Paris during the German advance in September 1914.

12. *Taillefer* (1903) choral Ballad for solo voices, chorus and orchestra by Richard Strauss.

13. This could have been any Symphony up to No. VI finished in 1904.

14. None other, of course, than Maurice Maeterlinck, the librettist of *Pelléas et Mélisande.*

15. Gustave Doret (1866-1943) Swiss composer, conductor and writer on music. He wrote operas, cantatas, orchestral pieces and songs after studying with Joachim in Berlin and Massenet and Saint-Saëns in Paris. One of his best known works is his setting of René Morax's *La Fête des Vignerons* (1905), and several of his operas were based on plays by Morax.

16. Antoine Baïf founded in 1571 in Paris an 'Academy of poetry and music', with Thibaut de Courville, to encourage this style of composition, and Claude le Jeune was associated with him.

17. Albert Carré had been an enlightened Director of the Opéra-Comique and, with Messager, was largely responsible for the production in 1902 of *Pelléas et Mélisande*.

18. Firmin Gémier, Shakespearian actor and producer.

19. Gabriel Astruc, the impresario and founder-designer of the *Théâtre des Champs-Elysées* which struck a new note in theatre design when it was first opened in 1913.

20. Jean Marnold, influential music critic and editor of the *Mercure Musicale*.

21. Louis Laloy, critic and musicologist, an authority on Chinese music and the friend and biographer of Debussy. He was for many years Secretary-General of the Paris Opera, and in 1936 was appointed Professor of the History of Music at the Paris Conservatoire. Co-editor, with Marnold, of the *Mercure Musicale*.

22. Later to become a pioneer of avant-garde music, Varèse was only 24 when Rolland wrote this letter and had not yet composed any of his controversial works, most of which were first performed in the U.S.A. where he went to live after the first world war.

23. Giovanni Tebaldini (1864-1952) Italian musicologist and composer had published in 1909 a paper in the *Rivista Musicale Italiana* under the title: 'Telepatia musicale', pointing out thematic similarities between the opera *Cassandra* by Vittorio Gnecchi (1876-1954) and Strauss's *Elektra*, accusing Strauss of plagiarism, since *Cassandra* was produced in December 1905, four years before *Elektra*'s *première* in Dresden in 1909. See also article by Romain Rolland in the 'Bulletin Français' de la S.I.M., June 1909.

24. See *Introduction*, Note 4.

25. Dupont (1878-1914), a pupil of Widor, wrote several operas of which the first to bring him success was *Cabrera* which won the prize founded by the Milanese publisher Sonzogno in 1904. The *Heures Dolentes* are a set of 14 piano pieces written at the end of his

life during his last illness. [See also p. 225 in *Romain Rolland and Music*.]

26. Hugo von Hofmannsthal.

27. This was Strauss's contribution to the *Liber Amicorum* which was published in 1926 in Zürich, sponsored by Georges Duhamel, Maxim Gorki and Stefan Zweig, in celebration of Rolland's 60th birthday. The text is by Goethe, and the dedication is as follows:

'Romain Rolland

To the great poet and highly esteemed friend
The heroic fighter against all the wicked powers
working for the destruction of Europe
With the expression of my deepest sympathy
and sincere admiration
Richard Strauss

January 29th, 1926'

*   *   *

My acknowledgments are due to Dr. F. W. Sternfeld for his help in translating and elucidating the texts in Notes 7 and 27 above. [Editor.]

PART II

*Fragments from
Romain Rolland's Diary*

II

FRAGMENTS FROM
ROMAIN ROLLAND'S DIARY

22nd January, 1898.

Richard Strauss concert at Lamoureux's.—A young man,
tall and thin, curly hair, with a tonsure which begins at the
crown of the head, a fair moustache, pale eyes and face.
Less the head of a musician than that of any provincial
squireen.—I had luncheon with him at the Wagners' in
Bayreuth in 1891.—He conducted Beethoven's Symphony
in A major, the Prelude to *Lohengrin* and the overture to
Die Meistersinger, and his symphonic poem *Also sprach
Zarathustra.* He conducts waywardly, abruptly, dramatically,
in the same style as Wagner. He introduces pauses into
Beethoven's symphony, speeds up and changes the tempi,
—the rhythm very pronounced, with a kind of excitable
and disjointed roughness. The wild gaiety, the staggering
drunkenness of the last movement; the two last pages of
the first are rendered with a force which sounds a bit
freakish, but is all the same impressive. *Zarathustra,* which
should contain all the philosophical sentiments: nature,
religion, science, disgust, joy, irony, laughing lions—is
obscurely complex from an intellectual point of view.
Musically, it is powerfully orchestrated, and abounds in
original effects; but fundamentally it is rather vulgar. The
restlessness in it is Schumann, the melancholy Mendelssohn,
the nature Wagner, and the gaiety, inebriated Gounod.
(One of the principal phrases seemed to me to be an
unconscious parody of a tune from *Faust* set to a dance
rhythm). The first pages are powerful (in the spirit of
Parsifal), and the laughter of the orchestra, the madness of

111

the trills and little scales, hiccoughs and frenzied bursts of laughter seemed to me the most striking part of the work. Taken all in all, more a strong man than an inspired one. Vital force, nerves, a morbid over-excitement, a lack of balance which will-power holds in check, but which disturbs the music and the musician. It was enough to see him at the end of the Beethoven symphony, his great body twisted askew as if struck by both hemiplegia and St. Vitus's dance at the same time, his fists clenched and contorted, knock-kneed, tapping with his foot on the dais—to feel the malady hidden beneath the power and the military stiffness . . .

Well, well! I've got an idea that Germany will not keep the equilibrium of omnipotence for long—In her brain there are dizzy promptings. Nietzsche, R. Strauss, the Kaiser Wilhelm . . . there's Neroism in the air.

* * *

April, 1899.
Wednesday evening—Mainz.—Friday evening—Mainz—Berlin. I am upsetting the order of these notes so as to write about my visit to Richard Strauss immediately after seeing him. Charlottenburg. Knesebeckstrasse, No. 30. On the 4th floor of a new and elegant house, in a flat furnished with some taste—a large rough sketch for some German picture, interesting (nude man and woman).—Very young face; dark hair receding, very little hair on the forehead, which is rounded, full and rather handsome; very pale eyes; the moustache so fair as to be almost white. Speaks French with difficulty, but sufficiently. Tall, but holds himself with extreme lassitude. Childish and involuntary shyness in his smile and gestures; but one feels underneath a pride which is cold, self-willed, indifferent or contemptuous of the majority of things and people, and which must blame itself, when alone, for not having asserted itself more, for having given in yet once more in conversation to social conventions. (Rather what I am myself).—One feels that

he is furious that, as conductor of the Opera, he has to conduct a bad and pretentious opera by Le Borne,[1] more especially as this has prevented him from conducting and hearing his own concert in Cologne. But the Kaiser, who wants to show evidence of sympathy for French art, had to be obeyed. 'As if there weren't any other works more worthy of French art', he says, 'like d'Indy's *Fervaal,* Messager's operettes which have such pretty and unaffected things in them, or the works of Bruneau.' I ask him if it was he who conducted the performance of Perosi's[2] oratorio. Without speaking, but with a grimace of such profound disdain that everything is said, he indicates that it was not, and I do not feel like arguing.* Moreover, he goes on immediately: 'No, but it was I who performed Chabrier's *Briséis,*[3] which gave me a great deal of pleasure.' I tell him what an impression *Heldenleben* made on me in Cologne; and he gives me the piano score which has just appeared. We talk of his symphonic poems—he begins by mapping out for himself very precisely his literary text; and then he goes on to the music. It certainly seems, according to his reply to the precise question which I put to him, that the musical phrases never come at the same time as the poetical ideas, but afterwards. Nevertheless he considers it pointless for the public to follow his *Heldenleben,* for example, in a little booklet. It is sufficient, he says, to feel the two elements: the hero, and his enemies.—It was in December that he finished that poem: and since then he has not done anything; firstly, because one must let one's mind rest a little, and also because he can't do anything in winter. He sighs for the South; he has spent a winter in Egypt, and would like to live in Italy.

—To my question as to whether the symphonic poem attracts him in preference to other forms of music, he says not (perhaps out of self-esteem), and that he has also written an opera, *Guntram;* but that he cannot have it performed,

*He does not know Franck's *Béatitudes* or his *Psyché* any more than he knows Perosi, but only the *Chasseur Maudit,* and the *Quintet.* [Author's note.]

113

because it is considered too difficult. He says that the theatre world is completely different from the concert world. In the latter there are connoisseurs, in the other, only pleasure-seekers. Above all in Berlin, (and he seems to have an even worse opinion of Paris) they are nothing but bankers and shop-keepers. I talk to him of our efforts, or of our desire in Paris to set up in opposition to these pseudo-aristocracies a democratic art and public. But I sense distrust, or a negation, in his polite look as he listens to me. When the word 'people' is mentioned, this disciple of Nietzsche understands: rabble; worse, perhaps, than the pleasure-seekers whom it wishes to destroy.—Nevertheless, he seems to have some relations with young writers, if not personally with Hauptmann;[4] and he shows in his literary judgements the same contemptuous and innovating spirit. The tradition and the conventionalism of the Schauspielhaus, which he scornfully puts in the same category as Sarah Bernhard's acting, disgusts him; and here he has some slight esteem only for the Deutsches Theater, at least for its external form.

I also visit, for the musical committee, the critic Otto Lessmann, 27 Spreestrasse, Charlottenberg. An old man, very fussy, who gives me a letter of introduction to Strauss, whom he greatly admires.

20th May, (1899).

Musikfest at Düsseldorf.—I travel with the delegates from the Town Council to some Congresses on hygiene;—they are visiting Hamburg and Berlin.—Stout men; heavy, quite intelligent, but each one shut up inside himself, talking with satisfaction, and never listening to anyone else except reluctantly. What they tell me about the water of Paris takes any desire to drink it away from me forever. —My fever puts up with the high speeds and vibrating motion of trains, but is aggravated by these journeys.—

Düsseldorf. 1 o'clock in the morning.—The hotels are packed.—Music and war. Tonhalle and barracks. From my bed I can hear the psalms and the organ from the neighbouring Protestant church. Hussars, green jackets.—Things have a Germano-Dutch look, grey and red stone, cold, clean, well aligned, mirrors in the windows, avenues along the canals.—

Military monuments.—To the Emperor, on horseback, between two guardian spirits—Two bas-reliefs: 1806-7 (a Spirit of War, waving a torch, half-naked, near a prostrate woman; in the distance, a carriage in motion led by a postillion in a top hat on horseback); 1870-1 (the German States offering the crown to Prussia who, modestly blushing, hangs her head and lowers her eyes.) In front, the crowned eagle claws the world.—A little further away, monument to Bismarck, in bronze, put up in 1899. More allegory round the plinth; a helmeted warrior, half naked, breaking loose, like an Albion by Cornelius—Nowhere else do memories of war and of conquerors take up so much room.

Charming gardens (Hofgarten, Königsallee). Still waters, where trees recline, plunging their arms in them; large fountains, lilac in flower; trees, with red clusters on them which emerge from the ground, as if half the body was buried in it; white busts on marble columns, in the midst of the greenery, in honour of princesses; monuments of obscure meaning, of debatable forms, but which make an aristocratic effect; an impression of a little German Versailles, of a nice poetic, middle-class court, and always rather Dutch, too, with straight canals; and, parallel to them those avenues of thick chestnut trees, and that abundant greenery; and those two-storied houses, with their flagpoles.

At table, these stout men, heavy and vulgar, deep in their beards and glasses like honest spiders with round eyes, get up with every glass to drink a health. And they do so with such gravity, such respect for themselves and for the act they are performing—There's a complete change of tone and expression in their conversation. They are saying Mass.*

*See *La Révolte* in Jean-Christophe (Note written in 1924).

How much of the sixteenth century there is in present-day Germany. Morally and physically. Those big, clean-shaven profiles, prominent and laughing, red in hue, country gentlemen.

First concert.

Städtische Tonhalle.

Considerable impression, as great as Bayreuth.

Two churches—one church (seventeenth century) for the concert—a cathedral for the restaurant—an immense platform for the musicians. Fifteen rows from top to bottom. Thirty from right to left.—Choirs of men above, surrounding the orchestra. Choirs of women on either side below, pink and white dresses, blue ribbons, all ages; from little girls to old girls and even beyond.

The conductor's rostrum, draped in red velvet, with a golden lyre on the front, and all around, the whole length of the footlights, garlands of laurels, scattered with bunches of flowers, in clusters, violets, roses, narcissi, red flowers,—large bunches in some places,—and shrubs in the corners.

A dense crowd, almost entirely German, quite a few mis-shapen heads of musicians, skulls bulging on one side or the other. A few Belgians: the Kuhopffs (?), just the same little picture-book Englishmen as ever, Berthel,[5] pleased to see me, annoyed that I was there; for she had taken her rôle of reporter seriously, standing in for me. Strauss, to whom I speak, decidedly tall, taller than I am, I think, and in bad health, puny, his back rather round and not broad; bald on the top of his head; looks mild, timid and inscrutable. I don't think I shall succeed in talking to him here—he is too busy and surrounded; and is too little given to conversations.

The Bach fugue and the prelude to *Parsifal*—both relatively mediocre. The latter, in addition to the unpardonable slips of the orchestra, is conducted in a dramatic way, and the orchestra is too much in evidence. It makes for thunderous effects; all the intimacy of the scene disappears. But what beauty!

Bach's Cantata *Halt' im Gedächtniss Jesum Christi*—makes

116

one want to shout with pleasure. From the very first chorus, those giant strides, full-throated male voice choirs, organ, shrill trumpet. Union of a people in a single thought. That soul of thunder—The tenor's *aria* is sung in a pretentious and romantic way—Madame Schumann-Heink, admirable, the foremost singer of Europe, power, soul, style, —but how ugly she is, that girls' school headmistress, with her gold pince-nez on her coarse nose, her homely face, and her red arms—Curious *Aria* of Christ: *Friede sei mit euch:* Cf. Perosi.[6] The tender mystery which fills everything. The olympian and pastoral shades of the Friedenfürst. It re-appears three or four times. And the chorus replies. Joy, strength, fullness of existence. Full light. Painted in the full light. Supreme art, perfect and admirably healthy. The complete opposite to Bayreuth. All the means revealed; in-viting participation of the listeners, irresistibly, instead of the mystical moat which Wagner digs between his stage and his audience.

It doesn't seem as if there could be anything possible after it. And yet Bach is surpassed by Beethoven's *Mass.* I had heard it twice at the Conservatoire; I thought I knew it. I have got to know it this evening for the first time. I bow down.—One must study the connection, in Bach and Beethoven, between the *soli* and the choruses: the former conscious voices, the latter the powerful and obscure life of the soul. The *Gloria* demented, like a storm at sea. Music full of flashes of lightning, athletic and frenzied will-power, wild, stormy, which stops, is shattered, in order to plunge forward again even more madly.—(The typical romanticism of the Germans. Classical music is our inven-tion). It's the singing of the Last Judgement.—At times it seems as if Beethoven is hanging on with both hands over the abyss, and singing.—And in the final bars, that sudden shimmering change of key, that C major in the key of B, like a patch of light on a storm.—

The *Credo:* the song of a people victorious over doubt, superior to others, triumphant, and still in battle, in the intoxication of action.—That mixture of fury and tenderness.

Again the Revolution and the Empire in this *Mass*.
Blows, and smiles.

Why the *Mass* sounds fuller here than in Paris. The organ,
the . . . * of the harmoniums. Then in addition to the
excellent quartet, the choirs use the full volume of their
voices. Beethoven wrote these feats of strength to be executed
by strong chests, and not by puny whipper-snappers sparing
themselves.

Oh the moral force of such a people, the union of wills!
Why should they need the theatre? It is obvious that for
them opera is not a need, but an artificial art; that it is in
choral and instrumental music that their communal and
natural vocation lies.

The mob during the interval. Jovial but inconsiderate
crush to get a sandwich or some synthetic scented champagne.

A total of $\begin{cases} 591 \text{ choristers} \\ 128 \text{ instrumentalists} \end{cases}$
and the soloists.

In the morning, rehearsal from 9—1.

Liszt's *Orpheus*.[7] Don't understand. A noble mind, but
so cold, so little sincerely carried away. Noble ideas and
cultivated passions in a worldly mind. All the same, there
is purity in the idea, and very subtle orchestration.—But
there is a manifest relationship between this music and
that of Strauss (who conducts): the spirit, themes, orchestration (*Tod und Verklärung*).—It must be admitted that if
great men can be loved by everyone, the intermediaries
between great men are more specifically national. They
are not understood by foreigners.

Heldenleben.—First movement, young, joyous, highly-
strung, confident. Second: derisive laughter and dancing
gait of the woodwind and bassoons. Phrase from St-Saëns's
Hercule.—Third [love] movement weaker—violin concerto.
—Fourth: magnificent cavalry charge, artillery, and all the

*Illegible word.

118

trappings of war. The finest battle in music. A real impression of combat.—Weak transitions between the movements, and weariness at the end.—

Strauss's person: something childish in his physiognomy, and something sickly in his thinness, his baldness, his round back, the worn-out and anaemic expression of his face.— He conducts with a stroke that is supple, brisk, with sudden slackenings and clean endings.—

Cf. What there is that is childish in him and in V. d'Indy.

Beethoven's *Triple Concerto.*—With so many virtuosi it's a pity such a meagre result is achieved (Hungarian dance movement).

Brahms' *Rhapsody.* [8] The impression that remains is how German it is, how moving it seems. And more and more how it fits the words. Its main charm comes from that. German Gluck. Each sound is expressive.

Always the same greatness, which is correctly pathetic, and bleak.

Mendelssohn's *Walpurgisnacht.*—Its boring minor key. The movement isn't bad, but there's no prayer in it. The conductor, Buchs, incites his troupe to curvet and jump, with whoas! like a circus groom.

All that scratches, and gnaws, and pants.

Mendelssohn's effort to be passionate. Impression produced by the monotony in the design. Movement, but no colour.

Garden round the Tonhalle.—And the continual eating!

These big, bearded Germans, with well-kept horses' tails on their chins, above which they seem to lord it,—treating themselves to libations, keeping steady through their tall glasses of champagne,—drinking in the calm,—with a mixture of solemnity and comicality—the smile of a flunkey being made to drink a health.

The jolly little girls whose smiles reveal two teeth too many.*

What a concentrated, serious air, all introvert, a little

*See *La Révolte* in *Jean-Christophe.* (Author's) Note written in 1924.

crushed, I, a Frenchman, have amongst these expansive and noisy Germans. Victory has changed the rôles.

The Rhine, in the mist, grey and peaceful, between its low, green banks, level with the water. Grey and red houses on the banks.—An enormous iron bridge, with two arches, like the halves of a wheel.

Ponds, in which houses are mirrored, in the town. Lilacs, fruit trees, beside little canals.

The Germans too respectful towards a quantity of things: towards their drinking glasses, towards their beards, towards themselves; one meets imbeciles who habitually call one another 'Excellency'.*

Triumph of *Heldenleben* at the concert. It seems there to have acquired a double intensity. I see people tremble, almost stand up at certain passages. At the end, in the ovation which it receives, wreaths are presented, trumpets sound, women wave their handkerchiefs.—It would be a colossal work, if a literary error didn't break up the movements, at the apogee of effect, in order to describe other scenes.—How the dissonances are attenuated by Strauss's conducting, envelopped in *p*. And what thunder in the triumphs and the formidable charge, which make the earth shake and hearts leap.—The Germans have found their poet of Victory.

Quantity misleads as to quality. These assembled masses lend grandeur to no matter what. I recognize in that the reason for one of the weaknesses of German taste.

Strauss tells me that Alexander Ritter,[9] Wagner's nephew, by marriage, has written two operas, and is the first to have introduced the Wagnerian system into the *Lied*.

Humour and highly-coloured psychology of *Don Quixote* —an inferior work, incidentally.

Nothing can be more dangerous for the Germans than a great man like Strauss. For he will end by driving them mad.

There is remarkable intelligence in *Don Quixote*. The two figures of Don Quixote and Sancho are excellent, the one

*Idem.

120

with his air of stiffness, languid, swash-buckling, the aged Spaniard, with something of the troubadour in him, always changing his ideas and always coming back to the bee in his bonnet; the other, with his breeziness and his bantering proverbs.—These are really sketches, scenes in miniature, rather than real descriptions.

Strauss' *Lieder* are rather weak, in the manner of Gounod. The Germans are in ecstasies. When this terrible hero wishes to lay bare his amorous heart, he's a child, a little trite and very sentimental. Madame S. plays to the public, displays her bosom, and her smile, feels at her ease here . . .

The melodies in Cornelius's *Der Barbier von Bagdad* are rather commonplace, but it is very well contrived, very lively, quite funny, and must make an enormous effect on the stage.

At the end, an ovation in Roman style—trumpets, waving scarves, a rain of bouquets on Strauss—Hoch! Strauss! Wreaths.—The young hero feels at home, he is familiar, sometimes angry with the musicians, sometimes jovial. Not being able to persuade his friend Becker[10] (the 'cello in *Don Quixote*) to come and take a call, he takes his instrument from him and presents that to the public.

We no longer have the same status that we used to have in the past with these people. Little do they care if there is one Frenchman more or less. They have the arrogance to think that their opinion alone counts in the world. They say to you: 'How strange, I would never have believed what good taste you have.' (That is to say: Like me).—Victory has passed this way—Victory may pass this way again.—Individually each of them is still quite timid, not very sure of himself—It's in the mass that they are powerful and narrowly conceited—Poor things! We used to be the same.—Let them enjoy their youth!

Melancholy beauty of the Rhine, which flows languidly towards the sands of Holland, towards its mysterious death. The town floats on the bank like a Dutch town. In the distance one sees, as at Antwerp, the boats going upstream across the meadows, as the river meanders on its sinuous

121

way. One can understand poor Schumann succumbing to the lure of the river, inviting him to such an easy death, to silence, to oblivion.

* * *

1st March, 1900.—Richard Strauss, passing through Paris, where he has come to conduct two concerts, invites himself to luncheon with us. He is younger in the face than last year. A face without a wrinkle, unblemished and clear, like that of a child. A big shiny forehead, pale eyes, a fine nose, frizzy hair; the lower part of the face is slightly twisted; the mouth often makes an ugly pout, from irony or from displeasure. Very tall and with broad shoulders; but his hands attract one's attention, delicate, long, well-kept, and with something rather sickly and aristocratic about them, which doesn't correspond to the rest of the individual, who is plebeian on the whole, and rough and ready. He behaves very badly at table, sits by his plate with his knees crossed, lifts his plate near to his chin in order to eat, stuffs himself with sweets like a baby, etc. His tone and his manner change completely, according to whether he is speaking to us, or to Henry Expert[11] and Robert Brussel, who come after luncheon. Cordial and good-natured with us, he is curt with the others; he scarcely listens to them, turns towards Clotilde:[12] '*Was?*' he says, '*Ach! so, so*'; and that's all.

His conversation shows me how right I was to see in him the typical artist of the new German empire, the powerful reflection of that heroic pride, which is on the verge of becoming delirious, of that contemptuous Nietzscheism, of that egotistical and practical idealism, which makes a cult of power and disdains weakness. In addition to this he has certain dispositions which I had not seen clearly before, and which strictly speaking belong more to the people of Munich, the south Germans: an elemental vein of the clownish humour, paradoxical and satirical, of a spoilt child, or of Till Eulenspiegel.—In order not to consider some of his ideas odious, one must bear this in mind.

He declares that he is absolutely indifferent to the Transvaal war, that at the beginning he took sides, but was on the side of the English—'I am very fond of the English,' says he; 'they are very agreeable when one is travelling. For example, when I was in Egypt I was very glad that the English were there, instead of the Egyptians; one is always sure of finding clean rooms, every comfort —etc.' That's one point of view for judging the history of humanity. 'The Boers are a barbarian people, backward, who are still in the seventeenth century. The English are very civilized and very strong. It is an excellent thing that the strongest should prevail.' But what about the weak? The Egyptians, the Boers, what if they suffer? 'Oh! I don't know anything about it; I don't think about it; Egypt doesn't exist when I am not there.'—But what if the strong were only strong on the surface, if there was in the weak a moral force superior to that of their conquerors, and perhaps a source of genius, even of artistic genius, more alive than the English colossus, with its mediocre and moribund heart?—'Perhaps you're right, I expect you're right; but I prefer to think what I think.'

He tells me about his relations with the Emperor. His first interview.—The Emperor summons him, frowns as he looks at him: 'You're yet another of these modern musicians?' He bows. 'I have heard Schillings' *Ingwelde;*[13] it's execrable; there's no melody.'—'Forgive me, your Majesty; there is melody, but it is hidden beneath the polyphony.'—He looks at him with a stern eye: 'You are one of the worst.' Another bow.—'The whole of modern music is worth nothing; there's no melody.' Same game. 'I like *Freischütz* better.' 'Your Majesty, I too like *Freischütz* better'—'Verdi's *Falstaff* is a detestable thing.'—'Your Majesty, one must bear in mind that Verdi is eighty years old, and that it is a splendid thing, after having created *Il Trovatore* and *Aïda,* to renew oneself again at the age of eighty, to create a work like *Falstaff*, which has genius in it.'—'I hope that when you're eighty you'll write better music.' Nothing more to be said.

Another time, during some festival, the Emperor, turning to a musician next to Strauss, pointed to the latter and said of him in a loud voice so that he could be heard: 'That fellow's a serpent which I've harboured in my bosom.'

Strauss says that the Emperor wants to impose his will everywhere, but wherever he meets with resistance, he withdraws in silence; which is even worse than his despotism. But the majority, instead of standing up to him, give in, and encourage his tendency to believe himself omniscient. He is surrounded by academic cliques which prevent him from trying to understand modern art, both in painting and in literature. In literature, he has just refused the Schiller prize to Hauptmann. In painting, when visiting the last Exhibition and having arrived at the entrance to the galleries showing modern painters, A. von Werner said to him: 'Sire, now here are the galleries of children's diseases.' The Emperor said: 'One does not go to look at children's diseases.' And he turned on his heel without even casting a glance at the pictures.

He complains of the strictness and the moral hypocrisy in Berlin. 'Why shouldn't one have the right to say whatever one likes when one knows it's true?' He maintains that it has been predicted that one day he will lose his head.

He retains the old stock ideas about the French: the Frenchman cannot go beyond certain limits; but within these limits, he is perfect.—No one felt these limits better than Berlioz, who is a French musician in the highest sense of the word; he created all the music which was suitable for Frenchmen.—If one were to say to him that there are also very profound people in France, men like Descartes, or Pascal, he would toss his head, wouldn't believe a word, and not for the world would he put himself to the inconvenience of revising an idea so convenient for Germanic self-esteem.—He knows César Franck extremely vaguely, and has not so far had the curiosity to read the score of his *Béatitudes*.—I spar with him a bit over his admiration for Liszt,—the first, according to him, to have opened up new ways in music, since Beethoven,—to have taken from Beethoven not his formalism, but his living spirit. In order to explain the small hold that his works have over me, he says that they are symphonies written by a virtuoso of genius and that they should be performed by the orchestra, as he does on the piano, with extreme fantasy. He admires Liszt's *Dante* and *Faust* above all.—I question him about Schillings, one of whose pieces he is conducting on Sunday. He praises him, but with a certain patronising disdain. 'He's a very discriminating musician, but doesn't succeed in completely freeing himself from a certain constraint. He is constantly afraid of doing something vulgar. I don't like that: one must go ahead unhesitatingly, one must be sure that there is nothing vulgar in one, that there can be nothing vulgar in one.'—What is very curious is his contempt for Handel, in whom he sees nothing but music which is formal, monotonous, cold and English; an elephants' dance. In the end he excuses himself for this by saying that Handel is the god of all the musical conservatives in Berlin and that, as a reaction, he is led to think worse of him than is justified. His paradoxes almost always originate in analogous reasons. I muse on what he has just said about Schillings, and I don't consider that it's much better to be afraid of thinking the truth because mediocre people think the same.

He says that he has only composed some small things since last year. He says, smiling as he does so, that he thinks he is suffering from senile decay.—He wants to write a ballet.—The tragic vein seems to him to have been exhausted by Wagner.—Moreover, he is attracted by comedy, nay, by buffoonery; and while he is in Paris, like the good German he is, he revels in little slap-stick theatres; the day before he had been to the *Maris de Léontine;* he is entranced with it. He repeats, with ponderous merriment, jokes which are not at all funny, which seem to him to be killingly witty.

He also takes a great interest in painting, visits the Louvre, takes pleasure in the study of antique drawings, of Renaissance and French medieval sculptors; and wants to go over Versailles with me.—He shows very little curiosity about ancient music, and is totally lacking in the great encyclopaedic spirit of classical geniuses. He is a modern, very proud of being a modern, indifferent to all that is eternal and universal in human thought.

I reflect on the remarkable persistency with which almost all Germans today affirm the moral greatness of Might, and its legitimate supremacy over Right. I don't think that this would be the case if these Germans did not feel very conscious that they have violated and are violating justice, and are determined not to renounce the advantages of their iniquitious actions.

I would like to recall the exact words of his phrase: 'I don't like weak people who complain about the strong, when they are no stronger than they are.'

Saturday's dress-rehearsal.—X., who is like a ponderous Levantine, helps him to make himself understood to the musicians to whom Strauss splutters in very bad French. Both of them perched on very high stools like that of Diafoirus[14] and looking like monkeys on top of a ladder. X. treats his musicians with the boorishness of a schoolmaster brow-beating a class.—Strauss is above all bent on making the separate parts stand out clearly from each other; he has no original observations or feeling about the *Symphony in C minor;* he seems above all to be interested in the polyphonic parts; he makes the opening rather violent, takes the andante rather fast, the scherzo a little slow.— There's nothing that he conducts better than his own *Heldenleben.* I have no doubt that in his heart of hearts he takes only a very mediocre interest in old music, whatever it may be. He is essentially a modern; he is too much so. In that, he is unbalanced. No one in the hall except, at the end, X. . . , who comes and compliments him; and, naturally, on all that is worst in *Heldenleben:* woman, love. (I felt tears coming into my eyes!) Strauss, very taken up with *Louise* which he heard the day before, invites me to go to it with him on Monday, together with Clotilde and my sister.

126

Concert on Sunday, 4th March.—Hall very full. Behind me, de Blowitz, coarse and unspeakable, who snorts, and clears his throat, at every beat. He asks his neighbours if Richard Strauss is Johann's son; and during *Heldenleben* at the malicious talk of the hero's enemies declares: 'A village feast',—and at the beginning of the battle: 'The arrival of the Hussites.'—A very large crowd, and very warm acclamations at the end. But a good half of the hall is indignant about or scandalised by the work; and if it does not boo, it is from shyness, or politeness.—We go and say a few words to Strauss on the stage. He is quite blithe and frisky, and wants one to say that it was very fine. Charpentier comes, with emotion and respect in his voice, and tells him: 'You are a giant.' To which he replies: 'Well, Monsieur Charpentier, is that what the antagonists are like, in Montmartre?' with tremendous laughter. X. makes flat and stupid jokes, at which his familiars split their sides. I ask Strauss if he would like to come with us to the Théâtre Français or to a music-hall. 'A music-hall! A music-hall!' —'Because this week *Oedipus Rex* is being performed . . . ' '*Oedipus Rex?* What's that?' 'It's by Sophocles.'—'No, don't let's have any Sophocles! No Sophocles! The Palais-Royal!'

Monday 5th (March)

At the Opéra-Comique—performance of Charpentier's *Louise*, first tier box. The play is greatly superior to what I had expected. Much that is bad and insincere; but also much that is very good too, that is alive and intelligently dramatic.— Strauss arrives at the third act. He has spent the day at Versailles, then in rehearsing a quartet; then he 'has eaten too much fruit, he has a stomach ache'. He talks a lot about it like a child, and from time to time makes piteous grimaces, while holding his hands on his stomach. But when the music begins, he forgets everything, he follows it through a lorgnette with delight; above all in the fourth act, from the beginning of the duet (when Paris is lit up at the foot of Montmartre), up to the arrival of the Muse's procession; he inclines his head, cups his hand behind his ear, talks to himself in German,

127

looks at me or speaks to me, laughs with contentment like a child, and at the good bits, at unusual orchestral effects or modulations, puts his tongue out slightly, as if to lick his lips at a tit-bit. It's true that the orchestra has some excellent passages, sparkling with life, with rhythm, and with colour. But I do not hide from Strauss that I don't consider that the melodies differ much from those of Massenet, and that the emotion seems to me almost always inflated and false. 'But, my dear fellow,' he tells me, 'that's how it is in Montmartre. The French are like that. Large gestures, exaggerated eloquence, emphasis and ranting. We in Germany know that you are like that. It's very good like that and very true to life. Every nation has its defects. Those are yours. You don't like that, do you?'—'No, not at all; you might even say that I hate it.'—'Yes, but one must consider it true, all the same.' I tell him, but in vain, that there are in France, and always have been, accents of emotion side by side with noisy ranting, and deep feelings beside gesticulating rhetoric. He won't listen, or won't believe a word. His mind is made up, like that of all Germans. 'The French are exaggerated and grandiloquent. Not so the Germans. They are simple, and say things plainly as they are. Everyone knows that.'—But in the last act, when the music becomes high-flown, he looks at me a little mockingly and says to me: 'You don't like that, do you?' —But he considers this act as a whole 'terrifying' as he says, (*schrecklich*), that is to say, extraordinary; 'it's never been done before'.—He has written to Berlin at once to have the opera produced.—I admit, what's more, that there is, above all in the first and the fourth acts, some greatness, simplicity, and emotion which does not come so much from the effect as from the intelligence of the characters. The father is very remarkably drawn.—After the performance I suggest to Strauss that he should come and have something at a café. And as he has no self-control, although he is unwell, he accepts; but he hasn't taken a dozen steps when he is seized with stomach ache again, and he says with a grimace to me in the street: 'No, I think it would be more prudent to go to bed. The old chap must have a rest.' (speaking of his stomach).—

He is badly dressed in a frock-coat which is much too short and which rides up at the back; and his long legs look as if they are giving way. Nothing heroic about him. Oh! how far from a hero!—I am even afraid that he may never come back to being one again.

Thursday 8th (March).

The day of the fire at the Théâtre-Français—(Clouds of smoke are coming out of the windows on the 2nd, 3rd and 4th floors. On the roofs the silhouettes of firemen, and of gentlemen in top hats, an immense crowd all around). Chamber music concert, at the *Journal*, 100, rue Richelieu. Strauss contributes a sonata for piano and violin, a quartet for strings and piano, a *lento ma non troppo* from the violin concerto, and three songs. He is at the piano. He has charming fingers, very gentle, caressing and light; but he does not play at all like a composer; he has no strength, or character; he looks bored and indifferent. Moreover, apart from two dreamy and calm melodies, with a Beethovenian feeling about them, his music is not very interesting: they are youthful works, quite agreeable, classical, nay Mozartian, with some interesting modulations,—but without great originality.—In the artists' room, where people come to congratulate him, he holds me back; he wants to go out with me; he seems to have some affection for me. We walk a little way along the street. He speaks of the fire with his usual contemptuous indifference towards the French. 'It would be better,' he says, 'if all your theatres were burnt down. They're a public danger.' At a shop window we stop for a long time in front of photographs of the poor pretty little Henriot girl, who was burned. Strauss asks in a sulky tone, as if we ought to give him the answer: 'Why is it that young girls are always burnt, and not the old ones?'

Friday morning.

I go to fetch him at his hotel (Bellevue, Avenue de l'Opéra) in order to conduct him to the Louvre, part of which he already knows. I show him the eighteenth-century galleries, the royal apartments, and the drawings. He is very interested to get to know French Rococo. He has real taste in painting, and a fashionable taste, what's more. He greatly admires Chardin, whose workmanship he compares to that of Velasquez, (the painter whom he most admires). Fragonard amuses him; he appreciates the great Taraval; Boucher disappoints him a little. He is not hard on Greuze; he has a little too much sympathy for Vernet's landscapes, and he acknowledges great Watteau's superiority; he says that the *Embarcation* is a sort of '*Märchen-malerei*'. The happiness and the talent for living which the eighteenth century exudes flatter him agreeably.— He is clearly less attuned to our nineteenth-century painters, and to Delacroix in particular, but nevertheless he likes his Algerian women. Millet, Chintreuil and Daubigny please him.—He has even less sympathy for the painters of the Empire period, especially for Gérard, in which he is right, and also for David, in which he is wrong. I notice that everything which has a tendency to heroism, all painting which is tragic or in the spirit of Corneille, leaves him cold or bored.— From time to time he feels tired, and sits down. He talks to me about Napoleon I, for whom he has a great affection, but whose features disappoint and displease him. He considers them to be those of an actor, that his expression is cold and displeasing, and completely lacks the power of sympathy, which every truly great man has (like Wagner, whom, moreover, he has never seen, and Goethe. I make reservations about this).—We go through the Dieulafoy galleries, which he greatly admires. He sings the praises of slavery, talks of Cheops, who decreed that the whole nation should spend sixty years building his pyramid, and says that his wife considers that to be a very good thing. Needless to add that he is not a great supporter of socialism, of which we talk next, and in which he does not believe.—Finally I leave him among the drawings, in which he revels, (he says that they give him more pleasure than the paintings, because they are more sincere, more spontaneous)—in front of the big *Jeu de Paume* cartoon. He says a few words about Robespierre, which reveal a rather surprised and intrigued respect for that man's power over his contemporaries.

In the evening he comes to dinner. X kept him for 3 hours, playing him his new opera. 'Il joue et chante très mauvaise' (sic). This time he is completely unaffected and calm, and really likeable,—(although Clotilde—but not I—was shocked by the rather boorish lack of ceremony of his manners).

He has made the acquaintance of Hauptmann,[15] not long ago. 'He is', he says, 'an inarticulate being'. He stutters, and can't find the words he wants, he doesn't finish his sentences, he holds his head in his hands; one can't get anything out of him, nor find out what he thinks. For instance, he got him on to the subject of music, and of Beethoven, but did not succeed in understanding what his feeling was. However, he managed to make out that he doesn't like Wagner, that that genius's brutality was too uncouth for his neurasthenia. (He speaks with calm pleasure of this brutality which, in the same act of *Götterdämmerung*, makes Siegfried repeat two love scenes with two different women, and of the violent music which expresses them.) Hauptmann is an unhappy soul, who remains crushed beneath the weight of his thought and of the inclination, which does not succeed in curbing it, to go to the limits of his will; he is the hero of *Die versunkene Glocke*, he is Henschel,[16] all his impotent and weak heroes who torment themselves.

One of the questions which most preoccupies Strauss is that of the Censorship, the powers of which are daily extended and augmented in Berlin, and that of all the redoubling of puritanism, and the feudal reaction which, under pressure from the Centre Party, threaten the freedom of Art. For instance, quite recently a picture by Boecklin had to be taken out of a shop-window as being indecent. 'It's the Middle Ages.'— 'Fortunately, in music you can say everything, no one understands you.' He tells us how, when listening to Bach's B minor Mass recently, which is so free, so audacious, so independent in each one of its parts, he said: 'How fortunate that those words are there, to mislead people! Without that, to be logical, one should not allow it to be performed.' He compares this work to the Gothic cathedrals, in which the artist poured out his freedom of thought on all sides, in every corner, without anyone noticing it; writing was not allowed; so one

131

carved. Joking a little, he foresees the return of heretics being burned at the stake in Berlin.—Haven't they already wanted to tidy up Wagner's works, to make Siegmund and Sieglinde cousins and not brother and sister?

This lack of freedom is one of the reasons which confines him to pure music. He would very much have liked to write for the theatre. He has a weakness for his *Guntram*. He has made a libretto for a new opera. Above all he would like to set to music a ballet scenario, which has been brought to him. But the theatre is a prey to routine, to convention. One must be strong like Wagner to rise above it; and what good has Wagner's victory done? He realises now that what is suitable for opera is not Wagner, but Auber, Meyerbeer, etc. That's what they want. It's no good going against it. One is wrong to persist.—The subject of this ballet which tempted him, and which the *maître de ballet* in Berlin has turned down 'as not serious!' is the *Dance of the Stars*. A king, a tyrant, surrounded by his women, his jesters, his ministers, his poets, his scholars, —wants to be put amongst the stars. No one can carry out his wish. The poet declares that only poets have a place there. The magician can indeed make the stars come down to earth; and they do in fact appear; but the king cannot join in their dance. The tyrant becomes frenzied and threatens everyone; but he suddenly disappears into the ground, together with his court; and the stars rise slowly into the sky, carrying away the jester, the poet, and the magician—art, humour and knowledge, in their sacred dance. And the ballet finishes in the infinite space in which worlds disappear.—I can understand that ending fascinating a symphonist.

In the carriage, going to the Vaudeville where we are to spend the evening, he says to me naïvely, nicely: 'You were right in what you wrote about me: I am not a hero; I haven't got the necessary strength; I am not cut out for battle; I prefer to withdraw, to be quiet, to have peace. I haven't enough genius. I lack the strength of health, and will-power. I don't want to over-strain myself. At the moment I need to create gentle, happy music. No more heroic things.'

I question him about the Hero's wife (in the symphony)

which so greatly intrigued the audience,—some considering her a depraved woman, others a flirt, etc. He says: 'Neither the one nor the other. It's my wife that I wanted to portray. She is very complex, very much a woman, a little depraved, something of a flirt, never twice alike, every minute different to what she was the minute before. At the beginning, the Hero follows her, goes into the key in which she has just sung; but she always flies further away. Then, at the end, he says: "No, I'm staying here." He stays in his thoughts, in his own key. Then she comes to him.' In any case this very long, very developed section serves as a foil, an intermediary, between the two outbursts at the beginning and at the battle. 'It would be impossible to continue at such a pitch.'

Of conductors, he naturally prefers Mottl,[17] whose style is rich and strong (better in opera than in symphonies). He has a high opinion of Richter. But in spite of their great talent, he does not greatly appreciate those whom he calls the 'prima donnas' of the orchestra: Nikisch, who uses make-up on his hands; even Weingartner. He does not at all like Siegfried Wagner, whose *Bärenhäuter* seems to him a wretched thing, commonplace and worthless, and who is himself unbearable because of his self-confidence. He is pleased not to be in Berlin at the moment, where his opera is being performed; for he would have been obliged to talk to him about it. He says that Chamberlain's[18] book, (however intelligent it may be), is full of deliberate errors, written at Madame Wagner's dictation: in particular, the chapter on patrons; Madame Wagner being unable to admit that anyone ever patronised or understood Wagner, apart from herself.—In Berlin he is the enemy of the conservatives' camp, of which the Mendelssohns are the patrons, and Joachim the god. I am happy to find myself with a German who does not make a cult either of Joachim or of Brahms. He considers that Joachim is a good violinist, and that Brahms has dignity, serious-mindedness, erudition, but that he is cold, and stuffed with the classics; and that it is ridiculous to exalt him as people have done. He maintains that it's a bad joke on the part of Bülow, who launched the saying about the three great B's: 'Bach,

Beethoven, Brahms.' He is the enemy of virtuosi, tenors, etc.—
In short, he seems to live in a rather isolated way in Berlin;
his best friend is W. Rösch, secretary of the society of contemporary composers. He is also friendly with Wolfrum of Heidelberg, who has just composed a Christmas oratorio, in which
he praises the combination of Bach's style and Liszt's feeling.
—He does not like society; nor does his wife. They always vie
with each other in not accepting invitations.—I ask him if his
little boy (who is three) will be a musician. He hopes not;
because he remembers the sorrow he caused his father, and
believes that of necessity his son, if he were to be a musician,
when he is twenty would consider him a Philistine. He did as a
matter of fact have to go through struggles with his family,
with his father who was very musical, but of the old school,
who went barely as far as the penultimate works of Beethoven,
and understood nothing of his son's invention. Indeed, until
he had achieved success he was always on the side of the
critics against him, endlessly telling him:' Can't you see? All
that's absurd, it's not music.' And since he is afraid of being the
same to his own son, he hopes he'll be a painter or a sculptor.

At the Vaudeville, Pierre Wolff's *Le Béguin* is being performed, an absurd comedy full of wit; there is so much, in fact,
that there ceases to be any; unbearable showing-off. A
typical Jewish comedy: witty words, utter immorality and
with something hectic and irritating about it. Strauss, who
hardly understands anything, is wearied by Réjane's acting,
by her perpetual movement, her hands constantly occupied
with her clothes, her hair, her bodice, etc.; at the end he
coldly admits that she has charm, and is naturally natural.
M. Bréal[19] is with us, and has a very bad opinion of him,
because Strauss does not know that Zarathrustra really
existed; he thought that it was Nietzsche's invention. (In his
mind, he really did want to express, right up to the end of the
symphony, the hero's inability to satisfy himself, either with
religion, or science, or humour, when confronted with the
enigma of nature.)

After the theatre, we have some beer in a Bavarian café in
the Avenue de l'Opéra.

Saturday evening.

An evening party at the Xs or the Zs, I don't exactly know which. An almost exclusively semitic gathering. They had got the little Rioton girl from the Opéra-Comique to come, and she sings some passages from *Louise*, from *Manon*, and a melody by Strauss. She's a nice little thing, simple, placid, both slimly-built and at the same time solid, a real little mountain girl (she comes from the Dauphiné), who in many ways resembles Thérèse Pottecher.—Strauss, rather peevish at being in evening dress and in the midst of pretentious people, behaves exceedingly badly. He settles himself beside me on an upholstered sofa with a lot of cushions on it in the shade of a palm tree, and he closes his eyes, as if to sleep. I'm not quite sure that he doesn't sleep a bit. From time to time he half opens an eye, and raps out to me a few malicious words about the rest of the company; about the men who are dancing attendance on the little actress 'like flies on a lump of sugar',—and about the little actress herself who doesn't lose an inch of her height, who holds herself straight, straight, 'like my wife'.—They succeed in extracting him from his cushions for a moment in order to get him to the piano. He accompanies one of his songs with a bad grace; then, immediately afterwards, he gets up: 'Now, that's enough'; he shuts the piano, and goes back into his corner.—We talk about Russian novelists. He has not yet read *Resurrection:* 'Is it religious?' he asks, 'I don't like it when it's religious.' But he knows Russian literature well, *War and Peace, Anna Karenina,* the novels of Gontcharov; above all, Dostoevsky, whom he adores, and whose *The Idiot, The Brothers Karamazov, The Insulted and the Injured,* he praises. But the Russian characters, especially the women, are far from attracting him. In taking leave of him I suggest that he should come with us to the Ball at the Ecole Normale; he makes a face, and says that he prefers to go to the 'Federball', to the feather ball, in other words his bed. 'Nevertheless, you must be fond of dancing?'—'Me? Oh, of course.'—And with his big, gawky body he essays an *entrechat* in the middle of the drawing-room.

135

Sunday, 11th March.

Second concert, at which he conducts, in a way that is extraordinarily alive, vigorous, quivering (and always with that quite special talent for kneading the orchestral dough, for unravelling the instrumental masses, for making lines and colours stand out)—together with the overture to *Tannhäuser*, *Heldenleben* a second time, and *Don Quixote* for the first time. Indignation from one section of the public. The good old French public which, the less musical it is, the more it is a stickler for musical good taste, does not tolerate a joke, thinks it is being laughed at, that people are disrespectful to it. The baa-ing of the sheep infuriates it. At the end, applause and cat-calls: 'Bravo!' and 'It's disgraceful!'—Strauss, placid and drowsy, seems indifferent to it all.—So far as I'm concerned, although I have clearly expressed my criticism concerning his descriptive style, I couldn't help finding a great deal of wit and intelligence in these character paintings, and also in the wife of the Hero, whom up till now I had liked less.—I recall Strauss saying: 'In music one can say everything. People won't understand you.' And I think of the ironic amusement he must derive from this means of painting with cruel and farcical sincerity his enemies, his friends, his family, even his wife, without them suspecting it.—Charpentier applauds a great deal. I am surprised at his isolation, intentional or unintentional, and at the change (*idem*) in his appearance. He is certainly a good deal more simple and serious than he was a few years ago.—I wait for Strauss at the exit in order to shake hands with him. But he goes out another way.—I send him a telegram.—He leaves the following morning at 8.30.

*   *   *

May, 1905.

Strasbourg.—First Alsace-Lorraine Festival.—At the re-hearsal, Strauss's *Sinfonia domestica* begins to inspire me with a kind of aversion. Lack of proportion between the subject and the means of expression. Lack of intimacy. This yelling household displays itself in the full light of day with no sense of decency. And I am also conscious of too much that is

136

reminiscent of *Heldenleben* and of the old Strauss.—The general impression is: 'If I had a wife like that, I'd divorce immediately.' . . . —But at the concert in the evening I am struck by the beauty of the orchestration which is so light, so supple and so finely shaded, compared to Mahler's compact mass. The first statement of the themes has a character altogether too deliberate, conventional, schematic. They have not, moreover, great value in themselves. That of the child is particularly uninteresting and abstract. (Note how much Strauss's tone changes when he speaks of the child. There is something serious, religious, about it—but also less sincere.) The child's games are rather noisy, and not very interesting either. He's a young Hercules, that baby; and the whole house reverberates with his parent's conversations. (Note how, in this Symphony, Strauss keeps to the plan of an ordinary symphony in four movements.) The best part is the night, and the fugue at the end. In the night there is gravity, something dream-like, something rather unexpected and moving,—together with very bad taste.—The fugue, the quarrel, has an amazing comic liveliness about it. It's tremendous buffoonery, and it finishes with grandeur, in an apotheosis of the child, or of family life, which is a bit mendacious, very German,—but beautiful. The orchestra is superb. In this all the harshnesses fade away and blend, thanks to the combination of timbres. It's the work of a voluptuary—of an heir to the Wagner of *Die Meistersinger*.

But how one feels in Mahler the tiresome hypnotism of force, of German brutality, pulverising an Austrian temperament which is if anything dreamy and agreeable, a little whimsical, and basically soft. That makes the impression of Germanic heaviness stand out more than ever.

Unfortunate influences on all German artists: a) the theatre. They are almost all Kapellmeistern Direktoren of the operas in Berlin, Vienna, etc. Hence the character of their music, which is often melodramatic and in any case objective (this style does not suit them), too much show and effect. b) success in general. No sooner is a work written than it is performed. No longer any isolation, any long silences, any years lived with a work. The first idea that comes is accepted, liked. Cf. Beethoven forging the same themes all his life.

Present-day German artists are extra highly-strung. Mahler and his caricatures (shadow-theatre) of a hysterical cat. Strauss takes refuge in his power of apathy, of flabbiness. I am sure he has hours of waking sleep, of quasi-nothingness, like Rameau.

Strauss conducts Mozart's *Strasbourg Concerto* for violin. In an interesting, lively, but hectic way, in accentuating the rhythms to excess, at the expense of the melodic fluidity. Marteau plays simply.

Brahms' *Rhapsody*. *Stimmung für Männergesang-Verein*. Not without nobility, but conventional. Noble sentimentality.— Delirium of the public. The only thing encored.

October 1905.

During these holidays, I've had a fairly sustained correspondence with Richard Strauss about *Salomé*, the French translation of which he submitted to me. This enabled me to get to know better his amazing Germanic self-conceit concerning French music and literature, but also his perfect good faith, and his calm intelligence, devoid of second-rate vanity, capable of accepting all sincere criticisms, of being grateful for them, and of profiting from them. There's nothing petty about his pride; and if he succeeds in freeing himself from literary influences, and from the Wagnerian obsession, he is an artist who could rise very high. He knows how to criticize himself.

22nd November 1905.
Extract from a letter to
Mademoiselle Cosette Padoux in Bangkok.

. . . During these holidays I have had a fairly regular correspondence with Richard Strauss, concerning an opera which he has just written on Oscar Wilde's *Salomé;* he asked me to look through the French translation of it, which he has made himself. It is a very well-constructed work, very dramatic, but all in one breath, from beginning to end; and the subject, which the music powerfully translates, is an hysterical and morbid passion. It's a misfortune that Strauss who, so far as I am concerned, is the only German musician of genius at the moment, does not break away from the unhealthy atmosphere of his Berlin brotherhood . . .

* * *

25th March 1906.
Strauss has just conducted the *Sinfonia domestica* for the first time in Paris.—I go to fetch him the day before at his hotel (Hôtel Bellevue, Avenue de l'Opéra) to go to the rehearsal at the Châtelet.—It is rather cold. Some snow fell last night. Strauss, who has come in a spring suit, is shivering; in spite of the icy wind he made, the day before, a fairly long motor trip to Versailles: naturally, he has a heavy cold. He is as rash as a child, and like a child he grizzles afterwards. He grouses about the cold, about Paris, (almost as if Paris were responsible, and as if I were responsible for Paris). He has not thought of the remedy against the cold which consists in going to any shop to buy some warmer clothes: it's too simple an idea.

In the car, he starts all over again about French poetry and French recitative (I see that I talked to him for two months without him hearing: or at least, it went in one ear and out the other). Not without reason he upbraids the Parisian theatres for not giving anything but Gounod (*Faust, Mireille, Romeo*) and maintains that the most serious Frenchmen deep down still love Gounod above everything. I press him to tell me who these serious Frenchmen are: it's Bruneau.—He does not appear to appreciate Debussy, and his monotonous recitatives in triplets, at all. He is going to see him for the first time today; he is to lunch with him. I imagine that neither of them is particularly keen about it; they have the same indolence and the same pride.—Strauss says that *Salomé* is earning big takings everywhere in Germany, and he would very much like it to do the same in France.—I ask him if he has any work in hand.—No. Only military marches for the Emperor. 'That will please him.'—(There was a time when the Emperor and Strauss did not get on so well together.)

At the Châtelet. As we reach the stage, behind the curtain Mischa Elman can be heard playing the *andante* from Beethoven's Violin Concerto. Strauss growls. I ask him, 'What's the matter?'—'Oh, nothing! That piece. I would like to have written it.'

We listen to young Elman finishing his concerto, with amazing vigour and precision.—Strauss goes to conduct his *Sinfonia*. He seems to become more and more untidy as the years ago by. He conducts with his whole body,—arms, head and behind together; at moments he seems to dance on his knees; he crouches down; he makes tense and pulsating movements, like electric vibrations, with his hands. He gives explanations in very bad French gibberish, and sings out of tune passages that he wants played again; he cares nothing for ridicule; he always looks bored, sulky, half-asleep,—but nevertheless lets nothing escape him.—His music stirs me to my very depths. To me the finale is a flood of strength and of joy. One always wonders how *that* can have come out of *this*. But I should know better than anyone.

(Only, as always, there are too many 'hairs' in this music. It's as if sea-weed, or fibres, were twining themselves round a hero's torso.)

Afterwards, on the stage,—all the world and his wife were there: Bruneau, Pierné, d'Indy. I felt as if I was present at the meeting between Mendelssohn and Berlioz, after the *Damnation* at Leipzig. d'Indy: 'The entry of the double fugue was good.'—That was all.—Strauss, deferential to d'Indy, as Berlioz was to Mendelssohn: I would swear that, like Berlioz, he didn't fail to store up the saying in his memory.— And meanwhile Madame Colonne, fluttering round Strauss, was exclaiming 'It has love in it!' And, pinching his dangling arms in the too-wide sleeves of his summer overcoat: 'Your poor little arms! . . . Would you like me to lend you one of my husband's overcoats?'—And Colonne was saying to those around him: 'It's interesting, his symphony. Have you read the programme? Malherbe's[20] programme? It's admirable.'

—At the first night, Sunday 25th, a very big ovation. Since *Heldenleben* at the Thèâtre de la République, 5 or 6 years ago, Strauss has not had a success of that sort in Paris. (In the last few years it was a bit cool.) I even think that of all Strauss's works this was the one which most gripped the Parisian public.—I am not surprised at that. Whatever one may think of the first part of the *Domestica*, the end burns with joy, one can't resist it; I really think there's been nothing like it in symphonic music since Beethoven.

—Just now, looking at the big portrait of Strauss which I have at home and which Strauss gave me, I was thinking: it's very idealised; they've credited him with a character which he does not possess. Strauss, in real life, hasn't that vigour of expression; the impression he gives is pale, uncertain, eternally youngish, a little inconsistent.—But when seeing him close to, at the concert, conducting his orchestra, I was struck by the *other* Strauss: his face is ageing, hardening, shrinking; it is acquiring and retaining an intense seriousness, which not the slightest gleam of gaiety illumines for an instant. In profile, with his thick crown of hair, set very high up, and framing a monk's tonsure, with his enormous bulging forehead, his nose which appears small and short, and his sulky mouth, he looks like a barbarian from Asia, one of those Huns who founded a family in Germany.—But there is one thing which his portraits do not convey at all: that is the pale blondness of hair and complexion.

His wife and son are present at his Symphony which depicts them. The boy, rather nice, with a full, oval face and with very highly set and arched eyebrows. He seems very lively and gay.

November–December 1906

Gailhard is putting on Richard Strauss's *Salomé*. So far as the gallery is concerned, he appears to be animated by a pure love of art. In reality, a certain X is covering all the expenses of the production, in order that his mistress may take the principal part. But N., the prima donna, is getting worked up about it, and her adherents are protesting.—Now, one fine day both factions take it into their heads (how do they know it? I never said a word to them about it) that I am a friend of Strauss, and that he readily listens to me.—That is why, one fine day, there rings at my door an elegant young man, whom I scarcely know, who overwhelms me with protestations of friendship and of enthusiastic admiration, who volunteers to obtain for me the musical column in the ... in place of ... and who wishes at all costs to inveigle me to Berlin, in order to see *Salomé* and Strauss—in a word, who wants to butter me up, and make of me an unconscious instrument for persuading Strauss to take on the actress protected by X. Very cunning, all that; in any case I refused to make the journey. I only understood the ruse when, the next day, I saw Y rushing to me in his turn ... He, whom I had not seen for a year and who would never come on any serious business, made twice in two days the journey from ... to the Boulevard Montparnasse, in order to talk to me about the important interests of threatened Art, about his admiration for Strauss, about the shameful cabal which threatens to give the part of Salomé to an unworthy actress ... In a word, he was asking me to write to Strauss in order to thwart these plans (and to further his own; he didn't add that, but I added it for him.) Naturally, I have written to Strauss to draw his attention to the two cliques, and to warn him not to trust any of these honest Parisian advisers, but to judge for himself.

* * *

Sunday, 5th May 1907.
    First night of *Salomé* in Paris.—At the rehearsal at the Châtelet Strauss greets me in a friendly way, tells me he is unwell, is having some trouble with his heart, then suddenly: 'And there you go, publishing books against German music! You attack German music! But you haven't got any French music ... The smallest town in Germany has a concert hall, an orchestra, choirs, organs, better than you have here in Paris.' I say: 'Yes, but you have bad music played in them.' He protests.—'But it's true, it's true'—'In your country,' he says,

142

'it's a question of Monsieur So-and-So's mistress, or of Monsieur Someone Else's mistress, and which of the two will sing or dance a part.'—Well I know it. It was I who warned him, last December, about the double cabal at the Opéra.— I assure him that if I run down Germany, that is no reason for not doing the same to France. After all! If I run down France, there's no reason why Germany should be sacrosanct to me.

In the hall, during rehearsal. I am near Colonne and Pierné. Hours pass: Strauss lingers interminably on the same pages. Colonne says: 'A German never knows what time it is in music.'—'It isn't only the Germans,' says Pierné. 'What about Tchaikovsky!'—'Yes, the Russians, they've got a very large country, the steppes.'—Strauss flings himself about, yaps, trumpets. His stage-manager, Loewenfeld, flings himself about, takes all the parts. The actors in their everyday clothes, with bowler hats, a Roman sword at their waists, or a lance in their hands, fling themselves about, making great gestures. The actresses, in tailored suits and elegant hats, prostrate themselves in front of Loewenfeld, who represents the missing Herod (Herod and Salomé only arrive tomorrow, 3 hours before the dress rehearsal) or fan gas-stoves. Old Colonne groans: 'Isn't it stupid!—My Goodness! Is there anything as ridiculous as the theatre!'—'Yes,' I say to him, 'it's curious that a man like Strauss, who has such powerful means at his disposal as the dramatic symphony, such as he has transformed it, prefers all the conventions of an art as childish as the operatic theatre.' Colonne thinks, exactly as I do, that Wagner is much greater in the concert hall than in the theatre. We agree that his music is of the nineteenth century and his production, etc., of the fourteenth.—Basically, he hasn't much sympathy for the new music, old Colonne hasn't. He says: 'How odd it is that the decadence of two nations: France and Germany, should be incarnated in two men who represent it, the one with his effeminate refinement, and the other with his brutality!'—For all that, he affects to admire the *Domestica*, because he was the first to have it performed in Paris.—But he is not quite sure about that. He asks me: 'That's so, isn't it? That's right?' He draws a very odd parallel

143

between Strauss and young Dupont (Gabriel Dupont).[21] 'Moreover, he's very gifted, that young man; but he takes the same peculiar pleasure in making the notes shout one against another. There, just listen to that,' he exclaims at a passage of *Salomé*, 'all the notes of the scale at once!'

Pierné, very nice, very unassuming, and self-sacrificing (he has supervised all the rehearsals, and lets Strauss have the honour of the first night.) How strong the physical characteristics of people from Lorraine are! The same shape of face (head), the same reddish fair hair, pointed beard, the same look, same kindly, flinty way of talking, as his compatriot Marcel Dubois.

Dress rehearsal.—Three or four ministers, and the President of the Republic, the director of the Conservatoire, etc., etc. They would never have done that for Debussy. One can certainly see that Strauss is no Wagner: he has too much success too quickly. It's true that it's a reply to the proposals made a fortnight ago by Wilhelm II to Saint-Saëns, Massenet and to the opera at Monte-Carlo.—A gala audience. All the odious rank and fashion of Paris, doctors, third-rate actors, critics, and even musicians. I met X at the entrance, who tells me that this is the third time that he has come to hear *Salomé* (he heard it in Brussels), and that he hates it. A hatred which is more flattering than love, since he comes back in spite of it. Vincent d'Indy, between the Samazeuilh couple, mumbling with embarrassed timidity what little sympathy he has for the work. Z laughing at the domestic scenes between M. and Madame Herod.—The work is a torrent which bears along mud, flotsam, and foam with it, helter-skelter; its only merit is, I think, its frenzy; it's a mixture of base Italianism, of conventional Meyerbeer, of Wagner (*Tristan* and Beckmesser), and of Strauss, highly-strung and nervy, strained to hysteria. I find it repugnant, and I admire it. I admire it, for want of something better, whilst rather despising the man who has thus abused his artistic power.—At the end he appears on the stage, the man in question, in order to be applauded. The curtain is raised three or four times. But he is used to enthusiasms of a different kind. Someone whispers

144

to him: 'I am able to announce to you that the president intends to give you the Legion of Honour.'—'I've well deserved it', he replies.

Oh! the poor little women in tailored suits and elegant hats! What have they done to them!—They appear at the performance rubbed all over with black boot-polish, their poor little faces are black, black, and shiny,—horrible piccaninnies. —Mustn't they have cried about it?

Just back from the third performance of *Salomé*—(A full house. Men and women in evening dress even as far as the upper circle).—I find a note from Marnold[22] whom I introduced to Strauss. (He wants to translate *Feuersnot* and have it performed at the Opéra-Comique).—Marnold tells me that Strauss, who is still tired and unwell, would like to see us both the next day, and that 'he highly values my friendship and my advice"—which gives me pleasure, and makes me decide to write him my comments on the subject of *Salomé*. Essentially they boil down to this: 1) I regret that he has taken as repugnant and unwholesome a poem as Wilde's. I regret, in general, that he is influenced by the mirage of the decadent literature of Berlin.—2) I think that, in spite of his undeniable victory in the theatre, and his mastery of the stage, he has more to lose than gain in writing for the theatre; for he is essentially lyrical, and only feels, in a general way, his own personality (and what approximates to it); while he can only succeed in painting the external world, for which he has basically little sympathy, in an intellectual and arbitrary way.—3) I urge him, without ceasing to love power above everything, to prefer a power which does good, which communicates and inspires love, like that of the very greatest artists, like Beethoven.—To sum up, I confess that *Salomé* seems to me to be the most powerful of dramatico-musical works of today; but I add that he is worthy of better things than *Salomé*, and I beg him to rise above his victory and his partisans, and to separate his cause from that of contemporary decadent Europe, which is rushing madly towards suicide.

—(I must say that after having seen *Salomé* again and having digested my impression, I find Strauss's work less unhealthy

F

than I at first considered it. If one separates it from Wilde's poem, one has music which is no doubt morbidly neurotic, and verging on hysteria, but with very little sensuality about it, and which, without the magic of the instrumental richness, and the intellectual tension, would be on the cold side.)

Wednesday, 15th May

Saw Strauss in his hotel room (Hôtel Bellevue, Avenue de l'Opéra), I was with Marnold. Then Loewenfeld, the stage-manager of the Stuttgart theatre, and another German came. —Strauss was very nice, very good-natured, as perfectly simple and natural as ever; not a second of posing, not a single artificial word, not a premeditated gesture. I am always surprised how tall he is; he is thin, well-built; a tired face, still young, although the forehead (and part of the head) is very bald. He complains of his heart, and of excessive tiredness.— He doesn't lose much love over Paris, of which he has surely seen the worst sides. He again goes back over the story of the intrigues which surrounded *Salomé*, that the part should be given to such and such an actress, because she was so-and-so's mistress . . . One can understand that Strauss was disgusted.— . . . —Then he complains about the anarchy which reigns in France: 'I don't want to say anything about the Colonne orchestra,' he says. 'It played well.'— . . . —Thereupon, he starts railing against republics, which he can't bear: France, America. 'Is it even worse in America?' Marnold asks him, laughing. Strauss reflects for a moment, then says with a grimace: 'Yes, even worse.'— . . . —In his dissatisfaction with Paris he even incriminates its climate,—always raining—or, when it is fine,—dusty.

There is only one thing that finds favour in his eyes, as in those of Loewenfeld, and that is the staging at the Opéra-Comique, under Carré's direction. The other day he saw *Ariane et Barbe-Bleue* by Dukas.— . . . He is trying to get to know new French music, and I write down for him in his notebook the names of Sèverac,[23] Ravel and A. Magnard.[24]

(I even write to the last-named to send his works to Strauss.) Strauss reproaches our musicians with being too solely harmonists and not polyphonists: 'Polyphony,' says he, 'is music itself.'—'Why no,' Marnold exclaims immediately, 'It's harmony which is music.' I couldn't help laughing, seeing the eternal dispute between the choir-master and the dancing-master cropping up as always.

What gives me great pleasure is seeing Strauss (and Loewenfeld) taking up with uncommon vigour the defence of Berlioz against Marnold who, (very characteristic of our musical pedants in present-day France) declares that Berlioz is not a musician. 'He's a genius,' says Strauss. 'He has too much genius. He makes mistakes. What does it matter? It's like Boecklin.[25] You can pick out in his work an arm that's badly done, a movement that's incorrect. What does it matter? He has genius: that's all.' We agree entirely about this. About Berlioz and about Boecklin, I think like a German. At all events, I've not found a Frenchman who thinks like me. I really believe the French are incapable of feeling genius— except when it is accompanied with very great talent, which gets it by: (in this case, it's the very great talent that they like, it's not the genius).—Strauss has just re-edited Berlioz's *Treatise on Instrumentation*, with notes. He is indignant that none of Berlioz's operas are performed in France: neither *Cellini*, which overflows with life and imagination, nor *Les Troyens* of which he (and Loewenfeld) speaks solemnly and with deep emotion, nor *Béatrice et Bénédict*, which seems to him a little masterpiece.—Marnold makes a face. He does not hide the fact that Saint-Saëns seems to him a greater musician. ('Yes, he writes better,' says Strauss, 'but he has nothing to say.'), and for two pins he would prefer Gounod to Berlioz.

Strauss tells us some of his impressions of Spain, where he has conducted a few concerts. He admires Barcelona, where he conducted *Heldenleben*, heard his most difficult choral work sung, and where he was struck by the intense and multi-farious life. But Madrid seems to him barbarism itself. 'They massacre symphonies there,' he says, 'like bulls'. He tells us that the audience came to concerts to hear wrong notes. It was waiting for the scherzo of the *Eroica* with delight because it was sure the horn would be out of tune in it. But Strauss had rehearsed it well: the horn was not out of tune. Disappointed, the audience encore the piece. This time, the poor horn, tired, goes off the rails. The public, in delirium, starts to split its sides with laughter, and to hoot. Strauss, furious, turns round, tapping with his foot, and shouts: *'Was ist das?'* Deathly silence.—At the end the orchestra sends a deputation to him to thank him for having championed their cause.

Loewenfeld, intelligent, likeable, unobtrusive. It is deplorable to see with what gross stupidity our French artists (those we call artists in this country) receive foreigners. 'When I was introduced to Gailhard, in connection with *Salomé*,' Loewenfeld says, 'he treated me as if I was bringing him five francs. He began to talk about me, in French (knowing that I understand French). He said: 'This chap comes from Stuttgart.'—'Ah!', said the other, 'he'll give us a production the way they do in Stuttgart!'—When Marnold spoke to Carré, who is considered intelligent and well-read, about Strauss's *Feuersnot*, Carré seemed to consider the work to be that of a beginner: the name said nothing to him.—One wouldn't believe how much ill-feeling our stupid Parisians gratuitously pile up in the hearts of foreigners who have dealings with them. They don't suspect that these foreigners have as much—or more—shrewdness as they have, and that none of the offensive remarks made to them will be lost on them or forgotten.

I am very grateful to Loewenfeld for having said,—when I was criticizing the *Comédie-Française:* 'Ah! but Mounet-Sully is there. I saw him for the first time as Louis XIII in *Marion Delorme*. I don't like *Marion Delorme*. But Mounet-Sully is wonderful. He's the greatest actor I've seen.'

In order to have his revenge, X is writing to the papers.—
. . . This spitefulness and falsehood is extremely well received by the Parisian press, to which Strauss makes no complaint at all. *La Libre Parole* is conducting a violent campaign against Strauss, calling him a Jew— . . . It asserts that Strauss or his wife have grossly insulted France in Parisian drawing-rooms. As is natural, fine patriotic motives are called into play to

148

serve base interests— . . . In the meantime Strauss, who is contemptuous, spends four days in the forest of Fontainebleau, which enchants him.

Wednesday, 22nd May 1907.

Dinner at Marnold's house with Ravel. Strauss was to have come; but he was made to stay to dinner at Colonne's. This morning he played and sang his *Feuersnot* score to Carré, who accepted it.—Mademoiselle Marnold, a beautiful girl of seventeen, tall and well-developed for her age, full of life and laughter, with beautiful eyes and handsome features rather on the large side. She treats her father like an old pal of whom she makes fun with charming and easy impertinence.—I greatly appreciated Ravel. He is intelligent, free, and natural in everything he says. He criticises himself and criticises others with a great desire for impartiality, and with a clear-sightedness which is fairly rare in an artist. Yesterday he heard *Salomé*, which he considers a stupendous work, together with *Pelléas* the most outstanding work in European music for the last fifteen years. He is above all struck by the unparalleled richness of the rhythms and of the orchestration. Even Marnold, who was so hostile to Strauss up till now, and who so far knows *Salomé* only from reading the score, considers it to be a work of genius, from the harmonic point of view. Both of them, Ravel and Marnold, made a dead set at a subordinate passage: the hallucinatory sighing of the wind round Herod. It goes without saying that they are shocked by the bad taste, and the enormous gaps there are in it here and there. But Ravel, much more than Marnold, feels and admires the formidable unity of the work, which sweeps us along from beginning to end as the wind sweeps along a leaf. Marnold went so far as to reflect on French music, and so far as to say— (which, for him, is tremendous): 'There are moments when, after having heard *Salomé*, one finds all French music, even *Pelléas*, too finicky. Strauss has drive, a *Schwung*, which we all badly need.' That's what I call a *mea culpa:* those are my own ideas, aired by the person who, until now, has been their most resolute adversary.—But if the independents, like Ravel and Debussy, have sufficient intelligence and good faith to recognize (and perhaps to envy) Strauss's power, all the Schola,[26] as a whole, has risen against him. For this there are reasons which are as much moral as musical. I quoted X's saying, the other day; and Ravel was quoting that of Z, who said that 'those who admire *Salomé* deserve to be whipped'. There was talk of inviting Déodat de Séverac with us to meet Strauss. (Séverac is a friend of Marnold's and of Ravel's.) But Ravel says: 'No, it's not possible; Séverac won't come, or it would embarrass him; for that would compromise him with regard to the Schola'. Dukas alone, (whom the Schola has for the time-being made its champion) confessed on leaving after a performance of *Salomé*, 'that until then he thought he knew about orchestration, but he could certainly see now that he didn't.' (Talking of this, Ravel is very struck by the expressive use of the percussion in *Salomé:* it is something quite new to him.)

We talk of other musicians. Ravel defends Mendelssohn and Gounod against the reaction which crushes them today, the injustice of which is excessive. He does not hide the fact (which, for an ultra-modern musician, takes some pluck) that certain things of Mendelssohn charm him profoundly (*The Midsummer Night's Dream*, the overtures to *Meeresstille* and to *Melusine*, some of the *Songs without Words*). Above all, he defends *Carmen* against Marnold, who treats it with crushing contempt, saying that anything good in it is Spanish, and the rest is Jewish (for he has an obsession about the Jews, and maintains that Bizet must be one—which, after all, is not impossible). He is not so hard on Dukas either, although his *Ariane* seems to him, after *Salomé*, a 'useless' work, and he very much admires Mussorgsky's *Boris Godounov*.—There is talk, too, of his estrangement from Debussy, which appears to grieve him. It is obvious that it is all on the side of Debussy who has, I know, a violent antipathy for the music (or for the success) of Ravel. Ravel talks about him with a great deal of dignity and modesty, replying (to Marnold, who asserts that there must be a little jealousy on the part of Debussy) that Debussy has really no reason to be jealous of him, that there is nothing about his success so far that could cause him concern. And never a word of criticism escapes him about Debussy's art.—Only one wonders why Debussy remains without producing anything for so long; and Marnold expresses the thought that Debussy is played out, and that he is bitterly conscious of this.

After dinner we go to *Pelléas* to meet Strauss there. Carré has given a first-tier box to Marnold so as to give Strauss an opportunity of hearing the work, which he so far knows only from the piano score. Strauss arrives towards the end of the first scene. He takes his seat between Ravel and me. Marnold and Lionel de la Laurencie[27] are behind. Nikisch and various other foreign artists who have come either for *Salomé*, or for the Russian concerts, are in the audience. With his usual lack of restraint, regardless of social conventions, Strauss converses with no one but me, confiding to me his impressions of *Pelléas* in undertones. (Moreover, he mistrusts the others, after all the tittle-tattle in the papers.) He listens with the greatest attention and, looking through a lorgnette or my opera-glasses, he doesn't take his eyes off the actors and the orchestra for an instant.—But he doesn't understand a thing. After the first act (the first three scenes), he says to me: 'Is it always like this?'—'Yes.'—'Nothing more? . . . There's nothing . . . No music . . . It doesn't connect . . . It doesn't hold together . . . No musical phrases. No development.' Marnold tries to take part in our conversation, and says to him with his usual ponderousness: 'There are musical phrases; but they are not stressed, underlined, so that the general public notices them.' Strauss, rather hurt, but very calm, replies: 'Yes, but I'm a musician, and I can't hear anything . . .' We resume our conversation in an undertone. I try to make Strauss understand the restraint of this form of art, which is all in shades and half-tones, of its impressionism, delicate and poetic, using of little touches of colour in juxtaposition, unobtrusive and vibrant. He says to me: 'So far as I'm concerned, I'm a musician above everything else. Once there's music in a work, I want it to be the master, I don't want it to be subordinate to anything else. That's too humble. I don't say that poetry is inferior to music. But the true poetic dramas: Schiller, Goethe, Shakespeare, are self-sufficient: they don't need music. Where there is music, it must carry all before it; it must not come after the poetry. So far as I'm concerned, I have the Wagnerian system. Look at *Tristan*. There's not enough music for me in this. The harmonies are very subtle, there are good orchestral effects, it's in very good taste; but that's nothing, nothing at all. I consider it no more than Maeterlinck's drama, by itself, without music.' He starts listening again, very conscientiously, and makes an effort to notice and point out to me everything that he considers good in the work, as much out of a sincere desire to understand it, as out of consideration for me. But I can very well feel that this is more politeness than true esteem for the work. What is new in it escapes him. On the other hand, he doesn't let a single Wagnerian imitation pass without noticing it, and not in order to praise it. 'But it's just *Parsifal*,' he says to me at one passage. Nevertheless, the scene with the hair, the prelude to the cavern scene, and the scene following, give him a certain pleasure. It's clearly what he likes best in the whole score. But he always comes back to his rather scornful praise: 'It's very subtle.' I try to explain to him what is new in this type of art and the originality of the dramatic method, in which nothing is stressed, in which everything is inward and marked by a discretion worthy of Racine, He says: 'Yes, I understand. I agree with what you say about the method, about the novelty of the method. But with this method I would undertake to write quite different music to *Pelléas*.' I cannot, after all, break a lance for a form of art, when I realise its deficiencies better than anyone in France. I say to him: 'Look here, so far as I'm concerned, Debussy is a very great artist, more of a great artist than of a musician.' He takes me by the hand. 'There you are! That's what I think. A great deal of good taste, of subtlety, very well done, very artistic, pretty colours.'—'And poetic intuitions, too,' I tell him.—'I'll go as far as that: poetic intuitions. There. I won't say any more. We are in agreement.'—We are a little less in agreement than he would like to believe. For what com-

152

pletely escapes him (and that's very natural), is the principle thing about this type of art: the restrained and supple truthfulness of the recitative, of the musical speech, with its imperceptible tremors, certain inflections of which are so suggestive, and evoke profound and distant echoes in our hearts. The scene of the farewells, of the lovers, and of the death of Pelléas, seem to him to have misfired. Of course, he was waiting for the obvious scene, and he doesn't understand why Debussy didn't write it; he doesn't understand that Debussy's originality was precisely that of not writing it. I do my best to show him how new this is still, and a reaction against declamatory and extravagant art. He understands very well that it's a reaction. 'Yes,' says he, 'against Massenet and Gounod.' Not only against Massenet and Gounod. Also against Wagner. Also against Strauss. And I can't say it to him. (Perhaps deep down he does feel it.) But he seems to notice in this only an intellectual tendency, a bias towards simplicity, which comes as an interruption to musical development, and a hindrance to the expansion of spontaneous feeling. What is even more surprising, is that the last scene escapes him completely. I myself consider it the height of emotion and of art. I don't believe that anything so intense and with such economy of resources has been produced in music since Monteverdi. It is really Racinean art.—So far as Strauss is concerned, it lacks music.—I tell him (it's the contrary to Mozart's saying after *Don Giovanni*): 'If it had one single note of music more in it, it would be too much.'—He looks at me, shakes his head, and says: 'No, no . . .'

From time to time, what's more, he puts as much courtesy as possible into applauding, after every note, both the work and those interpreting it, whom he considers good. He reproaches the orchestra for not being sufficiently muted (and he's right). The bassoons are much too resonant.

After the performance we go to a café on the Boulevard, the Taverne Pousset. Strauss, Loewenfeld, Hermann, Marnold, Mme. Laurencie, Ravel, and myself. Strauss chose the furthest recess of the café, so as to be secure from indiscreet listeners. Even there, he is on his guard; he talks only with

153

extreme reserve. He is quite ready to tell me what he thinks; but he doesn't want to tell the others. He says that everything one says in Paris is in the newspapers the next day, but distorted. Therefore he is very discreet in his views. Nevertheless, he implies that *Pelléas* seems to him very interesting, but nothing more. He accepts my appraisal that it is 'a masterpiece of taste'; but so far as he's concerned, that is not saying much. A great German artist of today is far from suspecting the greatness there is in perfect harmony, equilibrium, good taste. He is hypnotized by power. Strauss says ironically: 'You Frenchmen are always afraid of saying something in bad taste.' (Which is true); and he sees, or thinks he sees this constraint in Debussy's work. He says: 'It's subtle, very . . . (gesturing with his fingers), very *gekünstet*, but it's never spontaneous; it lacks *Schwung*.' He adds furthermore (and this eulogy is perfectly reconcileable with his contempt for French music) that he very well understands that Debussy is quite a different type of artist to Dukas, and that he is the most original French composer.

Marnold says that he wishes Germany and France could get to know one another better, and that German composers could be sent for a period of several years instruction in France, and French composers to Germany: thus, the former would benefit from the harmonic genius of the French, and the latter from the German genius for *Schwung*. Returning to an idea which we have often discussed together, he says that Germany, France and Italy cannot do without each other; and that the greatest musicians are those who are nourished by those three musical civilizations.

That brings the conversation round to early music, in which Strauss takes prodigiously little interest. He says, curling his lip with slight disdain as he does so, that he knows nothing of Frescobaldi, nor of Monteverdi, nothing before Bach, and that it doesn't interest him. A few little things of Rameau. Someone tries to make him understand that there are works of genius dating from that period, and of a genius which is still quite modern, like Monteverdi's *Orfeo*. He listens politely, but with boredom. At one point Marnold talks to him about Bach, and about the way he wrote for trumpets and horns; he enters into certain technical explanations: about harmonics, etc. Strauss says to him: 'You are much more knowledgeable about my own craft than I am: I don't know anything about all that.' (There is irony behind this. But Marnold doesn't sense it.)—Then, as these conversations about early music bore him, he gets up and goes away.—The conversation continues between the French and Loewenfeld, who seems a pretty good braggart to me; (he tries to dazzle us by his knowledge of the scores of Monteverdi and of Lully; he picked the wrong thing: these Germans have no inkling of the musical erudition of the French of today; and Loewenfeld lost a splendid opportunity for not keeping some really asinine remarks to himself.) He is very taken up with staging Auber's *Le Domino Noir* again in Stuttgart; and he makes enquiries of each of us as to where he could obtain a first edition of Scribe. The first edition of the libretto of *Le Domino Noir!* That seems irresistibly comic to us.—An interminable discussion on the question as to whether the French are less known in Germany, or the Germans in France.—I leave them in the middle of it.

Strauss who talks to Carré about his idea of perhaps setting *Tartuffe* to music! 'Wretch! You should do no such thing,' he is told, 'There's nothing less musical than Molière.'

Marnold criticizes to Strauss the latter's musical motive for Jokanaan, which he considers very commonplace. Strauss, very astonished (these French must frequently astonish him a good deal) defends himself at first—'No, no, I don't think so.' Then he ends by saying: 'In any case, I didn't want to treat him too seriously. You know, Jokanaan is an imbecile. I have no sympathy at all for that type of man. In the first place I would have liked him to be a bit grotesque.'

I ask Strauss if he knows Mussorgsky's *Boris Godounov*. He tells me: 'No.' I say to him: 'It's an opera with genius in it.' He says to me: 'I don't know a Russian opera that has genius.' I reply to him: 'There's this one.' 'Ah!' says he. But he'll never look at it.

I have made Albéric Magnard send Strauss all his works;

and Marnold has left Ravel's works at his house. Perhaps he will look at them in Berlin. But here he doesn't look at a single page of them, and doesn't address a friendly word to Ravel.— He is an intelligent, strong man, and faithful in his affections, but he lacks broad and generous sympathy.

I ask him if he found my letter disagreeable. He grasps my hand as if to pulverize it: 'It gave me great pleasure.' he says. 'It was a very good letter. You know, I am the sort of man to whom one can say everything, and who listens with pleasure to all comments, who is grateful for them, when they are sincere and thoughtful, and when they come from someone in whom one has entire confidence. You are right. The text of *Salomé* is not good. I took it because I hadn't anything else, and because I had something to say. What was I to do? I can't write my libretti like Wagner.'—'You are not, I hope, giving up symphonic poems?' I ask him.—'No, but I haven't any on hand; in order to write one, there must be a need, a passion to be expressed; I don't want to write without that.'

L. de la Laurencie says something very true about Strauss, in connection with his inability to appreciate *Pelléas*. 'Of course, there's too little music in it for him. He has musical Bulimia.'[28]—I noted this German voracity the other day during a conversation. Someone was speaking to him about the possibility of performing his works at the Opéra-Comique. 'Yes', Strauss was saying, 'but what do you expect me to do with 70 meagre instruments! I need 110 at least.'—Debussy says of Strauss (whom he admires): 'He has the sound disease.' The noise disease.—It's rather true.—Like Berlioz, whom he in many ways resembles.

Thursday, May 28th.

Dinner at the house of a certain X who is, I don't know how, a friend of Strauss. One of those Jews who are good sorts, not very trustworthy, toadying and a bit sticky, whom it is impossible to shake off once they have stuck themselves to you. Rich, snobbish, a good musician what's more, and much in evidence in the artistic and political worlds of Paris.—I find there—(my sister accompanies me)—Strauss, Pierné and his wife, one of Briand's secretaries and his wife, the Z's Lord Speyer,[29] to whom the score of *Salomé* is dedicated, and Lady Speyer, Mary Garden (yesterday's Mélisande) and a rather pretty American woman, who has been playing (very badly) the part of the page in *Salomé*.—Strauss, with his broad forehead and his calm, vague eyes, like those of a young bull whose horns have not yet grown. We can hardly talk at all. He speaks to me again about *Pelléas*, from one end of the table to the other; he is bent on telling me that he was not insensible to the artistic qualities that there are in this work; he repeats that he is completely in agreement with me—(which I persist in doubting),—but that he does not want to argue with Marnold, because Marnold is incapable of arguing: he has only one idea in his head.—That shady customer, Z, still young, fat, and florid after two or three ups and downs of fortune, pays flat compliments and utters witticisms stupid enough to make one weep, which enchant the two actresses sitting on either side of him, their dresses cut so low as to show their navels.—Y says to me, joking (half), that he is going to sue me for having libelled him in the last volume of *Christophe*. —X has spent a wealth of wit, which exhausted him, in composing the menu for a dinner entirely devoted to Strauss. I give here this specimen of attic facetiousness: *Potage Feuersnot.—Truite Zarathustra.—Poularde Domestica.—Jambon de Prague à la Iochanaan.—Canard Eulenspiegel.—Salade Hérodias. —Asperges sauce Sieben Schleier.—Glace Salomé.*

This ice, which is this witty Maecenas's own invention, is all red and sprinkled with gory fruits.—During dessert, X's father proposes, in German, a ceremonial toast to Strauss. (Everyone speaks German). Strauss replies with a few casual words without getting up, saying that he is charmed by all the French, except by Mademoiselle Troukhanova[30] and that he drinks to all the French, except to Mademoiselle Troukhanova.

We have to leave at once after the dinner for the Sorbonne, where Paris University is at home to London University. X's car takes us with the Piernés (Pierné is conducting the Colonne orchestra at the Sorbonne concert). Madame Pierné is a

157

charming little blonde, with small and delicate features, a little Dresden china figure; she still seems quite young, although she already has a son of seventeen. Like her husband, she is very nice and very unaffected.—On the way, they talk to us about Strauss. . . . —Pierné adds that, so far as he is concerned, he has nothing but praise for him, and that Strauss has always been charming to him.

The French concert at the Sorbonne: Bizet, Lalo, Saint-Saëns, Fauré, seems pretty insipid and mediocre to us after the powerful or brilliant music which we have heard during the last few days. Saint-Saëns, himself at the piano, plays his own fantasy: *Africa*. This man of over seventy has the fingers of a virtuoso of twenty. His music, it must be added, is not of the slightest interest. He is the object of triumphal ovations. He has become the great musician of the Academes. And it is to them that he comes to gather laurels, now that musicians consider him almost as if he were dead—deader than Mendelssohn,—and perhaps even than Brahms.—It's odd that one can talk for hours, among musicians, of French music without even thinking of pronouncing the name of Saint-Saëns.

15th July 1907.
Extract from a letter to Mademoiselle Cosette Padoux, in Bangkok.
. . . I don't know if I spoke to you in my last letter—(I don't exactly remember now when I wrote it)—about all the Russian and German musicians we had here, last month: Strauss, Rimsky-Korsakov, Glazunov, Nikisch, etc.,[31] and about my conversations with them, especially with Strauss. Not one of them understands the others, and none of them understand anything about French music. The most powerful of them is Strauss: he is a volcano, too. His music burns, smokes sputters, stinks, and mows down everything before it. He is the decadent Attila of German music . . .

*   *   *

Extract from a letter to Paul Dupin[32]

. . . I am in the process of reading the score of *Elektra*, by Richard Strauss, which has just been performed in Dresden. The materials are, as usual, rather (or very) vulgar; but one is swept along by the torrent. The libretto is much more beautiful than that of *Salomé*. That legend of the Atridae is in any case unfailingly moving; it exudes horror and a tragic pity which grip one irresistibly from the beginning to the end. Strauss himself has been caught by it, (in spite of his nonchalance and Bavarian bantering which I, who know him well, come across endlessly in his ambling phrases and his eternal waltz rhythms, which he trails about everywhere with him, even at Agamemnon's: it's a very odd thing to see these German waltz rhythms transformed in his hands, and gradually translating with frenzied passion the transports of Elektra or of Clytemnestra). Joking apart, never has Strauss gone more deeply into the painting of the depths of the soul, of suffering. To me there does not seem to be in *Elektra* anything so extraordinary as the end of *Salomé*. But it is greater. In the scene of the recognition of Orestes by Elektra he touches the sublime. . . .

*   *   *

14th May, 1914.

At the Opéra, first night of the Russian season.—First performance of *Josephslegende* by Richard Strauss, Schumann's *Papillons* (as a ballet), *Scheherazade* by Rimsky-Korsakov (as a ballet—with Karsavina, Michael Fokine, etc.)—The production of *Joseph* is the most magnificent I have ever seen. In it however the stage-designer, José-Maria Sert, Bakst who designed the costumes, and Fokine, the choreographer, eclipse the musician, although the latter has adapted himself to them with the litheness of a monkey. A stage set of the Marriage in Cana, but in which the Christo-Venetian vision has taken on Babylonian proportions. Costumes by Veronese or Carpaccio, but all the colours exacerbated to the point

159

of flamboyance after passing through the brains of Muscovite artists, who are half Orientals. A mixture of the atmosphere of the Italian Renaissance with that of Scythian barbarity and Persian mirages. A production so perfect that the tissue of this long act (which lasts more than an hour) is not broken by any interruption, any failing of the action, even a fleeting one. Absolute harmony of the music with the slightest gestures or steps.—For the rest, the music seemed to me of mediocre quality, docile, rather commonplace, but always amusing, and of fine orchestral substance.—I admire Fokine's skill at translating any given music into a choreographic drama, as, e.g., in *Scheherazade*, the literary scheme of which he has totally transformed and succeeded in adapting exactly to a new drama of his own invention, without mutilating the score in any way.—That raises an odd problem of musical psychology which should be looked into. How can the music express two different actions so perfectly? In what does it express them, or suggest them? And what essential connection is there between these two authors?—My sister and I are in two dress-circle seats which Strauss had asked to be sent to me. In the row in front of us is Gabriele d'Annunzio, who boos Strauss's work when the curtain falls. His girlfriend, Ida Rubinstein, must have quarrelled with Strauss; she was to have interpreted the part of Potiphar's wife and withdrew, at the last moment.—Strauss, much aged, bloated, heavy and red . . .

October 1914.

Since the beginning of the war I had not heard speak of Richard Strauss. An article by Richard Specht in the *Pester Lloyd* of Budapest, 12th Sept. gives me news of him:

'When signatures were being collected for the famous Manifesto of German artists and intellectuals, Richard Strauss refused to give his. He said that he would joyfully send back his title of doctor *honoris causa* of Oxford University if, in exchange, a British dreadnought would be handed over or sunk; but declarations about things concerning war and politics were not fitting for an artist, who must give his atten-

160

tion to his creations and to his work; it is the business of those who make it their living or their career . . . Since then, he has voluntarily kept away from all manifestos, declarations, interviews, printed opinions, vocal fanfares, and particularly from any injurious appraisal of enemy conduct . . .'

End of January, 1917.

Letter from Dr. Hans Huber, director of the Conservatoire at Bâle (Bâle, 24th January).

Dear Sir,

Yesterday evening I was with Richard Strauss, who has been conducting his *Elektra* here, and who will next week conduct a revised version of his *Ariadne* in Berne. He told me how pleased he would be if he could meet you there on that occasion and have a talk with you. In such sad times, it would be a good thing if two such eminent men could, in a neutral country, stretch out a hand to one another.—I promised Strauss to write to you about this, and it would certainly be a great joy for all the artistic world if you would consent to make this little journey to Berne. I may perhaps be permitted to address this entreaty to you as an admirer of your works, and not only of *Jean-Christophe*, but also of the *Tragédies de la Foi*, of the *Triomphe de la Raison*, and of your *Angelo* (*sic*) . . .

DR. HANS HUBER.

I replied:

Friday, 26th January 1917.

Dear Sir,

I thank you for communicating Richard Strauss's friendly remembrances to me. I too would be very pleased to meet him; and if a touch of 'flu which I have at the moment allows me, I shall gladly go to Berne on one of the days when he is there. But I desire that our meeting should take place in private, for there is no point in making the wolves howl,— unless one wishes to: (and in that case one must choose the occasion and the moment). Would you be kind enough to let me know on what days Strauss will be in Berne, and what his address will be?

Yours very sincerely—and allow me to add my best regards to you as an artist.

ROMAIN ROLLAND.

Sierre (Valais)—Hôtel Château Bellevue

February 1917.

Richard Strauss writes to me from Zürich (12th February), when he is on the point of leaving Switzerland. He kindly suggests that I should go and stay with him for a while, at Garmisch, in Bavaria! He undertakes to obtain the authorisation . . . How little these poor Germans suspect what the state of mind is in Europe! Reverse the situation: a German invited to France, it would be like one of Napoleon's soldiers in besieged Saragossa!

* * *

Vienna. 10th May, 1924.

. . . On Saturday morning I want to get up and go out on an urgent errand to the Bank. But the weather is still awful, rain and wind; I catch cold again, and go back to bed once more when I come in. I spend the day in bed; but I don't want to forgo the concert in the evening. And this rashness serves me in good stead: for the music sets me up again, stops my bouts of coughing, gives me back internal rhythm.—The magnificent Philharmonic Orchestra, conducted by Strauss, plays *Zarathustra* and *Heldenleben*. *Zarathustra* seems very weak to me, —laughter without frenzy, the dance of the spheres reduced to a Vienesse waltz. But *Heldenleben* still produces in me the intoxication of the first days when I heard it, as a young man, at the Gürzenich in Cologne. What a bath of vigour and joy Strauss's orchestration is for me!—Strauss has aged little; and he is less heavy-looking than he was beginning to be in 1914, when I saw him at the performances of *Joseph* in Paris; he is tall, slim, cold, impassive, precise; he makes very few gestures; at rare moments of musical frenzy one discerns the intense nervous vibration which stirs him, and which suddenly makes the orchestra flare up: it's like an electric spark applied to gunpowder.—Some songs by him, in good old classical taste, are also sung.—On leaving we find Stefan Zweig,[33] who has come from Salzburg to spend three or four days with us.

Sunday 11th (May)

In the morning, a visit to the museum, with Zweig.—The Brueghels: the two-fold interest of art and of popular psychology, morbid, almost lunatic and famished.—Rembrandt: the proud gaze of an old and suffering face.—Rubens: Helen, the fat sufferer from arthritis; a love for swellings, puffiness, distortions of the beloved body.—Coreggio. —A panoramic excursion.—But what artistic futilities in these big museums, filing-cabinets for history!—Luncheon in the cellar near St. Stephen's.—Invitation from the Bürgermeister to a gathering in honour of Strauss.—The director of the Opera, Dr. Schalk, offers us his box for the performances.—In the evening, *Ariadne auf Naxos*. The comic parts are good and well acted; the polka sung by the comic singers does not fall flat.—But the general impression is a disappointment. I had heard tell about this work (from Zweig, from Bahr, from Annette Kolb, from all the Viennese élite),[34] as if it was Strauss's master-piece! It seems to me hybrid and cold. No over-all conception as regards either the general idea, the drama, the musical style or the production. Serious, or ironical? The two authors have thought so much about this that in the end they don't know themselves. *Ariadne*, twice re-written: it should be a third time. All those pastiches: that would be nothing; but Hofmannsthal, a slave to his virtuosity, ends up by taking them seriously. And Strauss can't. Instead of ending, as they should have done, with an ironic septet of the five comic and two tragic characters, the comic characters are eliminated and we are offered nothing but a pompous and frigid tragedy involving two bombastic persons. Lack of taste. Lack of life.—I feel that both Strauss's art and German music in general are stagnating. What confirms my impression is the fact that none

163

of the best Viennese judges notice it. Vienna: a big old provincial town. It has no inkling of new trends, of the accelerated rhythm, of the contribution of such people as Stravinsky, Honegger, etc., of this frenzy which we can no longer do without in music, especially operatic music.—I feel here that I am with distinguished old people half-asleep and habit-bound. The public here is, moreover, hard on the slightest faults which offend against these habits. The Zerbinetta, an excellent artist who takes this break-neck part with admirable virtuosity, is booed for a single wrong note in the last *aria*.

Monday 12th (May)

In the morning, tour of the National Library, with its great baroque ball-room,—of the music library, where Dr. Haas[35] does the honours. It would be a nice place in which to continue my journey to the country of Hasse and of Traetta.[36] *Epithalamium* by Orlando di Lasso. Beethoven's abuse. Strauss's *Rosenkavalier,* given in exchange for the site for a house.[37]—At the Albertina we are shown portfolios of drawings by Dürer and Altdorffer.

Visit from Madame Andrö, my translator for the *Voyage Musical,* who was greatly impressed by reading *L'Eté*.[38]

A letter from Richard Strauss invites me to come to see him; and I go to his flat, in the Mozartstrasse. I find him surrounded by a circle of ladies and boring society people. Strauss, serious, heavy, affectionate. Very preoccupied by nationalist follies, by our threatened European civilization. Civilization, for him, is concentrated in Europe, a little tiny Europe, three or four nations. And they are destroying themselves! He doesn't understand. He never has a smile on his face. No sudden bursts of gaiety, of fire, of unconscious 'raga-muffinery,' as there used to be in the past.—He is, moreover, tired by this succession of musical festivals, the end of which he is impatiently awaiting in order to escape, on Thursday, to Garmisch; and he has had heavy anxieties: his son, recently married, caught typhus in Egypt, and almost died.— The question of money also preoccupies him. In Vienna he is reproached for, and people speak ungraciously of, the place this preoccupation now occupies in his life . . . But no one has mentioned what Strauss told me today: all his fortune, the fruits of his work, deposited in England before 1914, has been confiscated; and at his age he has to make tours in America in order to better his circumstances once more.—His ballet *Schlagobers* has just been slated by the Viennese critics. Strauss appears affected by its failure. 'People always expect ideas from me, big things. Haven't I the right, after all, to write what music I please? I cannot bear the tragedy of the present time. I want to create joy. I need it.'—He appears to be absolutely indifferent to national questions and to national quarrels.—Madame Strauss, who flutters about hither and thither, and who kisses him on the head whilst stuffing him with pastries, affects the same detachment from the German fatherland (which astonishes me).—But what I have no doubts about is the pleasure which my coming to Vienna gives him. He greatly appreciates faithfulness and says with warmth, pointing to me: 'The best friend.'—He is working on a new libretto by Hofmannsthal,[39] about Helen and Menelaus coming back to Sparta after the Trojan war,—a continuation (or an interpolated episode) of the Second part of Faust: for, at the end, Helen goes off towards the Middle Ages, in order to meet Faust there.—But why does Strauss, who so well realizes his inaptitude for great subjects of thought, let himself be caught by them again?

In the evening, at the Opera, *Schlagobers* (the whipped cream of Vienna).—It is now clear to me that the righteous indignation of the Viennese critics, and even of the best dilettantes such as Specht, Stefan, etc., stems from personal motives; for the music is highly agreeable, and the production remarkable; there are real happy touches in it of colour, light and shade, notably in the scene of the riot, which conjures up visions of Brueghel and of Rembrandt. But the public, under the influence of the press, does not applaud. The cabal has given its orders. Strauss has caused too many wounds to self-esteem, even amongst his adherents. They are taking their revenge.

Tuesday, 13th (May).

Stefan Zweig invites us to luncheon, together with some Viennese friends, in a big hotel on the Graben (Kärtnerstrasse). A simple luncheon, and very cordial. At table I sit next to Arthur Schnitzler,[40] and the director of the *Neue Freie Presse,* Benedikt. The other guests are Paul Stefan, Richard Specht,[41] Felix Braun, Erwin Rieger, Trebitsch, and Hoheneimer (who is president of the Viennese P.E.N. club).

Stifling heat has, with no transition, succeeded the cold of the preceding days. Both are especially noticeable in Vienna, which is swept by winds and roasted by the sun.

In the evening, at the Opera, Strauss's *Die Frau ohne Schatten.* A long performance, from 6–10 p.m. The work is full of picturesque and poetical happy thoughts; it even at times displays a pretty melodic vein; but it suffers from the German disease of musical development, of repetition. And Hofmannsthal's libretto affirms that writer's theatrical incompetency. His obscure thought trails an icy shadow. It weighs down the passion. Strauss suffers from his collaboration. His old spirit has gone to sleep, it's as if his blood has thickened. Bavarian phlegm.

Wednesday 14th (May).

. . . In the evening, the last Strauss concert.—*Don Quixote* and the prodigious *Domestica.* A monument amongst classical masterpieces. The summit of the post-Wagnerian symphony. Strauss grows animated while conducting it, becomes the young Strauss once more, laughs with the timpani, takes pleasure in the joy he is unleashing.

Chatted with Edward Dent and with Guido Adler.[42]

Thursday 15th (May).

In the morning, a visit from the poet Paul Neubaur, who has come from Prague to see me. Small, rather mannered. Intelligent. Appears to be sincerely devoted.

Arrangements with the Czech Embassy for our departure on Sunday.

In the afternoon, from 3 p.m.–6 Hertzka, the director of

Universal music publishing house, comes to take us in his car for a drive around Vienna. We go to Kobenzl, that kind of Viennese Meudon, from where one overlooks the vast panorama of Vienna and the Danube, through a beautiful *viale dei colli*, among the young woods of springtime. Opposite, the pleasant and picturesque lines of the Kahlenberg. It is a magnificent day. Everywhere the lilac is in flower.—As we go down again we pass the cemetery at Grinzing once more, in order to pay our respects to Mahler's grave, very simple, two columns, the name, without titles, with no date; the grave is neglected, except for a bunch of faded flowers, ivy. He liked this part of the world, and planned to retire here after his stay in America.—Then, to Hertzka's house and to the school of agriculture, founded and run by his wife, at Grinzing. Vast grounds bought before the war, and built with taste. Forty girl pupils. (Madame Hertzka is away at present, at the Congress of the Women's League for Rights and Freedom, in Washington). Hertzka, long grey hair and beard, very nice, reticent, and full of attentions. His *Universal* publishing-house has existed for twenty-one years—for seventeen years he has been at the head of it. And now he has publishing houses in London and in New York. The *Universal* of Vienna is the centre of new music, it organizes big international auditions; and Hertzka is the real head of the international publishing-house.—Tea out of doors. Still with the 'Schlagobers' (whipped cream) which, in Vienna, is mixed with everything. The young prefects from the school come to call on us, some bringing in their aprons a swarm of chicks, others some ducklings, others kittens, others two little kids, and armfuls of flowers. Hertzka shows me his fine musical facsimile editions of Bach, Beethoven, Wagner . . .

—I have written to Strauss in order to tell him what pleasure *Schlagobers* gave me, and to console him for the 'injustice' of the critics.— X loses no time in publishing my letter, as if it had been addressed to another friend; the word 'injustice' is misread: never mind that! They print: '*l'imprudice** de la

*Meaningless word—misprint for 'injustice'. Tr.

167

critique', and even in capital letters, as if this unknown word had a startling meaning—and an insulting one, for Viennese critics. Immediately a journalist turns up to congratulate me on the vigour of my fine expression . . . 'As you have so well said: the 'imprudice' of the critics . . .'—And now here I am, saddled with a barbarism and all the critics of Vienna at my heels!

20th May 1927.

Performance of Richard Strauss's *Der Rosenkavalier* in Geneva. (Orchestra and Company of the Dresden Opera, conducted by Fritz Busch.—The Marschallin: Meta Seinemeyer; Octavian: Elisa Stuenzner; Sophie: Marguerite Nikisch; Baron Ochs: Ludwig Ermold; Valzacchi: Hans Lange; Annina: Elfriede Haberkorn; Faninal: Rudolf Schmalnauer.) No outstanding artist, but an excellent ensemble; very well sung and acted; the two best interpretations: Baron Ochs and Octavian.—It was the first time that we had heard the work, although we have a particularly soft spot for it. And we recognize that this soft spot was merited. Of all the works of Richard Strauss, none will do more to keep his name alive then *Rosenkavalier* (and the *Domestica*). He has put the best of himself into it—as a man and as a musician. The flower of his poetry (too hidden, too wasted, in the rest of his music). The first meeting of the two children, in the second act; the exquisite delicacy, the youthful awakening of an innocent love; some passages depicting the amorous intoxication of an adolescent, at the beginning of the 1st Act; the beautiful trio so tinged with emotion, and the purity of the duet which bring the work to an end, are worthy to take their places in the classical treasure-house of the Webers and the Mozarts. But never did any musician have the good fortune, which fell to Richard Strauss, to work on a libretto like Hofmannsthal's. Even without the music, it's a feast to be relished. What subtlety of touch, what grace, and what malice! It is almost too rich and too delicately shaded to be fully expressed in the operatic theatre: the listener loses more than half of it; one must read it in order to fully appreciate it.—I take off my hat to those little idiots, the critics of Geneva, who preach to him! They reproach him with mixing up his styles and, while bound to evoke the memory of Molière, they think that they are crushing him beneath that name. They have no idea that they are dealing with one of the most perfect artists who has ever handled the German language,—and that the *Rosen-kavalier* is perhaps his masterpiece for the theatre.—Since divine Mozart's *Nozze,* never has music been so nobly served.[43]

(Naturally, I also see the longueurs, and the errors of taste, —and above all that false style of 'sung recitative'.—But what do I care, if I can gather in these fields a bunch of the purest and most delicate flowers of music and poetry!)

NOTES

DIARY

1. Fernand Le Borne (1862-1929), Belgian critic and composer. The opera in question may well have been *Mudarra,* produced in Berlin on April 18, 1899.

2. Dom Lorenzo Perosi (b. 1872), composer of Church music and at one time musical Director of the Sistine Chapel in Rome.

3. Unfinished opera (one act only completed), first performed in Berlin on January 14, 1899. (See also Note 3. Introduction.)

4. Gerhardt Hauptmann (1862-1945), German dramatist, author of, among other things, *Die versunkene Glocke* (1896), a fantastic play which Ravel at one time intended to set to music.

5. Berthel Bamberger, niece of Louis Bamberger, German statesman. Louis Bamberger was the brother of Mme. Michel Bréal, mother of Clotilde Bréal, Romain Rolland's first wife.

6. See Note 2 above.

7. First performed under the composer's direction in 1854 as an introduction to the first Weimar performance of Gluck's *Orfeo.* (Symphonic piece.)

8. For contralto solo, male chorus and orchestra (1870).

9. See Note 2. Introduction.

10. Hugo Becker (1863-1941), famous cellist; professor at the Hochschule in Berlin; partner in trios with Ysaÿe and Busoni.

11. Famous French musicologist, author of numerous scholarly works, notably *Les Maîtres Musiciens de la Renaissance Française* (23 vols.) and a catalogue of French and Flemish works of the 15th and 16th century (2 vols.) (1863-1952).

12. Rolland's wife. (See Note 5 above).

13. Max Schillings (1868-1943), German conductor and composer, musical director at Stuttgart, and Director of State Opera in Berlin from 1919 to 1925. He wrote four operas, of which *Ingwelde* (1894) is the first.

14. Characters (father and son) in Molière's *Le Malade Imaginaire;* term signifying an ignorant and arrogant medical pedant.

15. See Note 4 above.

16. A character in one of Hauptmann's novels.

17. Felix Mottl (1836-1911); Famous Wagnerian conductor; Director of the Munich Opera.

18. Houston Stewart Chamberlain (1855-1927). An ardent Wagnerian who settled in Germany and married Wagner's daughter Eva. Author of *Richard Wagner* (Munich 1896) and *Richard Wagner, German Artist, Thinker and Politician*, Leipzig.

19. Rolland's father-in-law.

20. Charles Théodore Malherbe (1853-1911), French composer and musicologist. Author of books on Wagner, Tchaikovsky, Auber, etc., one time archivist of the Paris Opéra.

21. See Note 25, *Correspondence*.

22. See Note 20, *Correspondence*.

23. Déodat de Séverac (1873-1921). A pupil of d'Indy and a composer of great originality and charm. His works include two operas, orchestral and chamber music, songs and a number of piano suites and pieces among which *En Languedoc*, the region of which he was a native, is typical.

24. See *Correspondence*, letter from R.R. of November 10, 1904, and Note 11.

25. Arnold Boecklin (1827-1901), Swiss painter.

26. The famous *Schola Cantorum*, founded in 1894 by Charles Bordes, Alexandre Guilmant and Vincent d'Indy, and characterised by a certain austerity of outlook and the highest standards of training and proficiency.

27. La Laurencie (1861-1933), distinguished French musicologist, former President of the Société Française de Musicologie.

28. English: Bulimy ... 'morbid voracity' (Chambers's Twentieth Century Dictionary).

29. No doubt, Sir Edward Speyer (1839–1934). German-born patron of music and musicians domiciled in Britain.

30. Russian ballet dancer; created *La Péri* of Paul Dukas (1912).

31. This was on the occasion of the first concerts of Russian music organised by Diaghilev in Paris in 1907. The programmes included excerpts from Rimsky-Korsakov's operas *Mlada, Sadko,* and *Tsar Saltan,* and the second act of *Boris Godunov,* all of which were new to Paris and created a sensation.

32. Paul Dupin (1865-1945); French composer, entirely self-taught, the originality of whose works attracted Rolland; and in return Dupin wrote an orchestral Suite inspired by *Jean-Christophe.* (See also p. 225 in *Romain Rolland and Music.*)

33. Stefan Zweig (1881-1942); German novelist, and librettist of Strauss's opera *Die schweigsame Frau,* produced in Dresden under the Nazi regime in 1935. This collaboration made Strauss unpopular with the authorities, since Zweig was a Jew and had had to leave Germany.

34. Annette Kolb (1875-) novelist; Hermann Bahr (1863-1934) writer.

35. Robert Haas; Austrian musicologist (b. 1886), Director of National Library in Vienna, editor of Bruckner's symphonies.

36. Johann Adolph Hasse (1699-1783); Prolific German composer, pupil of Alessandro Scarlatti, author of numerous operas which had great success in Italy during his lifetime, but are now entirely forgotten. Tommaso Traetta (1727-1779), Italian composer; wrote church music and 40 operas; worked in Naples, Parna, Venice, St. Petersburg and London, but only his name has survived.

37. These somewhat cryptic entries no doubt refer to exhibits in the music library: a work by di Lasso; some letters of Beethoven, perhaps, containing abuse; the score of *Rosenkavalier.*

38. *L'Eté:* a chapter, or section, from Rolland's novel *L'Ame enchantée.*

39. This was *Die ägyptische Helena* (1928).

40. Famous Austrian playwright and novelist (1862-1931).

41a. Paul Stefan (1879-1943); Austrian music critic and author; one of the founders of the I.S.C.M. (International Society for Contemporary Music), correspondent of the *Neue*

Zürcher Zeitung and *Musical America* and author of books on Mahler, Schoenberg, Schubert, Toscanini etc., and translations into German from Tacitus, Daudet, Verlaine, Sainte-Beuve, Theodore Dreiser, Papini and Verdi (Letters).

41b. Richard Specht (1870-1932); Austrian music critic, author of books on contemporary composers, including Richard Strauss.

42a. Edward Dent (1876-1957) the distinguished English musicologist; sometime Professor of Music at Cambridge University and first President of the International Society for Contemporary Music.

42b. Guido Adler (1855-1941). Austrian musicologist, Professor at Vienna University where he founded a famous Institute for musical history comprising a valuable collection of musical instruments and library. General Editor of *Handbuch der Musikgeschichte*—(1924), an outstanding contribution to musicology.

43. But cf. Rolland's criticism of Hofmannsthal on p. 163.

PART III

Two Essays:

I. RICHARD STRAUSS

II. FRENCH MUSIC AND GERMAN MUSIC

I

RICHARD STRAUSS*

The author of *Heldenleben* is no longer a stranger to Parisians. Each year, on the conductor's rostrum at Colonne's or at Chevillard's concerts, we see his tall, thin silhouette with its abrupt and imperious gestures reappear, his pallid face a little feverish, his eyes uncommonly clear, vague and at the same time intent, his mouth that of a child, his moustache so fair as to be almost white, his frizzy hair forming a crown above the bald temples, and his forehead round and bulging.

I would like to sketch here the strange and dominating personality of the man who is considered in Germany as the heir to Wagner's genius,—of the man who has had the double audacity of writing, after Beethoven, another Heroic Symphony, and of depicting himself as the hero of it.

Richard Strauss was born in Munich on 11th June, 1864. His father, a famous virtuoso, was first horn in the royal orchestra. His mother was the daughter of Pschorr, the brewer. He was brought up surrounded by music; from the age of four he played the piano, and from the age of six he composed little dances, *Lieder*, sonatas, and even overtures for orchestra. It is possible that this extreme artistic precociousness was not without influence on the feverish character of his talent, that it strained his nerves to excess, and gave his mind a rather morbid over-stimulation. Since

*An article which appeared in the *Revue de Paris* on 15th June, 1899, and was reprinted in *Musiciens d'Aujourd'hui*.

175

then he has been composing all the time. At high-school he composed choruses for tragedies by Sophocles. In 1881 Hermann Lévi made his orchestra perform a symphony by the young student. At the University he spent his time in writing instrumental music. Bülow and Radecke played it in Berlin, and Bülow, who became fond of him, summoned him to Meiningen in 1885 as Musikdirektor. He spent 1886-1889, with the same title, at the Hoftheater in Munich. From 1889-1894 he was Kapellmeister at the Hoftheater in Weimar. He returned to Munich in 1894 as Hofkapellmeister, and in 1897 he succeeded Herman Lévi there. Finally he left Munich for Berlin, where he is at present conducting the Royal Orchestra.

Two facts in his life should particularly be remembered: the influence of a man to whom he owes the deepest gratitude: Alexander Ritter; and his journeys to the South. He made the acquaintance of Ritter in 1885. This musician, unknown in France, and who has been dead for several years, was Wagner's nephew; he wrote two well-known operas: *Fauler Hans,* and *Wem die Krone?* and he was, according to Strauss, the first to introduce the Wagnerian system into the *Lied*. He is often mentioned in the correspondence of Bülow and of Liszt. 'Before I met him,' says Strauss, 'I had been brought up in strictly classical discipline; I had subsisted exclusively on Haydn, Mozart, and Beethoven, and I had just been through the stage of Mendelssohn, Chopin, Schumann and Brahms. I owe to Ritter alone the fact that I came to understand Liszt and Wagner; it is he who showed me the importance, in the history of the art, of the writings and the works of these two masters. It is he who, by dint of years of lessons and affectionate advice, made of me a musician of the future (*Zukunftsmusiker*), and put me on the path along which I can now walk independently and alone. It was he who initiated me into the ideas of Schopenhauer.'

The second influence, that of the South, which seems to have left an indelible impression on him, dates from April, 1886. It was then that he visited Rome and Naples for the first time, and returned with a symphonic fantasy called: *Aus Italien*. In the spring of 1892, following an acute attack of pneumonia, he made a long journey, lasting a year and a half, to Greece, Egypt and Sicily. The serenity of these blessed countries filled him with an eternal regret. Since then, the North weighs on him; 'the horrible grey on grey of the North, phantom ideas with no sun*'. When I saw him one icy April day in Charlottenburg he told me with a sigh that he could not compose anything in winter; he is nostalgic for the Italian light. This nostalgia has penetrated his music, in which one feels one of the most tormented souls of deep Germany and, at the same time, an unceasing yearning for the colours, the rhythms, the laughter, the joy of the South. Like the musician dreamt of by Nietzsche†, it seems as if 'he must have in his ears the prelude to a deeper, mightier, and perhaps more perverse and mysterious music, a super-German music, which does not fade, pale and die away, as all German music does, at the sight of the blue, wanton sea and the Mediterranean clearness of sky—a super-European music, which holds its own even in the presence of the brown sunsets of the desert, whose soul is akin to the palm-tree, and can be at home and can roam with big, beautiful, lonely beasts of prey . . . I could imagine a music of which the rarest charm would be that it knew nothing of good and evil; only that here and there perhaps some sailor's home-sickness, some golden shadows and tender weaknesses might sweep lightly over it; an art which, from the far distance, would see the colours of a sinking and almost incomprehensible *moral* world fleeing towards it, and would be hospitable enough and profound enough to

*Nietzsche.
I hope I will be forgiven for annotating this essay with Nietzsche's ideas, which are constantly reflected in Strauss, and throw such sharp light on the soul of the modern German.
†Id.—*Beyond Good and Evil*, 1886, XVI, 255. Trans. Helen Zimmern. [Vol. XII of *Complete Works*, ed. by Dr. Oscar Levy. Edinburgh and London, 1909.]

receive such belated fugitives.'—But the North, the melancholy of the North, and 'all the sadness of the populace', the moral anguish, the thought of death, the tyranny of life, always come to weigh afresh on this soul craving for light, and to force it into feverish musings and ruthless combats. And, doubtless, it is better that it should be so.

Richard Strauss is at the same time a poet and a musician. These two natures coexist in him, and each tends to dominate the other. The equilibrium is often upset; but when his will-power succeeds in keeping it, the union of these two forces both aimed at the same objective produces effects of an intensity which has not been known since Wagner. Both have their origin in heroic thought, which I consider to be even more rare than poetic or musical talent. There are other great musicians in Europe; but this one is, in addition, the creator of heroes.

Where there are heroes, there is drama. With Strauss there is drama everywhere, even in those of his works which seem the least likely to contain it: in certain of his *Lieder*, in his pure music. It bursts out in his symphonic poems, which form the most important part of his work. These poems are *Wanderers Sturmlied* (1885), *Aus Italien* (1886), *Macbeth* (1887), *Don Juan* (1888), *Tod und Verklärung* (1889), *Guntram** (1892-93) *Till Eulenspiegel* (1894), *Also Sprach Zarathustra* (1895), *Don Quixote* (1897), and *Heldenleben* (1898)†.

I shall not dwell on the first four, in which the spirit and style of the composer are in the process of formation. *Wanderers Sturmlied* (*Traveller's song during a storm*) Op. 14, is a setting of a poem by Goethe for six voices with orchestral accompaniment. Written before Strauss met Ritter, it is written after the manner of Brahms, with rather conventional skill and introversion. *Aus Italien* (op.16) paints with

*Not a symphonic poem in reality, but an opera. Tr.

†This article was written in 1899. Since then the *Sinfonia Domestica* has appeared (1903). It is discussed in the following chapter: *French Music and German Music* (Note by Romain Rolland).

exuberance the impressions made by the Campagna, by the ruins of Rome, by the shores of Sorrento, and by the life of the people in Italy. *Macbeth* (op.23) inaugurates, without much brilliance, the series of musical transpositions of literary subjects. *Don Juan* (op.20), a great advance, translates with inflated fervour the poem by Lenau, and the romantic madness of the hero who dreams of embracing the whole of human pleasure, and who dies conquered and in despair.

Tod und Verklärung (*Death and Transfiguration*) op.24*, marks considerable progress both in thought and in style. It is still today one of Strauss's most moving works, and the one which is composed with the most noble unity. It is preceded by a poem by Alexander Ritter, of which I will give a free outline.

In a poverty-stricken room, lit by a night-light, a sick man lies helpless on his bed. In the midst of a silence laden with terror, death is approaching. From time to time the poor man dreams, and is soothed by his memories. His life passes before him again: his innocent childhood, his happy youth, the struggles of his maturity, his efforts to attain the sublime goal of his desires, which always escapes him. He continues to pursue it and thinks he is about to embrace it at last; but death stops him with a thunderous 'Halt!' He struggles desperately and, even while in the throes of dying, is bent on realising his dream; but the sledge-hammer of death shatters his body, and night spreads over his eyes. Then there resound in heaven the words of salvation to which he vainly aspired on earth: Redemption, Transfiguration.

Richard Strauss's friends have sharply protested against the orthodoxy of this ending, and Seidl†, Jorissenne‡, and Wilhelm Mauke§, assert that the subject is more lofty: it is the eternal suffering of the soul struggling against its internal

---

*Composed in 1889, performed for the first time in Eisenach in 1890.
†*Richard Strauss, Eine Charakterskizze*, Prague, 1896.
‡*R. Strauss, Essai critique et biologique*, Brussels, 1898.
§*Der Musikführer: Tod und Verklärung*, Frankfurt.

demons, and its deliverance, through art. I shall not enter into the discussion, while nevertheless believing that this trite and frigid symbolism is much less interesting than the struggle against death, which can be felt in every line of the work. A work which is relatively classical, and in sentiment generous and majestic, almost Beethovenian. The realism of the subject: the dying man's hallucinations, his feverish shudders, the pounding of the blood in the arteries, the hopeless death struggle, are transfigured by the purity of form. It is realism of the same type as the C Minor Symphony, and of Beethoven's dialogues with Fate. Remove the whole programme, and the symphony remains clear and poignant, because of the cohesion of its inner emotion. For many musicians in Germany, *Tod und Verklärung* remains the summit of Strauss's work. I am far from sharing this opinion. The composer's art has subsequently developed prodigiously. But it is true that *Tod* marks the summit of an epoch in his life, and is the most perfect work in which a period is summed up. *Heldenleben* will be the second stage, the second and highest peak of the following period. How much the force and richness of feelings have grown since! But he has never recaptured the delicate and melodious purity of soul, the youthful grace, which still shines in *Guntram,* the work which follows, and which seems to peter out after that.

From 1889 onwards, Strauss was conducting the Wagnerian dramas at Weimar. Obsessed by them, he turned his attention to the theatre, and wrote the libretto for an opera: *Guntram*. Illness interrupted this work, which he continued in Egypt. The music for the first act was written between December 1892 and February, 1893, between Cairo and Luxor. The second act was finished in June, 1893, in Sicily. Finally he finished the third act in Bavaria, at the beginning of September, 1893. There is, however, no trace of oriental feeling in this music, but there are occasionally Italian melodies, a soft light, a rather bleak calm. In it I feel above all a convalescent spirit, a spirit which is languid rather like a little girl, who dreams with a soft-hearted smile and with tears always ready to flow. It was doubtless because of these indefinable impressions of convalescence that Strauss has retained a secret affection for this work— or so it seemed to me. In it his fever has subsided. Certain parts of it are impregnated with a tender feeling for nature, which is reminiscent of Berlioz's *Les Troyens*. But too often the music is empty, and conventional; and Wagner's tyranny makes itself felt in it, which is rare in Strauss's other works. The libretto is interesting. Strauss has put much of himself into it, and one can witness the crisis which threw this generous, tortured and proud mind into confusion.

Strauss had just been reading a historical study on an order of mystic *Minnesänger,* which was founded in Austria during the Middle Ages in order to combat the corruption of Art and to save souls by the beauty of song; they called themselves *Streiter der Liebe,* Warriors for Love. Strauss, at this epoch full of neo-Christian aspirations and under the influence of Wagner and of Tolstoy, was fired with this idea; and of one of these *Streiter der Liebe* he made his hero: Guntram.

The action takes place in the thirteenth century in Germany. The first act represents a glade, near a small lake. The peasants have revolted against the nobles, and have just been crushed. Guntram and his master Friedhold are distributing alms to them. The band of conquered men flees through the woods. Remaining alone, Guntram surrenders himself to his dreams in the joy of springtime, the innocent awakening of nature. But the thought of the misery hidden beneath this beauty crushes him. He thinks of man the sinner, of human suffering, of the civil war. He thanks Christ for having led him to this unfortunate country, then kisses the cross and decides to go to the very heart of Sin, to the tyrant's court, to take the divine revelation to him. At this moment Freihild, the wife of Duke Robert, the most cruel of the nobles, appears. She abhors those who surround her; life is hateful to her, and she wishes to drown herself. Guntram prevents her from doing so. When he realises that she is beloved by the people and the only benefactress of the poor, the pity with which his grief and her beauty inspire him is transformed unbeknown to him into deep love. He tells her that God has sent him in order to save her; and he goes to the castle, whither he feels himself called by the double mission of saving the people —and Freihild.

In the second act the nobles are celebrating their victory, in the Duke's castle. After the grandiloquent flatteries of the official *Minnesänger*, Guntram is invited to sing. Discouraged in advance by the baseness of these men, feeling that he will speak in vain, he hesitates, and is on the point of leaving; but Freihild's sadness holds him back, and it is for her that he sings. His voice, calm and restrained at first, speaks of the melancholy he feels in the midst of this celebration of force triumphant. He takes refuge in his dreams; in them he sees shining the gentle face of peace. He describes it lovingly, with a childish tenderness which becomes more and more impassioned when he pictures the ideal life of free humanity. Then he depicts war, death, the waste-land and the night which spread over the world. He speaks directly to the prince; he shows him his duty, and the people's love which would be his reward; he threatens him with the hatred of the poor, who are being driven to despair; finally he urges the nobles to rebuild the towns, to free the prisoners, to come to the help of their subjects. He concludes amidst the deep emotion of those present. Duke Robert alone senses the danger of such outspoken words, and orders his men to seize the singer; but the vassals take Guntram's side. In the midst of this struggle it is learned that the peasants have revolted again. Robert calls his men to arms. Guntram, who feels he has the support of those surrounding him, has Robert arrested. The Duke defends himself; Guntram kills him. A complete change of heart then takes place within him, of which we shall have the explanation only in the third act. In the scenes which follow he does not say another word; he lets fall his sword; he lets his enemies regain their authority over the masses; he allows himself to be put in chains and taken to prison; whilst the band of nobles goes off boisterously, to fight the rebels. But Freihild, full of cruel and unaffected joy, Freihild, freed by Guntram's sword, gives way to her love for him, and wants to save him.

The third act, which takes place in the castle prison, is unexpected, hesitant, and very curious. It is not the logical continuation of the action. One feels in it an upheaval in the poet's thought, a moral crisis which was still shaking him at the time when he was writing, an agitation which he had not succeeded in shaking off; but the new light, towards which from now on his life was to be directed, shows through clearly. Strauss was too far advanced in the composition of his work to escape the neo-Christian renunciation which was to conclude the drama; he could only have avoided it by completely recasting the characters. Therefore Guntram spurns Freihild's love. He realizes that he, like the others, has fallen under the curse of sin. He was preaching charity to others, and he himself was a prey to egoism; when he killed Robert, it was far less in order to free the people from a tyrant, than in order to satisfy instinctive and bestial jealousy. He therefore renounces all his desires and, withdrawn from the world, expiates the sin of being alive. But the interest of this act does not lie in this expected ending which, since *Parsifal,* has become rather commonplace. It lies in a scene obviously inserted at the last moment and which clashes sharply with the action, but does so with uncommon grandeur: the dialogue between Guntram and his one-time companion, Friedhold.*
Friedhold, his friend, his instructor, comes to reproach him for his crime and to bring him to appear before the order which will pass judgment on him. In the original version, Guntram gave in and sacrificed his passion to his vow.

*Some people consider that Friedhold represents Alexander Ritter's ideas, as Guntram does those of Strauss.

But during his journey in the East, Strauss suddenly conceived a horror for this Christian annihilation of the will, and Guntram, like him, rebelled. He refuses to submit to the rules of his order. He breaks his lute, the symbol of vain hope in the redemption of humanity by means of faith. He rejects the noble but vain dreams in which he believed, and which vanished in the light of life. He does not abjure the vows he made in the past; but he is no longer the same man who made them. When he was without experience he was able to believe that man should be subject to rules, that life should be controlled by laws. One hour enlightened him. Now he is free and alone, alone with himself. 'Alone I can allay my suffering. Alone I can expiate my crime. Only my own internal law can direct my life. My God speaks to me through myself alone. My God speaks only to me. *Ewig einsam.*' It is the proud awakening of individualism, of the powerful pessimism of the *Uebermensch*. Such a sentiment gives to negation itself, to renunciation, the character of action: it is one more violent affirmation of the will.

I have dwelt somewhat on this drama because of the real value of its thought, and above all because of its autobiographical interest. Henceforth Strauss's mind is formed. The circumstances of life will develop it, but without making any major changes. *Guntram* was the cause of bitter disappointments to its author. He did not succeed in having it performed in Munich. The orchestra and the singers rebelled against music which they declared to be unplayable. It is even said that they obtained from an eminent critic a formal certificate, which they brought to Strauss, certifying that *Guntram* was not made to be sung. The main difficulty was the length of the principal part which, with its reveries and dissertations, by itself takes up the equivalent of an act and a half. Some of its monologues, like the song in the second act, last half an hour at a stretch. *Guntram* was nevertheless performed at Weimar on 16th May, 1894; and shortly afterwards, Strauss married Freihild, Pauline de Ahna, who created the part

184

of Elizabeth (in *Tannhäuser*) at Bayreuth, and who has since devoted herself to the interpretation of her husband's *Lieder*.

But Strauss always resented his lack of success in the theatre, and reverted to the symphonic poem, in which he showed more and more marked dramatic tendencies, and a spirit growing daily more arrogant and contemptuous. One has only to hear him speak—and with what cold disdain!—of the theatre public, 'a band of basely pleasure-seeking bankers and shopkeepers,' to feel the hidden wound of this successful artist, to whom the theatre was closed for so long, and who, by an added irony, was obliged to conduct at the Berlin Opera the musical banalities which were imposed on him by a bad taste which was truly 'Royal'.

The first large symphony of the new period was *Till Eulenspiegel's lustige Streiche, nach alter Schelmenweise, in Rondeauform* (*Till Eulenspiegel's Merry Pranks, after the old legend, in Rondo form*) op.28*. In this his contempt in so far only expressed in witty banter, which scoffs at worldly conventions.—In France we know little about the figure of Till, the devil-may-care scoffer, the legendary hero of Germany and of Flanders. Therefore for us Strauss's music loses much of its meaning, for it claims to remind us of a series of episodes of which we have never heard: Till going through the market, thrashing the good wives; Till in a priest's habit making a boring sermon; Till paying court to a young woman who rebuffs him; Till chaffing some pedants; Till condemned and hung. Strauss's tendency to represent, in a few musical sketches, sometimes a character or a dialogue, sometimes a situation, or a landscape, or an idea, in other words the most diverse and changeable impressions of his wayward mind, is very marked in this work. It is true that he relies on certain popular themes, the meaning of which must be easily understood in Germany;

---

*Composed 1894-95, first performed at Cologne, in 1895.

G*

and that he develops them not quite, as he asserts, in strict Rondo form, but with a certain logic: so that, apart from a few sallies, which are indecipherable without a programme, the work as a whole has, in spite of everything, musical unity. This symphony, much relished in Germany, seems to me less original than the others. It might be taken for very subtle Mendelssohn, with uncommon harmonies and more complicated orchestration.

There is much more grandeur and originality in the following poem: *Also sprach Zarathustra, Tondichtung frei nach Nietzsche* (*Thus spoke Zarathustra, free composition after Nietzsche*), op.30*. The sentiments are more broadly humane, and the programme which Strauss set himself does not peter out in minute picturesque or anecdotal details, but is sketched with a few expressive and majestic strokes. Strauss asserts his freedom with regard to Nietzsche. He wished to depict the different stages of development which a free spirit goes through in order to reach the *Uebermensch* [Supermen]. These are purely humane ideas, and are not at all peculiar to a system of philosophy. The sub-titles of the work are: *Von den Hinterweltlern* (*Of religious ideas*), *Von der grossen Sehnsucht* (*Of the supreme aspiration*), *Von den Freuden und Leidenschaften* (*Of joys and passions*), *Das Grablied* (*The song of the tombs*), *Von der Wissenschaft* (*Of knowledge*), *Der Genesende* (*The convalescent, or the soul freed from its desires*), *Das Tanzlied* (*The song of the dance*), *Nachtlied* (*Night song*). In it man is seen, at first crushed by the enigma of nature, searching for a refuge in faith; then, rebelling against ascetic ideas, plunging madly into the passions; soon sated, nauseated, tired to death, he tries learning, then rejects it, and succeeds in freeing himself from the anxiety of knowledge; finally he finds his release in laughter, master of the world, the blissful dance, the dance of the universe, into which all human sentiments enter: religious beliefs, unsatisfied desires, passions, disgust, and joy. 'Lift up your hearts, brothers, high, higher! And don't forget your legs,

*Composed 1895-6, first performed at Frankfurt-on-Main in November, 1896.

either! I have canonized laughter; supermen, learn to laugh!'* Then the dance moves away, and is lost in the ethereal regions. Zarathustra disappears dancing beyond the worlds. But he has not solved the enigma of the world for other men: therefore, in contrast to the harmony of light which characterizes him, is set the sad note of interrogation, with which the poem closes.

Few subjects offer such rich material for musical expression. Strauss has treated it with power and flexibility; he has been able to keep unity in this chaos of passions by contrasting man's *Sehnsucht* with the impassive power of nature. As to the boldness of the style, it is scarcely necessary to remind those who heard the symphonic poem at the *Cirque d'Eté*† of the inextricable 'fugue of knowledge', and the thrills of the wood-wind and the trumpets which express Zarathustra's laughter, and the dance of the universe, and the audaciousness of the conclusion which, in the key of B major, makes the final note, the note of interrogation, a C natural repeated three times.—I am far from considering the symphony to be without defects. The themes are not of equal value: some of them are common-place, and in general the execution is superior to the conception. I shall return later to certain defects in Strauss's music. But here I only want to consider the flood of overflowing life, the fever of joy which makes these worlds whirl round.

Zarathustra showed the progress of Strauss's contemptuous individualism, of a mind which 'hates the dogs of the populace and all that unsuccessful and sombre breed— that laughing storm, that stormy spirit which dances on swamps and on sorrows as if they were meadows'‡. This spirit pokes fun at itself in the *Don Quixote* of 1897, *fantastische Variationen über ein Thema ritterlichen Charakters* (*Don Quixote, fantastic variations on a chivalrous theme*) op.35. This symphony marks, I believe, the ultimate point which can be reached by programme music. In no other work does Strauss display

*Nietzsche.
†Parisian concert-hall.
‡Nietzsche, *Zarathustrâ.*

187

more intelligence, wit, and prodigious ability; and there is no other work—I say it in in all sincerity—in which so many forces are expended at such a complete loss, for a game, a musical joke, which lasts for forty-five minutes and compels the author, the performers and the public to do such hard work. It is by far the most difficult of these symphonic poems to perform, owing to the complexity, the independence and the fantastic caprices of the parts.—One can get an idea of what the author demands of the music from a few extracts from the programme:

The introduction represents Don Quixote deep in reading romances about chivalry; and, as in old Flemish or Dutch miniatures, we must not only see in the music Don Quixote's features, but we must also read the books which he is reading. Here, the romance of a knight who fights a giant. There, the adventures of a Paladin who dedicates himself to the service of a lady; or those of a squire who gave up his life to the fulfilment of a vow in order to redeem his sins. Don Quixote's brain grows confused—as does ours—with all this reading; he becomes mad.—He goes away, accompanied by his squire. The two figures are wittily drawn: the one inflexible, languid, an old Spaniard quick to take offence and something of a troubadour, whose ideas wander but always come back in the end to the bee in his bonnet; the other, round, jovial, a wily peasant who talks shrewd nonsense, whose bantering proverbs are translated into music by short-winded phrases which always come back to the point of departure.—Their adventures begin; and now we have the windmills (trills from the violins and woodwind), and the bleating army of the great emperor Alifanfaron (tremolo from the woodwind). And we have too, in the third variation, a dialogue between the knight and his squire, in which we are supposed to guess that Sancho is questioning his master about the advantages of the chivalrous life, which seem questionable to him. Don Quixote speaks to him of glory and honour; but Sancho does not care about that. And in reply to these high-sounding words he always counters with positive gain, rich meals at someone else's expense, hard cash. Then the adventures begin again. The two companions fly through the air on wooden horses. And chromatic passages on the flutes, harps, and timpani, as well as a 'wind-machine' (*Windmaschine*) convey the illusion of this dizzy journey, 'while the double-basses' tremolo on the root bass shows that the horse has never left the ground'*.

I will say no more. This is enough to show the kind of fun the author was having. When one hears the work, one cannot help admiring the virtuosity of the style and of the orchestration, and Strauss's sense of the comic. It is all the more surprising that he limits himself to illustrating the text†, when he is so capable of creating his comic and dramatic material out of nothing. In my opinion, *Don Quixote*, a feat of skill, an amazing exercise, in which Strauss has made his style more flexible and has enriched it, shows progress only in so far as the composer's technique is concerned, but is a step backwards for his mind, which seems in this work to adopt decadent conceptions of art as a plaything, art as a trinket, designed for a frivolous and affected society.

With *Heldenleben* (*A hero's life*), op.40‡, he rises again and with a stroke of his wings reaches the summits. Here there is no extraneous text which the music endeavours to illustrate or to transcribe. Instead here is great passion, a heroic will-power which develops throughout the whole work, crushing all obstacles. No doubt Strauss did sketch himself a programme; but he said to me himself: 'You needn't read it. It's enough to know that it is about a hero at grips with his enemies.' I do not know how far that is true, and if some of it would not remain obscure for those who follow it without a text; but this saying of the author seems to prove that he has understood the

*Arthur Hahn, *Der Musikführer: Don Quixote*—Frankfurt.

†Strauss has indicated on the score at the beginning of each variation which chapter of *Don Quixote* he is quoting.

‡Completed in December, 1898. First performed on 3rd March, 1899, at Frankfurt-am-Main—Published by Leuckart, Leipzig.

dangers of the literary symphony, and that he is moving nearer to pure music.

Heldenleben is divided into six chapters: *The Hero*; *the Hero's adversaries*; *the Hero's companion*; *the battlefield*; *the Hero's peaceful labours, his withdrawal from the world*; and the *ideal consummation of his soul*. It is an extraordinary work, drunk with heroism, colossal, irregular, trivial, and sublime. An Homeric hero is struggling amid the derisive laughter of a stupid crowd, a band of bawling, thick-headed ninnies. In a kind of concerto, a solo violin expresses woman's charms, coquetries, and her decadent perverseness. Raucous trumpets sound for battle; and then, how can one describe that fearful cavalry charge, which makes the ground shake and hearts leap, that tempestuous whirlpool, that storming of towns, that tumultuous tide, which is directed by an iron will?—The most splendid battle that has ever been painted in music! . . . At the first performance, in Germany, I saw people shudder when they heard it, suddenly rise to their feet, and make violent and unconscious gestures. I myself experienced the strange intoxication, the dizziness of this heaving ocean; and I thought then that, for the first time for thirty years, the Germans had found the poet of Victory. *Heldenleben* would, from every angle, be one of the masterpieces of music, did not a literary error intervene to cut short the fervour of the most passionate pages, at the apogee of the movement, in order to keep to the programme. A little coldness, tiredness perhaps, is also discernible at the end. The conquering hero realises that he has conquered in vain: the baseness and folly of men have remained the same. He masters his anger, and contemptuously resigns himself. He withdraws into the tranquility of nature. His creative force flows out in imaginative works; and here Richard Strauss, with a strange audacity, (which is only justified by the genius of his *Heldenleben*), represents these works by reminiscences of his own symphonic poems: *Don Juan, Macbeth, Tod und Verklärung, Till, Zarathustra, Don Quixote, Guntram,* even his *Lieder,* thus identifying himself with the hero of whom he has been singing.—Sometimes the storms conjure up in his mind the memory of his combats; but he also remembers his hours of love and joy; and his spirit is soothed again. Then the serene music develops and with powerful tranquility rises to a triumphal chord which seems to place a crown of glory on the hero's brow.

There is no doubt that Beethoven's thought often inspired, stimulated and guided that of Strauss. One feels, in the tonality of the first movement, (in E Flat), in the general drift, an indefinable reflection of the first *Eroica* and of the *Ode to Joy;* and also in the last movement, which is in addition reminiscent of certain of Beethoven's *Lieder*. But Strauss's hero is very different from Beethoven's; the old-time and revolutionary characteristics have become obliterated; and, with Strauss, the hero's enemies, like the external world, occupy much more room! The hero has much more difficulty in breaking free and in conquering. It is true that his triumph is more frenzied. If the worthy Oulibicheff claimed that in a dissonant chord in the first *Eroica* he recognised the burning of Moscow, what on earth would he find in this? How many towns burnt down! How many battle-fields! And then, there is in *Heldenleben* a scathing contempt, an ill-natured laughter, which Beethoven almost never has. Not much kindness. It is the product of heroic contempt.

If one considers this music as a whole, one is at first struck by the seeming heterogeneousness of the styles. North and South blend together in it; one feels the attraction of the sun in the melody. There was already something Italian in *Tristan;* how much more there is in the work of this follower of Nietzsche! Constantly the phrases are Italian, and the harmonies ultra-Germanic. Not one of the least attractions of this art is that of seeing, amidst the storms of German polyphony, the veil of lowering clouds, of heavy thoughts, being rent, and the smiling line of Italian shores appearing, with dances taking place by the seaside. These are not just analogies. It would be easy and superfluous to point out precise reminiscences of France or of Italy, even in the most advanced works: in *Zarathustra*, in *Heldenleben*. Mendelssohn, Gounod, Wagner, Rossini, Mascagni rub shoulders in them in a strange way. But these dissimilar elements blend in the work taken as a whole, controlled and assimilated by the author's thought.

The orchestra is no less composite. It is not a compact and dense mass, Wagner's Macedonian phalanx. It is broken up, divided to the utmost degree. Each part aims at independence, and follows its own whim without appearing to take any notice of the others. It seems sometimes, as when reading scores by Berlioz, that when performed it must produce an incoherent and broken effect. And yet, how full it is! 'It sounds good, doesn't it?' Strauss said to me, smiling, after he had just conducted *Heldenleben*.*

It is the subjects, above all, that seem unpredictable, ruled by a disordered imagination, alien to any logic. After all, have not these poems, as we have already seen, the ambition to express by turns, and indeed, simultaneously, literary texts, pictures, anecdotes, philosophic ideas, the author's personal feelings? What unity can one expect from the story of Don Quixote's or of Till Eulenspiegel's adventures? And yet, that unity exists, not in the subjects, but in the mind that deals with them. What saves these descriptive symphonies is the fact that, together with their very diffuse literary life, they have a musical life which is more logical and more concentrated. The musician keeps the poet's caprices within bounds. The fantastic Till disports himself 'according to the old rondo form', and Don Quixote's madness is expressed in 'ten variations on a chivalrous theme with introduction and finale.' It is in this that Strauss's art, one of the most literary and des-

*Here is the composition of the orchestra in these last two works of Strauss:

    In *Zarathustra:* 1 piccolo, 3 flutes, 3 oboes, 1 cor anglais, 1 E Flat clarinet, 2 clarinets in B, 1 Bass clarinet in B, 3 bassoons, 1 double-bassoon, 6 horns in F, 4 trumpets in C, 3 trombones, 2 Bass-tubas, timpani, bass drum, cymbals, triangle, tubular bells, bell in E, organ, 2 harps, strings.

    In *Heldenleben:* 8 horns instead of 6, 5 trumpets instead of 4, (2 in E flat, 3 in B): in addition, side drums.

criptive which exists, differs from others of the same kind: by the substantiality of the musical texture, in which one discerns the thoroughbred musician, nurtured on the masters, and classical in spite of everything.

Thus, throughout this music, a strong unity is imposed on disordered, often ill-assorted elements. To me this seems to be a reflection of the author's spirit. The unity is not in what he feels, but in what he desires. In him emotion is much less interesting than will-power, above all much less intense; and often it lacks personality. In his work the restlessness is at times reminiscent of Schumann, the religious feeling of Mendelssohn, the voluptuousness of Gounod and the passion of Wagner*. But the will is heroic, dominant, passionate and powerful to the point of sublimity. It is because of it that Richard Strauss is great, at present unique. One feels in him the force which dominates men.

It is through these heroic aspects that he is the heir of part of Beethoven's and of Wagner's thought. It is through them that he is one of the poets—perhaps the greatest—of present-day Germany, which recognises itself in him, as its hero.—Let us examine this hero.

He is an idealist who has limitless faith in the sovereign power of the spirit and of art the liberator. His idealism is at first religious, as in *Tod und Verklärung*, full of childish illusions in *Guntram*, tender and compassionate as a woman. Then he becomes irritated and indignant at the baseness of the world and the obstacles which he encounters. His contempt grows; he becomes sarcastic (*Till Eulenspiegel*); with the years of struggle he loses all patience and, more and more bitter, his contemptuous heroism develops. How his laughter stings and lashes in *Zarathustra!* How his will crushes and slashes in *Heldenleben!* Through victory he has become conscious of his power: now, his pride no longer knows any limits; he becomes hysterically uplifted, like the nation which it reflects he can no longer distinguish the

*In *Guntram* it even seems as if the author deliberately and openly had recourse to a phrase of *Tristan*, as if he could find nothing better to express passionate desire.

reality in his immoderate dream. There are morbid germs in present-day Germany: a mania of pride, a belief in itself and a contempt for others which are reminiscent of France in the seventeenth century. *Dem Deutschen gehört die Welt* (The German owns the world) pictures displayed in shop-windows in Berlin calmly state. When it reaches this point, the mind begins to rave. If you like, every genius raves; but the ravings of a Beethoven are concentrated in himself and create for his own joy. The ravings of many contemporary German artists are aggressive; they have a character of destructive antagonism. The idealist to whom 'the world belongs' is easily subject to vertigo. He was made to rule over his own inner world. The whirlpool of external images which he is called on to master maddens him. He reaches the point of raving like a Caesar. Germany had scarcely reached the mastery of the world when she found the voice of Nietzsche and of his hallucinated artists from the *Deutsches Theater* and of the *Secession*. And now here is the grandiose music of Richard Strauss.

Whither do all these frenzies lead? To what, then, does this heroism aspire?—This bitter and taut will no sooner arrives at its objective,—or even before it does so,—than it falters. It does not know what to do with its victory. It despises it, no longer believes in it, or grows tired of it.*

Like Michelangelo's *Victory*, she has put her knee on the captive's back; she seems ready to finish him off. Suddenly, she stops, she hesitates, she looks the other way, her eyes vacant, uncertain, with an expression of distaste, overcome with dismal boredom.

This is how, so far, Richard Strauss's work appears to me. Guntram kills Duke Robert and immediately lets fall his sword. Zarathustra's frantic laughter ends in an avowal of despondent impotence. Don Juan's frenzied passion sinks into nothingness. Don Quixote, on his deathbed, repudiates

---

*'The German mind which, only a short time ago, had possessed the will to dominate Europe, the strength to control Europe, has come, by way of last will and testament to abdication.'—Nietzsche, *An Attempt at Self-Criticism*, 1886.

his illusions. And in the oblivion shed over him by an indifferent nature, the Hero himself is resigned to the uselessness of his work.—Nietzsche, speaking of the artists of our time, smiles at 'these Tantaluses of the will, rebels and enemies of law, all collapsing finally at the foot of Christ's cross'.—Whether it is the Cross or the Void, all these heroes abdicate, are overcome with repugnance, with despair, or with the resignation which is sadder than despair. That was not how Beethoven kept his melancholy at bay. Sombre adagios mourn in the middle of his Symphonies; but at the end there is joy, and triumph. His work is the triumph of the vanquished Hero. That of Strauss is the defeat of the conquering Hero.—This uncertainty of will could be analysed even more clearly in contemporary German literature, in particular in the work of the author of *Die versunkene Glocke*. But it is more striking in the case of Strauss precisely because it is more heroic. All that display of superhuman will, in order to end in renouncement, in 'I don't want it any more!'

This is the canker of German thought,—I speak of the élite, which illumines the present and anticipates the future. I see an heroic nation, intoxicated with its triumphs, with its immense wealth, with its numbers, with its power, which clasps the world with its huge arms, and stops, crushed by victory,—wondering, 'Why have I conquered?'

II

FRENCH MUSIC
AND
GERMAN MUSIC

In May, 1905, there took place in Strasbourg the first *Musikfest* of Alsace-Lorraine. This was a great artistic achievement. Its object was to bring together at a 'musical festival' two civilizations which, for centuries, have been colliding with each other on the soil of Alsace, with the thought of fighting, rather than of understanding one another.

The official entertainments programme underlined this intention of the organizers:

'Music fulfils the highest of missions: it aspires to be a link between nations, races, and states which are, in so many things, strangers to each other; it aspires to unite what is separated, to make peace between that which is hostile . . . No country is more fitted to this task than Alsace-Lorraine—that ancient thoroughfare of the nations in which, since time immemorial, have been exchanged the material and intellectual goods of the North and South —and, above all Strasbourg, a town built by the Romans, which has remained a centre of spiritual life . . . All the great intellectual currents have left their traces in the people of Alsace-Lorraine. Thus they were predestined to play the part of intermediary between epochs and between nations . . . The East and the West, the past and the present meet and shake hands here. In festivals of this sort it is not a question of seeking a victory for this or that aesthetic tendency. It is a question of gathering together all that is great, majestic and eternal in the art of different epochs and of different nations.'*

*Published originally in the *Programmbuch* edited by Dr. Max Bendiner, of Strasbourg, and reproduced in *Musiciens d'Aujourd'hui*.

It was a noble ambition for Alsace, that eternal battle-field, to wish to inaugurate these European Olympic Games. In fact, what was set up as a competition between nations became reduced to a struggle, in the musical field, between two civilizations, two arts: French music and German music. For that matter, these two arts represent at present all that is truly alive in European music.

Such tournaments are fascinating. They could also be as useful to one of the rivals as to the other. Unfortunately, France pays no attention to them. It should be the duty of our musicians and critics to follow these international gatherings attentively, to make sure that the conditions of battle there are fair,—by this I mean: that our art is represented as it should be,—and to derive instruction for us all from the results. But they do nothing; they remain wrapped up in their Parisian concerts, where everyone knows each other too well to be able, nay, to dare, to criticize each other freely: thus, our art is wilting in an atmosphere of cliques, instead of seeking the fresh air and the fruitful rivalry with foreign art, which the majority of our musical critics prefer to ignore rather than to know. Never have I so much regretted this indifference as at the Strasbourg festival where, in spite of the unfavourable conditions in which, because of our negligence, French art was presented, I sensed what its force might have been, had it not wished to hold aloof from the battle.

Absolute eclecticism reigned in the choice of programme. In it were to be found jumbled together the names of Mozart and Beethoven, of Wagner and Brahms, of César Franck and Gustave Charpentier, of Richard Strauss and of Mahler.* French singers,—Caseneuve and Daraux,—

*Here is the programme precisely as it was for the three days:
1. Saturday, 20th May:
   Weber: *Oberon* overture (conducted by Richard Strauss);—César Franck: *Les Béatitudes* (conducted by Camille Chevillard);—Gustave Charpentier: *Impressions d'Italie* (conducted by Chevillard);—Three melodies and ballads by Jean Sibelius, Hugo Wolf and Armas

French or Italian virtuosi,—Henri Marteau and Ferruccio Busoni,—took part in the concerts, side by side with German, Austrian and Scandinavian artists. The orchestra (the *Strassburger Städtische Orchester*) and the choirs, formed by amalgamating various *Chorvereine* of Strasbourg, were conducted by Richard Strauss, Gustav Mahler and Camille Chevillard. But the names of these renowned *Kapellmeister* should not make us forget that of the man who was really the moving spirit of these concerts: Professor Ernst Münch of Strasbourg, an Alsatian, who conducted all the rehearsals, who had all the hard work to do, and who, at the last moment, stood aside to make way for the foreign conductors, leaving all the honour to them. Professor Münch, organist at the church of Saint-Guillaume, is one of the men who have done the most for music in Strasbourg, where he has formed excellent choirs (the '*Choeurs de Saint-Guillaume*') and where he organises Bach recitals, with the help of another Alsatian whose name is well-known to musical historians: Albert Schweitzer, director of the Seminary of Saint-Thomas (*Thomasstift*), minister, organist, lecturer at the University of Strasbourg, author of interesting works on philosophy and theology, and a now famous book on Johann Sebastian Bach, which is doubly remarkable for us: firstly, because this work, published in Leipzig by a lecturer at the University of Strasbourg, is written in French; and then because he is the product of a harmonious mixture

Järnefelt (sung by Madame Järnefelt);—Richard Wagner: Final Scene from *Die Meistersinger* (conducted by Richard Strauss).
2. Sunday, 21st May:
Gustav Mahler: 5*th Symphony* (conducted by Gustav Mahler);—Johannes Brahms: *Rhapsody* for contralto, choir and orchestra (conducted by Ernst Münch); Mozart: *Strasbourg Concerto* for violin, in G Major, (Soloist: Henri Marteau, Conductor: Richard Strauss); Richard Strauss: *Sinfonia Domestica* (conducted by the composer).
3. Monday, 22nd May:
Beethoven Concert (conducted by Gustav Mahler): *Coriolan* overture; Piano concerto in G major (played by Ferruccio Busoni); *Lieder: An die ferne Geliebte* (sung by Edwig Hess);—*Choral Symphony*.

of the French and the German minds, and is reviving the study of Bach and of early classical music. So far as I was concerned, not the least interesting part of the Strasbourg festival was learning to know personalities of that sort, born on Alsatian soil, and who represent in the noblest manner the highest level of Alsatian culture, which benefits at the same time from all that is best in the two civilizations.

Monsieur Chevillard was alone in representing French musicians. And certainly, as conductor, there could not have been a better choice; but Germany had delegated her two greatest composers, Strauss and Mahler, who came to conduct their latest works in person: it would not have been too much to set off against the glory which they enjoy in their own country that of one of our own principal composers.

In addition, Monsieur Chevillard had been commissioned to conduct, not a work of one of our recent masters, such as Debussy or Dukas, whose style he excels in rendering, but *Les Béatitudes* of César Franck, the spirit of which, in my opinion, he is far from understanding. The mystical tenderness of Franck escapes him; he brings out above all what there is of the dramatic in the work. Therefore this performance of *Les Béatitudes* and, it must be added, a very lovely one, gave an inaccurate idea of Franck's genius.

But what was inconceivable, and rightly made Monsieur Chevillard indignant, was the fact that he was given to conduct not *Les Béatitudes*, but a selection from *Les Béatitudes*. And in connection with this allow me, with the future in mind, to recommend French artists who are invited to similar festivals never to accept a programme blindly, but to draw it up themselves, or else to refuse to take part. If people want to make a place for French musicians in German *Musikfeste*, it must be the French who choose the works which are to represent them. Above all, a French conductor who is brought from Paris to conduct a work, must not, on his arrival, find himself faced with a truncated score, from which an arbitrary choice has been made of a few extracts, and even the integrity of these was not respected.* This shows a lack of respect for the art: works must be played as they are, or not at all.

Finally, during this three-day festival in which they had paid us the compliment of devoting the first day to French music, it would have been proper for this sole concert to have been entirely reserved for it. But, no doubt in order to palliate the effect produced by the enthusiastic reception which was expected—and which was given—to this French music by a section of the Alsatian public in the presence of the Staathalter of Alsace-Lorraine, care had been taken to sandwich the French works between two German works; and by virtue of a choice which I will never believe—which no one in Strasbourg believed—to have been dictated by musical reasons, the German work which concluded the evening was the final scene from *Die Meistersinger*, with Hans Saschs' resounding couplet against *Wälsche Kunst mit walschem Tand*. This error of courtesy—which is, what is more, meaningless, when it had just been proved by this very concert that one cannot do without *'welche'* art—would not be worth mentioning, if it did not help me to prove to French artists who take part in these festivals how regrettable their indifference is; this error would never have been committed if they had taken care in advance to have the programme submitted to them, and if they had vetoed it.

Even leaving aside this little incident—which I point out in order that I may be the interpreter of those Alsatians present who told me how sorry they were about it,—our French artists should not have consented to letting our music be represented only by a mutilated version of *Les Béatitudes* and by Charpentier's *Impressions d'Italie*, a work which is clever and brilliant, but second-rate, too easily crushed by the immediate proximity of one of Wagner's most monumental scenes. If one wants to institute a tournament between German art and French art, I repeat,

*Five out of the eight *Béatitudes* were played; and cuts had been made in the third and the eighth.

let it be a fair one, and let Berlioz be opposed to Wagner, or Debussy to Strauss, and Dukas or Magnard to Mahler.

These, then, were the conditions of battle: they were, whether it was so wished or not, unfavourable to France. And yet, to an impartial observer, the result was full of encouragement and hope for us.

In art I have never been concerned with questions of nationality. I have never even hidden my preferences for German music; and I still today consider Richard Strauss to be the foremost musical personality of Europe. I am all the more free to speak of the remarkable impression I had at the Strasbourg *Musikfest* of the reorientation which is taking place in music: French music is silently engaged in taken German music's place.

' . . . *Wälsche Kunst und wälsche Tand* . . . ' How misplaced this abusive phrase seemed when one was listening to César Franck's genuine thought! There is nothing, or almost nothing, in *Les Béatitudes,* for art's sake. It is the soul speaking to the soul. As Beethoven wrote at the end of his *Mass in D:* '*Von Herzen . . . Zu Herzen*' ('From the heart . . . to the heart!') And, in fact, in the last century I know of no one but Beethoven who has had to such a degree this virtue of being true, of saying nothing but the truth, of speaking only for himself, without thinking of the public. Never has faith been expressed with such sincerity. Franck, together with Bach, is the only musician who has really *seen* Christ, and who shows it. I shall even venture to say that his Christ is more simple than Bach's, in whose work the grandeur of the thought is sometimes led away, by the richness of form and by a kind of knack of writing, to repetitions and tricks of virtuosity which weaken it. In Franck's work, it is Christ's speech in its absolute purity, with no external embellishment, in its living force, and the harmony between the music and this majestic speech, in which there resounds the conscience of the world, is wonderful. I once heard someone say to Madame Cosima Wagner that there was, in certain phrases of *Parsifal,* in particular in the chorus: *Durch Mitleid wissend,* a virtue that was in effect religious, the force of a revelation. I find this force more effective, and the virtue more evangelic, in *Les Béatitudes*.

What an astonishing contrast! At this German musical festival it was a Frenchman who represented not only austere music, nurtured on the very marrow of the classics, but also the religious spirit, the evangelic spirit! The rôles are reversed. The Germans have so much changed that today they have difficulty in appreciating this seriousness, this faith. I was observing the audience: they were listening politely, surprised, bored: what business had this Frenchman to have a profound and pious soul?

—'There's no doubt,'—Henri Lichtenberger, my neighbour at the concert, was saying; 'In Germany we are beginning to represent boring music . . . '

In the past it was German music which had this privilege in France.

Therefore, in order to dispel the austere grandeur of *Les Béatitudes*, it had been arranged that they should be immediately followed by Gustave Charpentier's *Impressions d'Italie*. The way the public relaxed, from the very first movement, was worth seeing. At last here was some French music as the Germans understand it! Of all our living musicians, Charpentier is the best loved, the only one truly loved in Germany. Both the general public and the musicians are for him. Shall I say that the sincere pleasure which the orchestration and the amusing vitality of his works gives them does not go without a certain contempt for French frivolousness—*welschen Tand?*

'Listen to that,' Richard Strauss said to me during the third movement of *Les Impressions d'Italie:*—'That's the music of Montmartre, grand phrases: "Freedom! . . . Love! . . ." which one shouts without believing in them . . . '

He thought it charming, what is more; and doubtless, in his heart of hearts, according to the only formula current in Germany, he was approving of this Frenchman. Strauss likes Charpentier very much, he has set himself up as his patron in Berlin. I remember one of the first performances of *Louise* in Paris, during which he gave vent to childish pleasure.

But Strauss and the majority of Germans are putting themselves on a false scent when they try to persuade themselves that this French frivolousness, which amuses them, continues as in the past to be the exclusive property of France. They love it so much only because it has become German,—and they do not suspect that.—In the past, German artists took no pleasure in it. How easy it would have been for me to point it out to Strauss in his own works! The Germans of today have almost nothing in common any more with those of the past.

I am not only speaking of the general public. The public of today is both 'Brahmist' (sic) and Wagnerian at the same time: it has no opinion, and it likes everything; it acclaims Wagner, and it encores Brahms; it is frivolous, basically, and at the same time both sentimental and brutal. Its most striking characteristic, since Wagner, is the cult of force. While listening to the end of *Die Meistersinger* I felt how such arrogant music, that imperial march, reflected this military, middle-class nation, weighed down with health and glory.

But the most remarkable thing of all is how much German artists are, from day to day, losing the understanding of their great classical masters, of Beethoven in particular. Strauss, who is very shrewd, and who knows his own limits precisely, does not willingly venture into this domain, although he feels Beethoven in a much more alive way than all the other German *Kapellmeister;* at the Strasbourg festival, besides his own symphony, he merely conducted the overture to *Oberon* and a Mozart concerto. These performances were, it must be added, interesting: a personality like his is too uncommon for it not to be amusing to rediscover it in the works he conducts. But what a bluff and hectic aspect charming Mozart acquired! What stressed rhythms, at the expense of melodic grace!—At all events it was in this case a concerto, in which a certain freedom of interpretation is permissible to a virtuoso of the orchestra.

But Mahler, less circumspect, ventured to conduct the full 'Beethoven concert'. And what can be said of that evening? I will not say anything about the piano concerto in G major, played by Busoni with his brilliant and superficial virtuosity, which let nothing of the work's greatness remain: it is enough for me to say that this performance enraptured the public. But German artists are not responsible for this. In the case of the wonderful cycle of *Lieder: An die ferne Geliebte*, bawled out by a tenor from Berlin at the top of his voice, and of the *Choral Symphony* which, for me, was an outrageous exhibition, it was otherwise. I could never have imagined that a German orchestra, conducted by the foremost *Kapellmeister* of Austria, could have been capable of such a misdeed. Incredible tempi. The *scherzo* with no impetus. The *adagio* taken post-haste, without lingering over a moment of dreaminess. Pauses in the *finale*, which interrupted the whole development: breaks in the thought. The different sections of the orchestra tumbling over each other. Constant uncertainty and lack of balance. I have, in the past, criticised Weingartner's neo-classical inflexibility. How much I appreciated his robust balance and his straining at accuracy, while listening to this neurasthenic Beethoven! —No, it is no longer Beethoven, or Mozart, whom we can hear in Germany today: it is Mahler or Strauss.

Gustav Mahler is forty-six years old*. He has the legendary looks of those German musicians of the Schubert type who have something of the schoolmaster or the minister about them: a long, clean-shaven face, dishevelled hair on a pointed skull, bald at the temples, eyes blinking behind glasses, a big nose, a large mouth with thin lips, hollow cheeks, and an ascetic, ironical and ravaged appearance. He is excessively highly-strung, and in Germany caricatures of him in a shadow-theatre have popularised his dumb show antics like a scalded cat on the conductor's rostrum.

Born at Kalischt, in Bohemia, a pupil of Anton Bruckner in Vienna, he is *Hofoperndirektor* (Director of Opera) in

*Written in 1905.

205

Vienna. I intend one of these days to make a more detailed study of the work of this musician, the foremost German composer after Strauss, and the principal representative of South German music.

The most important part of his work is a series of symphonies, the fifth of which he was conducting at the Strasbourg festival. The first, entitled *Titan,* dates from 1894. These symphonies are enormous edifices, massive and cyclopean; the melodies on which these works are constructed are badly hewn blocks, of mediocre quality, commonplace, impressive only because of the thickness of their foundations, and because of the persistent repetition of the rhythmic patterns, which are kept up with the tenacity of an obsession. These stacks of music, erudite and barbarous, with harmonies both coarse and refined at the same time, are notable above all for their bulk. The orchestration is heavy and strong: the brass is preponderant in it, adding its garish gilding to the opaque colours of the sonorous edifice. Basically, the thought is neo-classical, rather flabby and diffuse. The harmonic structure is composite; in it the styles of Bach, of Schubert, of Mendelssohn, blend with those of Wagner and of Bruckner; owing to a marked predeliction for canon form, it is even reminiscent of Franck's writing: it is opulent and flashy bric-à-brac. In general, the most characteristic feature of these symphonies is the use of choirs with the orchestra.

'When I conceive a great musical picture (*ein grosses musikalisches Gemälde*),—' says Mahler, 'a moment always comes when the word (*das Wort*) is inevitably indispensable to me, as a prop to my musical idea.'

By means of this method, which Mahler has been well inspired to borrow from Beethoven and Liszt, and which it is incredible that nineteenth-century music has used so little, he has drawn striking effects, which are, perhaps, as much poetic as musical.

In his *Second Symphony, in G Minor,* after the three first movements, which are purely instrumental, a contralto voice is heard, singing words that are sad and ingenuous:

206

Der Mensch liegt in grösster Noth!
Der Mensch liegt in grösster Pein!
Je lieber möcht' ich im Himmel sein! *

The soul soars towards God, with a passionate cry:

Ich bin von Gott und will wieder zu Gott! †

And then comes an apocalyptic *finale*, in which—after a symphonic episode: *Der Rufer in der Wüste* (He who cries in the wilderness), to harsh and anguished strains,—the voices of the choir sing Klopstock's beautiful ode, the promise of the Resurrection:

Aufersteh'n, ja, aufersteh'n wirst du, mein Staub, nach kurzer Ruh! ‡

The law is proclaimed:

Was entstanden ist, das muss vergehen,
Was vergangen, auferstehen! §

And all the orchestra, the choirs and the organ sing the hymn of Eternal Life.

In the *Third Symphony*, known under the name of: *A Summer Morning's Dream* (*Ein Sommermorgentraum*), the first three, and the last movements are for orchestra alone; the fourth movement is a wonderful setting (one of the finest things Mahler has written), of Nietzsche's words:

O Mensch! o Mensch! Gib Acht! gib Acht!
Was spricht die tiefe Mitternacht? ‖

---

*Man lies in greatest misery;
  Man lies in greatest pain;
  How I would I were in Heaven!
†I come from God, and want to return to God.
‡Thou wilt rise again! Yea, thou wilt rise again, O my dust, after a little rest.
§What is born must pass away;
  What has passed away must rise again.
‖O Man! O man! Have care! Have care!
  What says the dark midnight?

The fifth movement is choral, sunny and tinged with emotion, based on a popular legend.

Finally, in the *Fourth Symphony*, in G Major, only the last movement is sung, and it has a humorous character: it is a kind of childish description of the joys of Paradise.

In spite of appearances, Mahler refuses to connect these symphonies with choirs to programme music. And doubtless he is right, if by that he means to say that his music has a value of its own, quite apart from any programme; but there is no doubt that it is always the expression of a definite *Stimmung*, of a conscious state of mind; and, whether he likes it or not, it is this *Stimmung*, much more than the music itself, which makes his music interesting. To me his personality seems more interesting than his art.

This is often the case in Germany: Hugo Wolf was an example of it. Mahler's case is really curious. When studying his works one is convinced that he is, in present-day Germany, one of the rarest types of a mind concentrated within itself, which feels with sincerity; and yet, the emotion and the thought do not succeed in expressing themselves in a truly sincere and personal way; they reach us through a haze of reminiscences, through a classical atmosphere. The cause of this is, I believe, Mahler's profession as director of Opera, and the musical saturation to which he is condemned by this profession. There is nothing more fatal for the creative mind than too much reading, above all when it does not choose it itself, and when it is forced to absorb excessive nourishment, the major part of which it is impossible for it to assimilate. In vain does Mahler defend his inner solitude: it is violated by his extraneous thoughts, which besiege him from every quarter and which his conscience as an orchestral conductor, instead of thrusting them aside, obliges him to receive and even to adopt. Feverishly active and burdened with heavy duties, he works without respite, and has no time to dream. Mahler will only be completely Mahler on the day when it will be possible for him to give up all his administrative duties, to shut up his scores, and to withdraw into himself and wait

without haste to become alone with himself once more.
—Unless it is already too late.

More than any other of his works his *Fifth Symphony*,
which he was conducting at Strasbourg, convinced me that
it is urgent that he should resort to this course. In this
composition Mahler has abstained from using the choirs
which were one of the principal attractions of his preceding
symphonies. He wished to prove that he was capable of
writing pure music; and in order to affirm this more
positively, like the other composers taking part in the
festival, he declined to publish an explanation of his work
in the concert programme: he therefore wished to be
judged from a strictly musical viewpoint. For him this test
was dangerous.

In spite of all my readiness to admire when hearing a
new work by an author of whom I have a high opinion,
I cannot consider that this test was favourable to him.
The *Fifth Symphony* is excessively long—it lasts an hour and
a quarter,—without any inner necessity justifying such
dimensions: it aspires to being colossal, and more often
than not it is empty. The themes are as stale as can be.
After a funeral march of conventional character and
tempestuous tempo, in which Beethoven seems to have had
the nonsense knocked out of him by Mendelssohn, comes a
scherzo, or rather, a Viennese waltz, in which Chabrier
holds hands with the elder Bach. The *adagietto* has a sickly
sentimentality about it. The final *rondo* starts off like an
idea of Franck's: it is the best movement; it is carried away
by a whirling intoxication out of which, amidst bursts of
joy, there arises a chorale; but it peters out in repetitions
which weigh it down and stifle it. In the whole work there
is a mixture of pedantic strictness and of incoherence: of
disjointedness, of sudden pauses which interrupt the
development, of redundant ideas which interrupt it without
any musical justification, of interruptions in its vitality.

Above all I fear that Mahler is unfortunately subject to
the hypnotism of force which is driving all German artists
crazy nowadays. His seems to me to be an uncertain spirit,

ironical, sad, agitated and weak, the spirit of a Viennese musician straining after Wagnerian grandiosity. No one has such a feeling for the grace of *Laendler* and delicate waltzes, of elegiac reveries, as he has. No one could perhaps rediscover better than he could the secret of the affecting and voluptuous melancholy of Schubert, of whom he sometimes reminds me in certain of his qualities as well as in some of his defects. But it is Beethoven whom he wants to be, or Wagner. He is wrong: he lacks their balance, and their Herculean strength. This was only too apparent when he conducted the *Choral Symphony*.

Be that as it may, and no matter what disappointment he may have caused me at the Strasbourg festival, I shall not venture to speak lightly or disrespectfully of him. I give him credit, sure that a musician of such high conscientiousness will one day create the work which he deserves.

Richard Strauss makes a perfect contrast to Mahler. He still has the look of a big absent-minded child with a sulky mouth. Tall, slender, fairly well-dressed and lordly looking, he seems to come from a more refined race than the other German artists around him. Contemptuous, indifferent to success, very exacting, he is far from having the same conciliatory and quiet relations with other musicians as Mahler has. He is no less highly-strung than him, and while conducting an orchestra he breaks into a frantic dance which follows the slightest details of his quivering music like clear water into which a stone has just fallen. But he has a great advantage over Mahler: he knows how to relax. Excitable and at the same time somnolent, he escapes from his state of nerves by his power of inertia; there is an underlying Bavarian indolence in him. I am sure that on emerging from his hours of intense life, during which his energy is used up in an excessive way, he has hours of quasi-vacuity. One catches glimpses of him at such times, his eyes vague and half asleep. That is how Rameau used to walk about for hours in his old age, without seeing, like an automat, and not thinking about anything.

At Strasbourg, Strauss was conducting his *Sinfonia Domestica*, the programme of which is one of the most daring challenges which he has so far offered to taste and common sense. He depicts himself in his own house, together with 'his dear wife and his boy'. (*'Meiner lieben Frau und unserm Jungen gewidmet.'*)—'I don't see,—Strauss used to say, 'why I shouldn't write a symphony about myself. I consider myself just as interesting as Napoleon or Alexander.'—Some people replied to him that that did not necessarily mean that others would share his interest. But I shall not resort to that argument: I can understand an artist of his ability talking about himself to us. What shocks me more is the way in which he talks about himself. The disproportion between the subject and the means of expression is too great. Above all, I do not like this display of all that is most secret in a man. There is a lack of privacy in this *Sinfonia Domestica*. The home, the living-room, the bed-chamber are open to all comers. Is that the feeling there is for the family in present-day Germany? I confess that the first time I heard this work it shocked me for purely moral reasons, in spite of the affection I have for its author. But later I did reconsider this first opinion, in view of the music, which is wonderful.

The programme is familiar:

The first movement depicts the three characters: the man, the woman and the child. The man is characterised by three themes: a theme full of spirit and humour, a dreamy theme, and a theme of enthusiastic and passionate action. The woman has only two themes: a capricious theme, and a theme which is loving and affectionate. The child has only one theme, which is calm, innocent, not very clear cut, and which will only acquire its full value in the development . . . Which of the parents is he like? The family is gathered around him and is arguing. The aunts say: 'He's just like his father!' (*Ganz der Papa!*). The uncles: 'Just like his mother!' (*Ganz die Mama!*)—The second movement of the symphony is a *scherzo*, which represents the child's games: terribly noisy games, the games of a gay Hercules; and the whole house echoes with the parents' conversations. How far removed we are from the good little children of Schumann, and their ingenuous family!—Finally, the child is put to bed; it is rocked to sleep; the bell chimes seven in the evening. Night falls. Dreams and anxieties. Love scene . . . The bell chimes seven in the morning.—The awakening. A merry argument. A double fugue, in which the man's theme and the woman's theme contradict each other with exasperated and farcical obstinacy; it is the man who has the last word. Apotheosis of the child and of family life.

Such a programme is more designed to lead the listener astray than to serve him as a guide. It falsifies the meaning of the work by only bringing out the anecdotal and rather burlesque side of it. And doubtless this side of it does exist. In vain does Strauss inform us that he did not wish to make a comic picture of conjugal life, but to extol the sanctity of marriage and of parenthood: he is so much of a humorist that the comedy carries him away in spite of himself. There is really only something solemn and religious about it when he is talking of the child: then the man's jovial brutality is softened, and the woman's provocative flirtatiousness becomes exquisitely refined. Everywhere else his irony and buffoonery gain the upper hand, sometimes attaining to power and liveliness of epic proportions.

But one must forget the tactless programme, which verges, and sometimes a bit more than that, on bad taste. When one succeeds in doing so, one finds oneself faced with a regular symphony in four movements, *Allegro, Scherzo, Adagio,* and a fugal *Finale,*—which is one of the finest works of contemporary music. It has the spirited exuberance of Strauss's preceding symphony, *Ein Heldenleben* (A Hero's Life), and it is superior to it in artistic construction; it can even be said that it is Strauss's most perfect work since *Tod und Verklärung* (Death and Transfiguration), with an opulence of colour and a virtuosity which *Tod und Verklärung* did not possess. One is dazzled by the beauty of the orchestra, which is so light, so supple, and so finely shaded, especially after the compact mass of Mahler's orchestra, that heavy bread with no yeast in it: here, it is all nerves, all life; nothing unnecessary . . . No doubt, the first statement of the themes has too schematic a character; Strauss's melodic vocabulary is, what is more, extremely restricted and not very elevated; but it is very personal: it is impossible to disassociate from him these vigorous themes, burning with a youthful ardour, which cleave the air like arrows, and twist in wayward arabesques. In the *adagio* of night there is, together with some very bad taste, a seriousness, a dreaminess, something moving and touching. And the fugue at the end is astonishingly lively. It is a mixture of colossal buffoonery and of an heroic pastorale worthy of Beethoven, of whose style it is reminiscent in its broad development. The final apotheosis is a flood of life. Its joy gladdens the heart. The most extravagant combinations of harmonies and the most unrelenting harshnesses fade and melt away, owing to the marvellous combination of timbres. It is the work of a sensual and powerful artist, of the true heir to the Wagner of the *Meistersinger*.

To sum up, these works make it apparent that, in spite of their seeming audacity, Strauss and Mahler are in the process of retreating surreptitiously from their advanced positions, and of deserting the symphony with a programme. Strauss's work would have everything to gain by being called *Sinfonia Domestica*, without any other indication: it is a regular symphony; and the same is true for Mahler's symphony. Strauss and Mahler are settling down; they are coming back to the scheme of the classical symphony.

But there are more important conclusions to be drawn from auditions of this kind. The first is that Strauss's talent is becoming more and more exceptional in the music of his country. With all his faults, which are immense, Strauss is unique for his powerful zest, his indestructible spontaneity, his privilege of remaining young in the midst of German art which is growing old; and his skill and artistry increase every day. Taken as a whole, German music exhibits grave symptoms. I shall not speak of its neurosis; I believe that

213

it is going through a crisis, and that it will sober down; moreover, I fear that torpor may follow this over-excitement. What is more alarming is the fact that, in spite of all the talent which still abounds in it, it has lost certain of its essential qualities. It scarcely has any melodic interest any more. One could search the works of Strauss, of Mahler, of Hugo Wolf, without finding a melody which has a truly original value in its own right, apart from its application to a text or to a literary idea and from its harmonic development.—But above all Germany is daily losing its inner depths; there is still some in Wolf's work, owing to his exceptionally unfortunate life; there is very little in Mahler's work, in spite of all his efforts to concentrate on himself; there is scarcely any in the work of Strauss, although he is the most interesting of the three. They no longer have any depth.

I have stated that I attribute this fact to the detestable influence of the theatre, to which almost all these composers are attached as *Kapellmeister,* directors of opera, etc. To it they owe the often melodramatic character, or at least entirely external character of their music—music for show, which constantly aims at effect.

Even more fatal than the influence of the theatre is the influence of success. These musicians have nowadays too many facilities for having their works played. A work is no sooner written than performed. There is no more isolation, no more long silences, no more years of living with a work. In addition, whatever the work may be, it is immediately supported by the formidable publicity organised around the principal German composers by their *Musikfeste,* by their critics, their press, their 'musical guides' (*Musikführer*) – those vindicatory explanations of their works, circulated in thousands, which set the tone for the sheep-like public.— Hence the ease with which a musician can be self-satisfied. He accepts the first idea which occurs. How different to Beethoven, forging the same themes all his life, putting his melodies back on the anvil twenty times before they reached their final form! That is just what someone like Mahler lacks. His themes have the rather commonplace appearance of some of Beethoven's ideas in their first drafts. But he does not get any further.

Finally, I want to mention the greatest danger which threatens music in Germany:—*there is too much music in Germany.*—This is not a paradox. I do not believe that there can be a worse misfortune for art than an uncontrolled superabundance of art. Music drowns musicians. Festival succeeds festival: the day after the Strasbourg festival, the Bach festival at Eisenach was beginning; then, at the end of the week, there was the Beethoven festival at Bonn. Concerts, theatres, choral societies, chamber music societies, take up the whole life of a musician. When will he have the time to be alone, to listen to the music within him? These torrents of tactless music penetrate into the last retreats of the soul, dilute its strength, destroy blessed solitude and the riches of secret thoughts.

It must not be thought that this excess of music is of very long-standing in Germany. At the time of the great classical composers this same Germany had barely a few regular concert institutions; and choral performances scarcely existed at all. The Vienna of Mozart and of Beethoven had only one concert organisation, and no *Chorvereine,*—no more than did the other towns of Germany. —Is the prodigious spread of musical culture in Germany which has been going on for a century in keeping with artistic creation? I do not think it is, and the contrast is making itself felt increasingly from day to day. They will learn to know *L'Apprenti Sorcier,* Goethe's ballad set to music with vigorous zest by Monsieur Dukas: in the absence of his master, the apprentice has let loose the magic powers; the flood-gates are open; no one can close them again any more; the house is submerged.

And so it is with German music. Musical Germany is in the process of being drowned under the flood of music.

APPENDIX

Romain Rolland and Music

ROMAIN ROLLAND AND MUSIC*

The music of the masters, and that of all those who pursue
a noble ideal with sincere enthusiasm, no matter from
whence they come nor to what school they are considered
to belong, have lost in Romain Rolland one of their most
understanding and highly-qualified supporters. A great mind
and a great heart, he spent his whole existence in following
the promptings of a generous and disinterested conscience,
without any concern for comment. He was not only one of
the masters of French musicology, but also a person of rare
qualities who, from his earliest youth remained closely
connected with an art which was for him, throughout the
trials of life, a tonic and a consolation. It is for this reason
that the numerous and vital pages which he devoted to
music, and which alone concern me here at present, have

*Romain Rolland's works on music:
Histoire de l'Opéra en Europe avant Lulli et Scarlatti (Fontemoing). 1895.
Vie de Beethoven (Hachette). 1903.
Musiciens d'autrefois (Hachette). 1908.
Musiciens d'aujourd'hui (Hachette). 1908.
Haendel (Alcan). 1910.
Voyage musical au pays du passé (Hachette). 1919.
Beethoven.—Les Grandes epoques créatrices (Editions du Sablier):
    I. De l'Héroïque à l'Appasionata (1 vol.); 1928.
    II. Goethe et Beethoven (1 vol.); 1930.
    III. Le Chant de la Résurrection (La Messe Solennelle et les
        dernières sonates) (2 vol.); 1937.
    IV. La Cathédrale interrompue (3 vol.): *a*) à La Neuvième
        Symphonie.—*b*) Les derniers quatuors.—*c*) Finita Com-
        oedia, 1943-1945.
Jean-Christophe (Albin Michel), 5 volume edition (1931) and 1 volume
    edition (1949).

such a special ring about them, which distinguishes them from so many works, the interest and utility of which are beyond dispute, but which belong to the realm of what is properly termed exegesis or documentation, than to that of creation proper.

As long ago as the thesis he wrote for his doctorate on *Les origines du théatre lyrique* (*The origins of Opera*) (1895) Romain Rolland gave evidence of the lofty principles which were to inspire his actions. In it he underlined music's powerful contribution to general history, since its aim is to express the very essence of the human spirit and its infinite diversity. Music adapts itself to the characters of all nations and of all times; since its birth in Italy it has appeared by turns in Germany, in France, in Russia, in Spain, indeed even in England. It is not necessarily confined by any formula or theory. In a way it is humanity's dream, which runs its course in spite of conflicts. Rolland made a study, already in a masterly way, of its successive manifestations at the epoch of the beginnings of opera. He was soon to return to the same questions again in the series of studies collected together under the title *Musiciens d'autrefois* (*Musicians of the past*), and added chapters full of substance on the Florentine School, Luigi Rossi's *Orfeo*, Lulli, Gluck, Grétry, and Mozart, whose respective characters and parts in the history of music were evoked with a penetration and breadth of ideas all too rare in this subject, in which too often the spirit of prejudice creates its havoc. These essays were written almost forty years ago. Read them again: you will see that they have lost none of their relevance.

I am tempted to say the same for the *Voyage musical au pays de passé* (*A musical tour through the land of the past*), which is less widely known, and which forms a natural complement to *Les musiciens d'autrefois*. Firstly you will find in it, under the title *Le roman comique d'un musicien au XVIIᵉ siécle*, a lively summary of a curious book by the composer Johann Kuhnau: *Der musikalische Quacksalber*, which was published in Dresden in 1700, and which describes the convalescence of musical Germany after the Thirty Years'

War, and the formation of its great classical style. An analysis of the diary of Samuel Pepys, an enlightened amateur of the time of Charles II, makes us understand the true essence of the English musical spirit at the time of the Restoration. These are followed by studies on the origins of classical style and music in the eighteenth century,—on Telemann and on Metastasio, whose value and importance, not often enough recognised, are underlined by Romain Rolland. The *Voyage musical à travers l'Europe du XVIIIe siècle*. (*A musical tour through eighteenth-century Europe*) then transports us successively to Italy, the cradle of opera and of the musical theatre, and to Germany, where instrumental and symphonic music made the great strides with which we are all familiar. I must be careful not to overlook the vigorously sketched and concise portrait of Handel, which serves in a way as a preparation for the book which Romain Rolland devoted a few years later to the author of the *Messiah* in the *Maîtres de la musique* series published by Alcan, and which is still today the most complete and solid work which we have in France on this subject. In it, before examining the works themselves in all their many aspects, he gives prominence to the great objectivity, the lofty impersonality, and the grand style which, no doubt owing to a life of travel, combines in itself so many other intimately assimilated styles, which characterize Handel's genius. He praises the force, the passion, the humour in him, combined with a sense of form and with a power of communication which, without in any way losing caste, is able to reach the soul of the masses. Finally, amongst other similar works which Romain Rolland has left, it will be sufficient for me to recall the full accounts of *L'Opéra au dix-septième siècle en Italie* (*Opera in Italy in the seventeenth century*), the *Origines de l'Opéra allemand* (*The origins of German Opera*) and *L'Opéra au dix-septième siècle* (*Seventeenth-century Opera*) which are among the best chapters of Albert Lavignac's *Encyclopédie de la Musique*, as well as the masterly introduction to the *Histoire de la musique* by the late Henry Prunières which, alas, remains unfinished.

I come now to *Les musiciens d'aujourd'hui* (*Musicians of Today*) which dates from about the same period as the *Musiciens d'autrefois*. It must be regretted that Romain Rolland, absorbed as he was to the end of his days by so many different tasks, was not able later to find the leisure to complete this work. In it he first of all discusses Hector Berlioz. Rolland praises to perfection that audacious genius coupled, as we know, to a vacillating and troubled soul; he stresses Berlioz's liberating rôle in French music of his epoch, and he praises his high poetic aspirations, doubtless superior to his gift of musical invention proper. Next comes Richard Wagner, in whose work Rolland does not gloss over certain incongruities of style and the lack of balance which, in his opinion, results from the predominance of the musical over the dramatic element proper in Wagner's works. This does not prevent him from having the highest opinion of the heroic dash, the happy joyousness, and the youthful force of *Siegfried,* the overflowing passion of *Tristan* —'a monument of sublime power which dominates all other poems of love—as Wagner dominates all other artists of the century—from the mountain heights'. In his opinion *Tristan* remains 'the highest summit of art since Beethoven'. It is not surprising that the pages which follow, devoted to Camille Saint-Saëns, are more moderate in tone. But they do do justice to the works, which are extensive, of this competent representative of the French classical spirit, to the perfect clarity of his message, in which something of the spirit of Mendelssohn and of Spontini survives. Vincent d'Indy likewise, in spite of the intransigence of some of his ideas, is appreciated by Rolland, both as a composer and as an animating spirit, with a remarkable independence of outlook and concern for fairness, and an all too rare sympathy for his powerful creative temperament, which is so often at odds with his aesthetic theories. Did not Romain Rolland himself make that 'faith in action', which he values and praises in the author of *Fervaal,* one of the principles of his own life? So far as Richard Strauss was concerned, he had the same understanding; he was the

222

first in France to recognise, to describe the character of Strauss's strong personality, of his proud independence, before rendering full justice, at the end of his life, to the extraordinary vitality which gives to the octogenarian master's recent works, sent him by a mutual friend at his own request, a renewed and passionate youth. Nor must I forget those pages written with emotion which revealed to France the infectiously attractive works and the tragic destiny of Hugo Wolf, or the soothing freshness of the Abbé Perosi's oratorios, and which also stated the profound reasons for the French triumph of Claude Debussy's *Pelléas et Mélisande:* the close synthesis of the score with the text, without one overlapping the other, as is sometimes the case with Wagner; the originality of the declamation closely moulded to the words; the subtlety of the harmonic language; the finely-shaded leavening of the orchestra; that 'essence of taste' which, in Romain Rolland's opinion represents, as do celebrated works by a Berlioz or a Bizet, one of the aspects of the musical face of France.

Two essays of a general nature conclude *Les musiciens d'aujourd'hui.* The first, motivated by an international festival held in Strasbourg, states certain truths, which unfortunately more often than not are still valid, about French music and German music, and about the way in which they were represented and defended on that occasion. In spite of the unfavourable conditions of the contest, in spite of the presence of such men as Richard Strauss and Gustav Mahler conducting the *Sinfonia Domestica* and the *Second Symphony in C Minor**, Romain Rolland points out that the experience was of an encouraging nature for French music 'which is silently engaged in taking the place of German music.' Romain Rolland devoted a long study, which first appeared in a foreign publication, to this cheering *Revival*, which dates from immediately after the war of 1870, and the principal cradle of which was the *Société Nationale,*

*Mahler in fact conducted his Fifth, not his Second Symphony at the Strasbourg Festival. Trans.

to the disinterested efforts of which he does full justice. This study still has its appeal today. In it he successively examines the rôle of opera houses, of symphony concerts, of the Conservatoire, of the *Schola Cantorum* (the fertile work of which he stresses, without concealing that its spirit is sometimes too particularist), of chamber music societies, and of the University, which held out longer against the introduction of music into its curriculum than did institutions of elementary education. Then he points out how excellent was the state of French music at that time, but also how shaky its prospects of duration were. 'The battle is not won for it. It will not be for a long time to come— so long as the taste of the general public remains unchanged —so long as the nation is not musically educated—so long as the links, which should unite the élite of a nation with the people, if the élite wishes to survive and to preserve its thought, are not re-established. It is the duty of the historian to point out to French artists that they must never disarm against the common enemy, which is more dangerous in a democracy than anywhere else: mediocrity. The road that stretches before us is still long and difficult. But when, turning round, with a glance we take stock of the path already trodden, we can have confidence. Who of us can contemplate without pride the task accomplished during the last thirty years? . . . A town in which out of nothing there has arisen one of the foremost symphonic schools of Europe, in which one of the keenest concert publics in existence has been formed, as well as an élite of great connoisseurs with catholic curiosity and all-embracing and free minds, who are the pride of France . . . It is impossible not to admire the nation which its very defeat has resuscitated, and the generation which has accomplished this magnificent work of the musical revival of the nation with unflagging perseverance and the faith which removes mountains.' A moving tribute, and one which, almost at the same time, the episodes in *Jean-Christophe* relevant to French music were to confirm and develop, notably in *La Foire sur la place* which, too, has lost nothing of its flavour.

In it there are—on the spirit of musical production of the epoch, on the monotony of the programmes of Parisian concerts, on the recruitment of critics, on the blunders of musical snobbery, on the excesses of choirs—appraisals the caustic implications of which equal those of the criticism with which, in the first part of *La Révolte,* Romain Rolland did not spare the German romantics and certain of their immediate successors. From it I glean in passing this profound view: 'Until then Christophe had believed that great ideas carry their light with them everywhere. He now became aware that no matter how ideas might change, men remained the same; and in the last resort nothing counted but men: ideas were what men were. If men were born mediocre or servile, genius itself became mediocre in passing through their souls, and the cry of liberation of the hero breaking his fetters became the act of servitude of generations to come.'

Let us return to France by mentioning the infectiously enthusiastic pages which Rolland's feelings for two musicians with whom life had dealt hardly, Gabriel Dupont and Paul Dupin, had inspired him to write. The author of these lines, in spite of the distaste he feels at speaking here of his own works, would be ungrateful if he had forgotten the spontaneous and warm way in which Rolland, whom he scarcely knew at that time, defended his *Sonata* for violin and piano, which was not accepted for the recitals of Eugène Ysaÿe and Raoul Pugno in 1904 without some assistance. I would like too to recall here the letter which he wrote to M. Paul Léon, at that time director of the Académie des Beaux-Arts, in order to protest against the vote of the Académie which refused the *grand prix de Rome* to Maurice Ravel in 1905: 'I am completely disinterested in this matter. I am not a friend of Ravel's. I may even say that I have no personal sympathy for his subtle and refined art. But fairness compels me to say that Ravel is not only a promising pupil. He is already one of the most prominent young masters of our school, which does not boast very many . . . Such a musician was a credit to the examination, and even if some unfortunate chance, which I would find it difficult to account for, resulted in his compositions being, or seeming, inferior to those of his competitors, he should nevertheless have been passed at the examination . . . I admire those composers who dared to pass judgment on him. Who will pass judgment on them in their turn? Forgive me for interfering in a matter which does not concern me. It is the duty of everyone to protest against a verdict which, even if it conforms to the letter of the law, is an offence to true justice and to art.'* Thirty-eight years later, at the time of Ravel's death, Romain Rolland, while once more pointing out his personal feelings about the limitations of Ravel's art, acclaimed in him 'one of the greatest artists of all time, a master of colour and of design'. Knowing the admiration which Rolland felt for Albéric Magnard, Alfred Bachelet, Guy Ropartz, and particularly for Paul Dukas, whom he considered unrivalled amongst composers of his generation, I have often regretted that no opportunity arose for him to express it in writing, as he did by word of mouth, with that loftiness of views and that forthright manner which were his alone.

* * *

But it was the appeal of the genius of Beethoven—who, according to that same Paul Dukas 'remains one of the most dazzling signs of the greatness of human destiny on the earthly horizon'—that was to enslave the passionate spirit of Romain Rolland from his youth onwards, and made him worship him unflaggingly until his dying day. In 1903 he published in Charles Péguy's *Cahiers de la quinzaine* the work which brought the *Cahiers* their first important success—his *Vie de Beethoven,* so packed with thought in its voluntary conciseness, and which later became famous. In the very first pages he states its significance: 'I give the

*Letter published by *La Revue Musicale* in its special number: *Hommage à Ravel* (December, 1938, page 178).

226

title of hero only to those who were great in heart.' As one of the greatest amongst these, the man whose life we are describing in this very article, said himself: 'I acknowledge no other sign of superiority than goodness. Where the character is not great, there is no great man, there is not even a great artist, nor a great man of action; there is nothing but a hollow idol for the vulgar mob: time destroys them together. Success is of little importance. It is a question of *being* great, and not of appearing to be so.'

Twenty-five years later he was completing the first volumes of the vast work devoted to *Les grandes époques créatrices* (*The great creative periods*) of the master of Bonn, the plan of which he had long been maturing, and which originally was to have consisted of five parts: the formative period, the heroic years, the acme of classical art, the great crisis, and the last Testament. But the length of time which the accomplishment of a task of this scope, as he conceived it, would have necessitated, and the demands of his numerous other activities and of his health which was, unfortunately, often frail, led him to concentrate first of all on essentials, in the hope of later summing up, in substantial comprehensive surveys, the history of the periods of formation or of maturity—a project which in the end he was unable to carry out. In the brief introduction to the first volume, he stressed how perennial is Beethoven's message, in his view so profoundly representative of an European age belonging to the past. He could only smile at the disapproval which he encountered amongst those newcomers 'who, tied like us to the turning wheel of time, imagine that only the past passes, and that the clock of the mind stops at their noon— who cherish the illusion that the new formula alone wipes out for ever the old formulas, and will not itself be wiped out, without seeing that even while they are speaking the wheel is turning and that the shadow of the past is already twining around their legs.' Have things changed a great deal in this respect? I leave it to you to decide . . .

It would, unfortunately, be impossible for me here to summarise adequately or in detail his *Les grandes époques créatrices,* and all the problems of aesthetics and of technique which they raise, and the fruitful lessons in ethics which they contain. That would call for a whole book . . . They show us to what an extent the powerful temperament, the great soul of a man like Beethoven remains representative of his century, and of the generous passions which shook it. In the immense output with which you are familiar and which includes all styles, Rolland does not only pick out the highest summits, the most significant turning-points, the most finished achievements. He also depicts the man as he was at the moment when he conceived them, and the environment which saw their birth. Thus, he opens with a striking portrait of Beethoven at the age of thirty, full of vigour and fervour, ready to obey the imperious voice of his inner genius, and who already, in certain of the piano sonatas, had fully shown of what he was capable. Next he describes the decisive crisis of 1802, and its glorious consequences; the *Eroica,* the *Appassionata, Fidelio,* the four *Leonora* overtures, the genesis of which Romain Rolland studies in detail with the assistance of Nottebohm's valuable *Sketch Books;* Rolland also added passages of no less import on Beethoven's deafness, on the influence of the sisters Josephine and Theresa von Brunswick, and of their cousin Giulietta Guicciardi.

Next, that concern for synthesis which was so characteristic, and which gives rise to so much protraction in his writings, led him, in connection with Beethoven's relationship with Bettina Brentano, that young and fascinating Egeria of great men, to consider the question of the relations between Beethoven and Goethe, which until then had been rarely studied, and to devote an intermediary volume to this question which, although closely linked to the others, is complete in itself. You will see, in *Goethe et Beethoven,* why two geniuses of the breadth and scope of those we are discussing can pass close to one other without seeing one other. 'And the one who loves most (Beethoven), only succeeded in wounding the other. And the other, who understands most, will never know the person closest to him, the greatest, his only peer, the only person worthy of him.' An interesting letter from Bettina, fully imbued with the Beethovenian spirit, completes this part of the work. It exalts the powers of genius which are freely expressed, and contrasts them with the empty formulas of the epigones and reasoners. Music must, by concentration of thought, free itself from the mechanism of the mind, and be nothing but the direct expression of the ultimate flow of life.

In 1937 there appeared in their turn the two volumes of *Le Chant de la Résurrection,* which opened with a new portrait of Beethoven at the age of fifty, at grips with the difficulties of life, with political crises, and foreign occupation. It illuminates, as it were, the psychological and musical analysis of those sample works which Romain Rolland selected as being particularly representative of this epoch of the great musician's troubled existence; prior to this he had given a masterly summary of the preceding period (1806-1809), prolific in masterpiece such as the Fourth, Fifth and Sixth symphonies, the last piano concertos, the Violin Concerto, the Trios (Op.70), and the *Coriolan* overture. These sample works are, first of all, the Sonata for piano, op.101, the song cycle: *An die ferne geliebte* (Op.98), the song *Resignation,* the importance of which, too often disregarded, is fully brought out,—then the monumental Sonata for piano, op.106, which dates from the same period as the first sketches for the Ninth Symphony, the Mass in D, and the three last sonatas, which are examined fully in chapters which, owing to the copiousness and soundness of their documentation, their breadth of tone, and the richness of views which abounds in them, are true models of their kind. I cannot do better than refer you to them, as well as to the short supplementary passages on the Eleven Bagatelles, the Brentano family, and the letter to the Immortal Beloved, which throw significant light on certain points which hitherto had remained obscure.

Lastly, before his death Romain Rolland was able, as he desired, to revise the final proofs of his commentary on *La cathédrale interrompue*—what human work is ever really finished?—which, in his view, is formed by the Ninth Symphony, the last Quartets, and the multifarious plans which haunted Beethoven's inspired brain to his last days, of which Rolland gives a striking account in the last volume: *Finita Comoedia*. In this final triptych, which itself constitutes the last panel and the worthy crown of the vast triptych of *Les grandes époques créatrices,* Romain Rolland does not only give us historical and technical studies worthy both of these imperishable monuments of musical history and also of a writer of his own high rank, but proves to us, by means of a detailed study of the successive sketches, how the Ninth Symphony, the final Quartets and the *Variations on a theme by Diabelli* at the same time evoke the past, illustrate the present, and foreshadow the future. He makes us feel, beneath the external categories of notes, of equivalent forms, the stirring of the inner forces which animate them, and which give them so great a power over our reason and our hearts. By reproducing Beethoven's opinions on the most diverse subjects and individuals, he pays a final tribute to that power of concentration, that natural generosity, that inexhaustible faculty of poetic invention and,—no matter what may have been said about it—of melodic invention—that power of a mind over which reason and the mastery of a great constructor hold sway. He sees in the force radiating from the heart of a man like Beethoven the secret of the unlimited powers of his art. On the ethical as on the aesthetic plane, he notes the phases of a Herculean struggle between the man and his destiny. To Beethoven's so often affirmed religious convictions he gives the space they merit, thereby giving proof of his respect for freedom of opinions, and he also gives space to the extraordinary understanding which a man like Wagner showed from his youth onwards for the very essence of Beethoven's genius. He praises that truth and simplicity progressively won, and that uprightness, that never-lacking sincerity, that invincible attraction towards the sublime art, 'the supreme aspiration of which is to dissolve in the Awakening.'

The future of a work such as this, the faithful reflection of the great figure it evokes and of the fine spirit which was pregnant with it for so long, is assured. Will not the works of Beethoven, which are above fashions, because of the unity of their conception, the prodigious variety of their aspects, the high level of their style which always stems from creative thought, and their continual progress towards new poetic horizons, remain eternal?

* * *

When Romain Rolland had returned to his native Burgundy, and was obliged to take care of his health—precautions to which his unremitting intellectual activity did not easily resign itself—absorbed as he was by other work such as his *Péguy*, in which he gives certain details about the initial publication of *La Vie de Beethoven* and of *Jean-Christophe* in *Les Cahiers de la quinzaine*, he nevertheless did not cease to take an interest in the art of sounds, which was always so closely connected with his intimate existence, —and to which he dedicated such a moving ode at the beginning of *La nouvelle journée* of *Jean-Christophe*. At his own request I had sent him the scores of the latest works of the great contemporary composers to whom he remained faithful, and he was reading them in his place of retirement in Vézelay. No matter what at that time the sadnesses of the moment may have been, he remained confident of that revival which he had already so eloquently extolled not so long beforehand. He believed that there is no night, however long it may be, without hope of dawn. For those he knew to be in sorrow, he would find precious words of comfort. He ignored partisan hatred and passions. Like his god Beethoven, he recognised 'no other sign of superiority than goodness'. His premature death—for he still had much to say—was for his friends and for French thought, a cruel bereavement, an irretrievable loss. Let us reverently honour his memory, and let us follow the example of his passionate devotion to great ideas and to great works of music.

GUSTAVE SAMAZEUILH.
(1945)

N.B. In his *Lettres à Malwida von Meysenbug,* recently published by Madame Romain Rolland in the series *Cahiers Romain Rolland* (Albin Michel), Rolland frequently expresses opinions full of substance on Gluck, Mozart, Beethoven, Wagner, Nietzsche, and the Abbé Perosi.

INDEX

A.

Adler, Guido, 166, 171 (note).
ägyptische Helena, Die, (Strauss opera), 7.
Ahna, Pauline de (wife of R. Strauss), 2, 184.
Aida, 123.
Allgemeinen Deutsche Musikverein, 20, 105 (note).
Alpensinfonie (R. Strauss), 9, 95.
d'Annunzio, Gabriele, xiii, 160.
Apprenti Sorcier (P. Dukas), 4, 215.
Arabella (Strauss opera), 8.
Ariadne auf Naxos (Strauss opera), 7, 9, 95, 96, 97, 100, 161, 163.
Ariane et Barbe-Bleue (P. Dukas), 4, 146, 150.
Astruc, Gabriel, 81, 106 (note).
Auber, Daniel François Esprit, (1782-1871), French light opera composer, 75, 132, 155.
Aus Italien (R. Strauss), 177, 178.

B.

Bach, J. S., 22, 116, 117, 131, 133, 134, 155, 202.
Bachelet, Alfred (1864-1944) French operatic composer; conductor Paris Opera 1914-1918, 71, 226.
Baïf, Jean-Antoine de, 42, 106 (note).
Bakst, Léon, (1866-1924), Russian painter, especially associated with Diaghilev Ballet.
Bamberger, Berthel, 116, 169.
Bamberger, Louis, 169.
Barber of Bagdad (opera by Cornelius), 121.

Barrès, Maurice, (French writer), xiii.
Bayreuth, xiv, 2.
Béatitudes, Les, (César Franck), 113, 124, 200, 201, 203.
Béatrice et Bénédict (Berlioz opera), 18, 147.
Becker, Hugo, 121, 169 (note).
Beecham, Sir Thomas, (1879-1961), English conductor, 10.
Beethoven, L. van, xii, xiii, 21, 84, 111, 117, 125, 131, 134, 138, 179, 191, 202, 227-231.
Benvenuto Cellini (Berlioz opera), 3, 12 (note), 147.
Berlioz, Hector, (1803-1869), 40, 75, 124, 140, 147, 156, 181, 192, 202, 222, 223.
Bernhardt, Sarah (1844-1923), 114.
Bizet, Georges (1838-1875), 40, 150, 158, 223.
Boecklin, Arnold, 131, 147, 170 (note).
Boer war, 123.
Boieldieu, Adrien (1775-1834), French light opera composer 75.
Boris Godunov (opera by Mussorgsky), 150, 155.
Borne, Fernand le, 113, 169 (note).
Bouffons, guerre des, 9, 12 (note).
Brahms, Johannes (1833-1897), 2, 18, 133, 134, 138, 158.
Bréal, Clothilde, (Mme. Rolland), 134, 170.
Brentano, Bettina (friend of Beethoven and Goethe), 228, 229.
Briseis (opera by Chabrier), 3, 12, 113.
Brueghels, 1) Pieter (1530-1600), 2) Pieter (1565-1637), Flemish painters, 163.

Bruneau, Alfred (1857-1934), French composer and critic; wrote operas on libretti by Zola, and a *Requiem*, 7, 33, 40, 113, 139, 140.

Brunswick, Josephine and Theresa von, friends of Bethoven, 228.

Brussel, Robert, French music critic, 122.

Bülow, Hans von (1830-1894), German pianist and conductor; married Cosima Liszt (later wife of Wagner), 2, 11, 176.

Busoni, Ferruccio (1866-1924), Italian composer and pianist, 199, 205.

Byrd, William (1543-1623), English composer, 26.

C.

Capriccio (Strauss opera), 8, 9.

Carmen, 3.

Carré, Albert, Director of Paris Opéra-Comique, 80, 106 (note), 146, 148, 149, 151, 155.

Chabrier, Emmanuel (1841-1894), French composer, 12, 113, 209.

Chamberlain, Houston Stewart (1855-1927), English writer on music; married Wagner's daughter Eva, 133.

Chansons de Bilitis (song-cycle by Debussy), 33.

Chardin, Jean Siméon (1699-1779), French *genre* painter, 130.

Charpentier, Gustave (1860-1956), French composer, 6, 7, 20, 33, 40, 127, 136, 201, 203.

Cheval, René (author of book on R. Rolland), x, xi.

Chevillard, Camille (1859-1923), French conductor and composer, 26, 199, 200.

Christus (oratorio by Liszt), 22.

Coeuroy, André, French music critic, 99.

Colonne, Edouard (1838-1910), French conductor, founder of *Concerts Colonne*, 53, 76, 78, 143.

Cornelius, Peter (1824-1874), German composer, author of *Barber of Bagdad*, 121.

Couperin, François ('Le Grand') (1668-1733), 9, 26.

D.

Dante Symphony (Liszt), 125.

Daphne (Strauss opera), 6, 9.

Daubigny, Charles François (1817-1878), French landscape painter, 130.

Debussy, Claude (1862-1918), 7, 26, 33, 35, 40, 44, 49, 86, 139, 144, 150-152, 154, 156, 200, 202, 223.

Delacroix, Eugène (1799-1863), French painter, 130.

Dent, Edward (1876-1957), English musicologist, first President of the International Society for Contemporary Music, 166

Don Giovanni (Mozart), 2, 153.

Don Juan (Strauss), 2, 179.

Don Quixote (Strauss), 2, 3, 120, 136, 166, 187-8.

Doret, Gustave (1866-1943), Swiss composer, 41, 106.

Dostoievsky, 135.

Duhamel, Georges, French writer, 5, 107.

Dukas, Paul (1865-1935), French composer, 4, 7, 20, 22, 26, 150, 200, 202, 215, 226.

Dupin, Paul, French composer, 159, 171 (note), 225.

Dupont, Gabriel, French composer, 94, 106 (note), 144, 225.

E.

Egypt, 123.

Elektra (Strauss opera), 7, 87, 88, 159, 161.

Expert, Henri, French musicologist, 122, 170 (note).

F.

Falstaff (Verdi), 123.

Fauré, Gabriel (1845-1924), French composer, 9, 158.

Faust Symphony (Liszt), 22, 125.

Fervaal (opera by d'Indy), 3, 113, 222.

Feuersnot (Strauss opera), 3, 18, 20-23, 28, 78, 87, 105, 145, 149.

Fokine, Mikhail (1880-1942), Russian choreographer, 159, 160.

Fragonard, Jean Honoré (1732-1806), painter, 130.

France, Anatole (1844-1924), French writer, ix, xiii.

Franck, César (1822-1890), Franco-Belgian composer, 113, 124, 200, 202.

François-Poncet, French Ambassador to Germany, 10.

Frau ohne Schatten, Die (Strauss opera), 6, 7, 100, 166.

Freischütz, Der, (opera by Weber), 123.

Frescobaldi, Girolamo (1583-1643), Italian organist and composer, 154.

Friedenstag (Strauss opera), 5, 6, 9, 10, 11.

Funck-Brentano, 48

Fürstner, Otto (Strauss's publisher), 87, 89, 90, 93.

G.

Gailhard, Pierre (1848-1918), French bass singer and part or sole Director of Paris Opéra (1899-1908), 80, 141, 148.

Garden, Mary (1877-1967) Scottish soprano [created *Mélisande* in Debussy's *Pelléas et Mélisande* in 1902], 157.

Gémier, Firmin, 81, 106 (note).

Gérard, Baron François (1770-1837), French historical painter, 130.

Gide, André (1869-1951), French author, ix.

Gillet, Louis (1876-1943), Art historian, Curator of Musée André-Jacquemart, 1.

Glazunov, Alexander (1865-1936), Russian composer, 158.

Gnecchi, Vittorio, 89, 91, 106 (note).

Goethe, Johann Wolfgang (1740-1832), German poet, xii, 5, 93, 130, 152, 228.

Gorki, Maxim (1868-1936), Russian writer, xiii, 5.

Götterdämmerung, 131.

Gounod, Charles (1818-1893), French composer, 40, 111, 121, 139, 147, 150, 153, 193.

Greuze, Jean-Baptiste, (1725-1805), French painter, 130.

Guercoeur (opera by Albéric Magnard), 26.

Guicciardi, Giulietta (friend of Beethoven), 228.

Guntram (Strauss opera), 2, 3, 10, 21, 79, 113, 132, 180-184, 193.

H.

Haas, Robert, 164, 171 (note).

Handel, 125, 221.

Hansel und Gretel (opera by Humperdinck), 3.

Hasse, Johann Adolph, German composer, 164, 171 (note).

Hauptmann, Gerhard (1862-1946), German novelist and playwright [Prix Nobel Literature 1912] xii, xiii, 114, 124, 131, 169, 195.

Hausegger, Siegmund von (1872-1948), Austrian conductor and composer, 22.

Heidelberg, 18, 29.

Heldenleben (Strauss Tone-poem), xv, 3, 9, 20, 34, 83, 85, 98, 101, 105, 113, 118, 120, 126, 127, 136, 137, 141, 147, 162, 175, 180, 189-192, 212.

Hercule (Saint-Saëns), 118.

Hitler, xvi.

Hofmannsthal, Hugo von (1874-1929), Strauss's librettist; Austrian poet and dramatist, 100, 107, 163, 168.

Huber, Hans (1852-1921), Swiss composer, 161.

Hugo, Victor (1802-1885), French poet, 47.

Humperdinck, Engelbert (1854-1921), German composer, xiii, 3.

I.

Ibsen, Henrik (1828-1906), Norwegian playwright, xiii.

d'Indy, Vincent (1851-1931), French composer and theoretician, Director of *Schola Cantorum*, wrote operas (e.g. *Fervaal*, 1897), symphonies, chamber music, a Treatise on Musical Composition and books on César Franck, Beethoven and Wagner; 3, 7, 16, 20, 26, 34, 113, 119, 140, 144, 222.

Istar, symphonic poem by d'Indy, 3, 12.

J.

Jean-Christophe (novel by Romain Rolland), viii, ix, xiii, xv, 6, 8, 11, 88, 97, 105 (note), 115, 119, 157, 161, 224, 231.

Joachim, Joseph (1831-1907), Austro-Hungarian violinist and composer, leader of famous Joachim Quartet, friend of Brahms and Schumann, 2, 133.

K.

Kaiser Wilhelm, 112, 113, 123, 124.

Karsavina, famous Russian ballerina, 159.

King Lear (Shakespeare), 83.

Kipling, Rudyard, xiii, 47.

Kolb, Annette, 163, 171 (note).

Krauss, Clemens (1893-1954), Austrian conductor specialising in Strauss operas, 9.

Kuhnau, Johann (1660-1722), German composer, 22, 220.

L.

Lalo, Edouard (1823-1892), French composer, 158.

Lalo, Pierre (1866-1943), music critic of *Le Temps,* 90.

Laloy, Louis (1874-1944), 86, 106 (note).

Landowska, Wanda (1897-1959), 26, 105 (note).

Lassus, Roland de (1532-1594), famous Netherlands composer, 164.

La Laurencie, Lionel de (1861-1933), French musicologist, 151, 156, 170 (note).

Le Jeune, Claude (1528-1600?), French-Flemish composer, 42, 106 (note).

Levi, Hermann (1839-1900), German conductor, directed *première* of *Parsifal* at Bayreuth in 1882, 2, 176.

Liber amicorum, 5, 107.

Liebe der Danäe, Die, (Strauss opera), 8.

Liluli, farce by R. Rolland, 100, 101.

Liszt, Franz (1811-1886), Hungarian composer, xiii, 2, 118, 124, 125, 176.

Lohengrin, 111.

Louise (opera by Charpentier), 3, 4, 6, 12, 127, 135, 136.

Lully, Jean-Baptiste (1632-1687), French composer, 155.

M.

Macbeth (Strauss), 2, 179.

Maeterlinck, Maurice (1862-1949), Belgian author and dramatist, 33, 49, 105 (note).

Magnard, Albéric (1865 - 1914), French composer, 26, 34, 105 (note), 146, 155, 202, 226.

Mahler, Gustav (1860-1911), Austrian composer, 28, 29, 137, 138, 167, 199, 200, 202, 205-210, 213, 214, 223.

Malherbe, Charles (1853-1911), 140, 170 (note).

Manifesto of German Intellectuals (1914), xiii, 5.

Marnold, Jean (1859-1935), music critic, 86, 87, 96, 106 (note), 145-151, 153-157.

Marteau, Henri, French violinist, 138, 199.

Massenet, Jules (1842-1912) French operatic composer, 128, 144, 153.

Massis, Henri, French writer, ix.

Mauclair, Camille (1872-1945), French author, critic and art historian, 90.

Maurras, Charles, French author and journalist, ix.

Meistersinger, Die (Wagner), 49, 111, 137, 201, 204, 213.

Mendelssohn, Felix (1809-1847), 119, 133, 140, 150, 186, 195.

Messager, André (1853-1929), French composer and conductor (directed 1st perf. of *Pelléas et Mélisande* in 1902), 7, 113.

Metamorphosen (Strauss), 8.

Metastasio, Pietro (1698-1782), Italian poet and librettist, 221.

Meyerbeer, Giacomo (1791-1864), German operatic composer, 75, 132, 144.

Meysenbug, Malwida von, xiii, xiv, 1, 11, 232.

Millet, Jean-François (1815-1875), French landscape painter, 130.

Molière, (Jean-Baptiste Poquelin-1622-1673) French dramatist, 155, 169.

Monteverdi, Claudio (1567-1643), Italian composer. 49, 153, 154, 155.

Montmartre, 127, 128.

Mottl, Felix (1856-1911), Austrian conductor, 133, 170.

Mounet-Sully, Jean (1841-1916), Famous French actor, 148.

Mozart, 138, 204.

Münch, Ernst, Alsatian organist and conductor, 199.

Mussorgsky, Modeste (1839-1881), Russian composer, member of the 'Big Five', author of *Boris Godunov*, 150, 155.

N.

Napoleon, 130.

Nietzsche, Friedrich (1844-1900), German philosopher, xiii, 11, 39, 112, 114, 177, 191, 194.

Nikisch, Arthur (1855-1922), famous Austro-Hungarian conductor, 17, 133, 151, 158.

Nobel Prize, x.

O.

Oedipus Rex (Sophocles), 127.

Orfeo Catala choir, of Barcelona, 88.

Orfeo (Monteverdi), 49, 154.

Orpheus (Liszt), 118, 169

Oulibicheff (or Ulibishev), Alexander (1794-1858), Russian amateur musician and author, 191.

P.

Paris als Musikstadt (by Romain Rolland), 25, 105 (note).

Parsifal (Wagner), 111, 113, 117, 169, 223.

Péguy, Charles (1873-1914), French writer, x, 226, 231.

Pelléas et Mélisande (Debussy), xv, 4, 33, 35, 44, 49, 88, 149, 151, 152, 154, 156, 157, 223.

Pepys, Samuel (1633-1703), English diarist, 221.

Perosi (Abbé Lorenzo (1872-1956), Italian composer, 113, 117, 169, 223.

Pierné, Gabriel (1863-1937), French composer and conductor (Colonne Orchestra), 7, 140, 143, 144, 157, 158.

Planck, Max, German scientist, xiii.

Praetorius, Michael (1571-1621), composer and scholar, author of *Syntagma musicum*, 26.

Prunières, Henri (1886-1942), French musicologist, 221.

Q.

Quixote, Don, (see *Don*).

R.

Racine, Jean (1639-1699), French dramatic poet, 48, 152.

Rameau, Jean-Philippe (1683-1764), French composer, 138, 154.

Ravel, Maurice (1875-1937), French composer, 7, 146, 149, 150, 153, 156, 225, 226.

Reinhardt, Max (1873-1943), Austrian theatrical producer, xiii.

Réjane, Gabrielle (1857-1920), French actress, 134.

Rembrandt (1606-1669), Dutch painter, 163, 165.

Revue d'histoire et de critique musicale, 18.

Revue musicale, 8, 12, 99.

Revue de Paris, 15, 21, 105 (note).

Rhapsody (Brahms), 119, 138, 169.

Rheingold, Das (Wagner), 23.

Richter, Hans (1843-1916), famous Wagnerian conductor, 133.

Rimsky-Korsakov, Nikolai (1844-1908), Russian composer, member of the 'Big Five', 158, 159.

Risler, Edouard (1873-1929), French pianist of German origin, 3.

Ritter, Alexander (1853-1896), Russian composer of German origin, 2, 11, 22, 120, 176, 178.

Robespierre, 130.

Rococo, 6, 130.

Rolland, Romain (1866-1944), vii-xvi, 1, 3-12, 87, 219-232.

Ropartz, Guy (1864-1955), French (Alsatian) composer, 226.

Rösch, Friedrich, 16, 134.

Rosenkavalier, Der, (Strauss opera), 7, 9, 94, 98, 99, 164, 168, 169.

Rousseau, J. J. (1712-1778), French philosopher and writer, 12.

Rubinstein, Ida (d. 1960), Russian dancer and patron of the arts, 160.

S.

Saint-Saëns, Camille (1835-1921), French composer, 118, 144, 158, 222.

Salome (Strauss opera), xv, 4, 7, 9, 12, 29, 33, 40, 41, 52, 53, 55-75, 78, 79, 81-85, 89, 90, 92, 93, 138, 139, 141, 142, 144-146, 148-151, 156, 157, 159.

Samazeuilh, Gustave (b. 1877), French composer and writer on music, xiv (note), 11, 144, 232.

Samson et Dalila (opera by Saint-Saëns), 3, 17.

Schalk, Franz (1863-1931), Austrian conductor, 163.

Schéhérazade, Ballet by Rimsky-Korsakov, 159, 160.

Schiller, Friedrich (1759-1805), German romantic poet, 152.

Schillings, Max von (1868-1943), German composer and conductor, 22, 123, 170.

Schlagobers (Ballet by Strauss), 6, 100, 165, 167.

Schnitzler, Arthur (1862-1931), Austrian playwright and novelist, 166.

Schola Cantorum, 26, 150, 170 (note), 224.

Schumann-Heink, Ernestine (1861-1936), Famous German-American singer, 117.

Schweigsame Frau, Die (Strauss opera), 8.

Schweitzer, Albert (1875-1965), Alsatian musician and doctor, 27, 199.

Sert, José-Maria (1876-1945), Spanish painter and stage designer, 159.

Serva Padrona, La, Opera by Pergolese (1710-1736), 12.

Sévérac, Déodat de, 146, 150, 170 (note).

Shakespeare, 83, 152.

Shaw, Bernard, xiii.

Siegfried (Wagner) 222.

S.I.M. Journal of the *Société Internationale de Musique,* 91-93.

Sinfonia domestica (R. Strauss), xv, 3, 26-29, 34, 53, 83, 99, 100, 136, 139, 140, 141, 166, 211-213, 223.

Société Nationale de Musique, founded in 1871 for the advancement of French music, 223.

Sophocles, 127, 176.

Souday, Paul, critic of *Le Temps,* ix.

Spanisches Liederbuch (song-cycle by Hugo Wolf (1860-1903)), 27.

Specht, Richard (1870-1932), Austrian music critic, 160, 165, 166, 171 (note).

Stefan, Paul, 165, 166, 171 (note).

Strauss, Josef, 2.

Strauss, Richard (1864-1949), vii, viii, xiii-xvi, 1-5, 7, 12, 24, 87, 111, 112, 114, 116, 118, 119, 120-122, 124, 126, 129, 134, 135, 137-142, 144, 146-148, 151, 153, 156-162, 164, 175-195, 199, 200, 203, 210, 223, 224.

Sudermann, Hermann (1857-1928), German novelist and playwright, xiii.

Symphonie sur un chant montagnard (d'Indy), 3.

T.

Taillefer (R. Strauss), 28, 105 (note).

Tannhäuser, 2, 136.

Tartuffe (Molière), 155.

Tchaikovsky, 143.

Tebaldini, Giovanni (Italian composer), 89-91, 106 (note).

Telemann, George Philipp (1681-1767), German composer, 221.

Thuille, Ludwig (1861-1907), Austrian composer, 22.

Till Eulenspiegel (R. Strauss), 3, 17, 185, 193.

Tod und Verklärung (R. Strauss), 2, 27, 83, 118, 179, 180, 193, 212.

Traetta, Tommaso, Italian composer, 164, 171 (note).

Tristan und Isolde (Wagner), 2, 152, 222.

Troukhanova, Russian ballet dancer, 157, 171 (note).

Trovatore, Il (Verdi), 123.

Troyens, Les (opera by Berlioz), 147, 181.

Turgeniev, Ivan (1818-1883), xiii.

V.

Varèse, Edgard, American composer, 88, 106 (note).

Velasquez, 130.

Verdi, 123.

Verklungene Feste: Tanzvisionen (R. Strauss), 9.

Verlaine, Paul (1844-1896), French poet, 47.

Vernet, Joseph (1714-1789) French painter, 130.

Vézelay, xvi, 5, 231.

W.

Wagner, Cosima, 2, 133, 202.

Wagner, Franziska, 11.

Wagner, Richard (1813-1883), xiii, 2, 11, 16, 40, 49, 77, 117, 130, 131, 132, 144, 153, 192, 193, 222.

Wagner, Siegfried (1869-1930), xiii, 2, 133.

Walküre, Die (Wagner), 82.

Wallenstein (3 symphonic overtures by d'Indy), 3.

Walpurgisnacht (Mendelssohn), 119.

Wanderer's Sturmlied (R. Strauss), 178.

Watteau, Antoine (1684-1721), French painter, 130.

Weingartner, Felix (1863-1942), Austrian conductor and composer, xiii, 133, 205.

Wells, H. G., xi.

West-östlicher Divan (Goethe), 101, 103.

Wilde, Oscar (1854-1900), xv, 4, 7, 12, 29, 37, 40, 52, 76, 77, 82, 83, 89, 138, 145.

Wolf, Hugo (1860-1903), Austrian composer, 27, 208, 214, 223.

Wolfrum, Philipp (1854-1919), Organist and musical director of Heidelberg University. A work of his, a *Christmas Mystery*, was given at the Hereford Festival in 1903. 8, 19, 20, 105 (note), 134.

Z.

Zarathustra, also sprach (R. Strauss), 2, 111, 134, 162, 186, 187, 193.

Zimmern, Helen, 177.

Zweig, Stefan, xiii, 5, 163, 171 (note).